Laughing Wolf

T0350035

MICHIGAN MONOGRAPH SERIES IN JAPANESE STUDIES
NUMBER 73

CENTER FOR JAPANESE STUDIES
THE UNIVERSITY OF MICHIGAN

Laughing Wolf

Tsushima Yūko

Translated by Dennis Washburn

Center for Japanese Studies
The University of Michigan
Ann Arbor   2011

English Translation Copyright © Dennis Washburn, 2011
All rights reserved.

Original Japanese text *Warai ōkami* Copyright © 2000 by Tsushima Yūko
All rights reserved.

Original work published in Japan by Shinchōsha, Tokyo, in 2000

*This book has been selected by the Japanese Literature Publishing Project (JLPP),
an initiative of the Agency for Cultural Affairs of Japan.*

Published by the Center for Japanese Studies,
The University of Michigan
1007 E. Huron St.
Ann Arbor, MI 48104-1690

Library of Congress Cataloging-in-Publication Data

Tsushima, Yuko.
  [Warai okami. English.]
  Laughing wolf / Tsushima Yuko ; translated by Dennis Washburn.
    p. cm. -- (Michigan monograph series in Japanese studies ; no. 73)
  "Original work in Japanese: Warai okami by Tsushima Yuko"--T.p. verso.
  ISBN 978-1-929280-69-8 (pbk. : alk. paper)
  I. Washburn, Dennis C. (Dennis Charles), 1954- II. Title.
  PL862.S76W3713   2011
  895.6'35--dc23

                                                                    2011025568

This book was set in Times New Roman.

This publication meets the ANSI/NISO Standards for Permanence of Paper
for Publications and Documents in Libraries and Archives (Z39.48—1992).

Printed in the United States of America

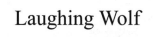

Laughing Wolf

Prelude

Hiraiwa Yonekichi, born in Tokyo in 1898, was the son of a bamboo wholesaler in the district of Kameido. When he was a child, his nurse read to him many stories by the popular Edo-period author Takizawa Bakin. One in particular, *The Marvelous Legend of the Crescent Moon,* made an especially strong impression on his young heart. This tale, which was first published in 1811, recounts the exploits of the great twelfth-century warrior Minamoto no Tametomo, a famously skillful archer who always kept two wolves, Yamao and Nokaze, by his side.

Later in life, when he was in his thirties, Hiraiwa began keeping wolves at his house—six Korean wolves, a Manchurian wolf, and two Mongolian wolves. He also cared for a number of other wild beasts, including two jackals, a bear, a musk cat, and a hyena. He had looked after domestic dogs long before he began taking in wild animals, and he was involved in establishing the Society for the Preservation of Indigenous Breeds as well. He founded the Center for the Research of Canine Behavior and presided over the Animals in Literature Society. In addition to all these activities, he left behind numerous writings related to canines, including his book *The Wolf: Its Ecology and History.*

Based on his personal experience, Hiraiwa wrote that wolves are deeply affectionate and wise, and can easily adjust to humans: "Just like dogs, all wolves prick up their ears, wag their tails, rub their bodies and roll over when they are happy. They occasionally whimper and lick your face, and will get so excited they end up peeing."[1] He gives examples of their behavior:

> I once tried going on a walk with one of the wolves. Even though I let it off its leash, the animal never strayed very far from me, and at one point it fixed upon a scent and refused to move. There was nothing I could do but pick up the wolf and take it back home as if I were carrying a child. I sweated profusely under the load, and the wolf, feeling utterly relaxed in my arms, fell into a sound sleep.
>
> Whenever my wolves sensed I was going out they would begin running around making a tremendous fuss ... Then, when I turned the corner on my street and disappeared from their sight, they never failed to call to me with their distant howls. This behavior always moved me.[2]

1. Hiraiwa Yonekichi, *Ookami— Sono seitai to rekishi* (The wolf: its ecology and history) (Tokyo: Ikeda shoten, 1981), p. 299. Revised edition printed in 1992 by Tukiji shokan. All the footnotes in the Prelude are by the translator. They do not appear in the original Japanese.
2. Hiraiwa, pp. 299–300.

In spite of his own experiences, Hiraiwa warns his readers that wolves cannot be raised as easily as dogs. They are extremely quick and agile, and their bite is powerful enough to shatter bones with one quick snap.

One behavior unique to the wolf is the way it stretches out its neck, lifts its mouth upward, and lets out a long howl in order to call to its companions over broad expanses. Many of these howls "begin first with a long, soprano-like *Aooooh*, then continue with a series of several shorter *Aoh, Aoh, Aoh* in the alto range. Finally, the melody ends with a closing *Oooh* in a voice that is almost bass. It is a beautiful, richly sonorous voice."[3]

Hiraiwa also discusses the wolf's speed, citing the observations of the American explorer Roy Chapman Andrews. In 1918 Andrews traveled from Ulan-Ude in Russia to the province of Tōshiyetü Khan in Outer Mongolia, where he spotted a wolf and gave chase in an automobile.

> … The tents were already in sight when a wolf suddenly appeared at the crest of a grassy knoll. He looked at us for a moment and then set off at an easy lope …
>
> The ground was smooth and hard, our speedometer showed forty miles an hour. We soon began to gain, but for three miles he gave us a splendid race.[4]

> … We swung toward the [wolves] which were trotting slowly westward, now and then stopping to look back as though reluctant to leave such an unusual exhibition as the car was giving them. A few moments later, however, they decided that curiosity might prove dangerous and began to run in earnest.
>
> … They separated almost immediately, and we raced after the larger of the two, a huge fellow with rangy legs that carried him forward in a long, swinging lope. The ground was perfect for the car, and the speedometer registered forty miles an hour. He had a thousand-yard start, but we gained rapidly, and I estimated that he never reached a greater speed than thirty miles an hour…. Leaning far out, Coltman fired quickly. The bullet struck just behind the brute, and he swerved sharply, missing the right front wheel by a scant six inches. Before Charles could turn the car he had gained three hundred yards, but we reached him again in little more than a mile….[5]

> … The wolf halted, too, and we could see him standing on a gentle rise with drooping head, his gray sides heaving. He seemed to be "all in," but to our amazement he was off again like the wind even before the car had started. During the last three miles the ground had been changing

3. Hiraiwa, p. 18.
4. Roy Chapman Andrews, *Across Mongolian Plains: A Naturalist's Account of China's "Great Northwest"* (New York: D. Appleton and Company, 1921), p. 51.
5. Andrews, pp. 57–58.

rapidly and we soon reached a stony plain where there was imminent danger of smashing a front wheel. The wolf was heading directly toward a rocky slope, which lay against the sky like the spiny back of some gigantic monster of the past.

... *For twelve long miles* he had kept doggedly at his work without a whimper or a cry of "kamerad." The brute had outgeneraled us completely, had won by strategy and magnificent endurance.[6]

Wolves are depicted in numerous works of literature, but Hiraiwa gives especially high praise to the account of the wolf-hunting scene in *War and Peace*, in which Tolstoy represents "a wolf just as it was, without the slightest embellishment."[7] One hundred and thirty borzoi hounds and twenty mounted hunters participated in this wolf hunt.

The count and Semyon leaped out of the bushes and to their left saw *a wolf, which, swaying softly, was moving at a gentle lope* to the left of them, towards the same bushes by which they were standing. The angry dogs squealed and, loosed from their leashes, raced toward the wolf past the horses' legs.

The wolf slowed his flight, turned his big-browed head towards the dogs awkwardly, as if suffering from angina, and, *swaying just as softly, leaped once, twice, and, with a wag of its tail*, disappeared into the bushes.[8]

.... They put a stick in the wolf's mouth, tied it with a leash like a bridle, bound his legs, and Danilo rolled the wolf from side to side a couple of times.

.... The hunters came together with their quarries and their stories, and everybody went to look at the seasoned old wolf, who, lolling his big-browed head with the stick gripped in his mouth, *looked with wide, glassy eyes* at this whole crowd of dogs and people surrounding him. When touched, he jerked his bound legs and *looked at them all wildly and at the same time simply*.[9]

Hiraiwa also cites a passage from Nishimura Hakū's *Enka kidan* (Strange tales from a misty landscape, published in 1773) as an example of how the figure of the wolf is depicted in Japanese literature.

I have frequently encountered wolves in both the mountains and plains of Mikawa. The mountain folk are accustomed to seeing them, and so

6. Andrews, pp. 58–59.
7. Hiraiwa, p. 26.
8. Leo Tolstoy, *War and Peace,* trans. Richard Pevear and Larissa Volokhonsky (New York: Alfred A. Knopf, 2007), pp. 498–99. Italics are Hiraiwa's.
9. Tolstoy, p. 502. Italics are Hiraiwa's.

they are not afraid. *So long as you don't provoke them, wolves generally won't bite people.* Once I came across a wolf on the road. I stood there, unable to move, wondering what I should do. The wolf, however, never hesitated at all, but just walked along casually, ignoring me as though it were traveling through a place where there were no humans. I had no choice but to withdraw to the side of the road and pretend not to look at him. The wolf leisurely proceeded along, just as he wanted, without so much as a glance back at me.[10]

It should be noted that Japan had long relied mainly on fish and grains for its food stocks, and so in contrast to societies based on livestock farming, which constantly suffered damage from wolves, the Japanese people were grateful to the animals and honored them as gods for getting rid of the wild boar and deer that damaged fields and paddies.

To illustrate this worship of wolves, Hiraiwa cites *Tōyū zakki* (Miscellaneous journal of travels to the east, published 1788) by the eighteenth-century geographer Furukawa Koshōken. Furukawa recorded his experiences in the village of Oinu-kawara in the feudal domain of Nanbu (the present-day town of Tōwa, which is north of Sendai in the district of Tome, Miyagi Prefecture).

It is said that the village was named Oinukawara because there are so many wolves in the region [text omitted]. *Deer live in the vicinity and damage the fields and paddies, so the residents consider the presence of wolves a blessing* and have no fear of them, unlike the people of the Ka-migata and Chūgoku regions of western Japan. If they encounter a wolf at night, it is customary to politely address the animal, saying, "Master Wolf, please be ever vigilant and chase away the deer."[11]

However, just around the time Furukawa was making his observations, rabies arrived from overseas and rapidly spread throughout Japan, affecting dogs first, then wolves, foxes, tanuki, and even cattle and horses. In *Enka kidan* Nishimura notes, "Sick wolves run wild, flying about like birds; and if they see a human, they snap at them fiercely. These wolves are able to travel tens of miles in a short period of time."[12] Because attacks on people occurred with increasing frequency, wolves sub-sequently came to be regarded even by the Japanese as a terrifying animal. Hiraiwa claims that rabies spread especially quickly among wolves because "they lived in packs."[13]

10. Cited in Hiraiwa, p.88. Italics are Hiraiwa's. Nishimura Hakū, *Enka kidan,* in *Nihon zuihitsu taisei,* vol. 4 (Tokyo: Yoshikawa kōbunkan, 1975).
11. Cited in Hiraiwa, p. 89. Italics are Hiraiwa's. The village name Oinukawara contains the Japanese word for dog, *inu.* Furukawa Koshōken, *Tōyū zakki* (Tokyo: Tōyō bunko, 1964).
12. Cited in Hiraiwa, p. 109.
13. Hiraiwa, p. 111.

Wolves came to be viewed as fierce, wild animals, and were inevitably hunted down with guns, which were becoming more technologically sophisticated.[14] At the same time, because of the development of firearms, the population of deer and other animals also drastically declined, and wolves began to suffer from a scarcity of prey. As the opening of land in the mountains and forests progressed, wolves gradually lost much of their hunting grounds. Moreover, Hiraiwa notes, "as wolves *came into contact with domesticated dogs*, distemper, which is highly contagious, invaded their territories and exacted a terrible toll."[15] He goes on to add, "there have been many stories told by those living in mountain villages around 1900 that a contagious disease spread among the wolf packs, and that occasionally they would spot a wolf carcass or a wolf lingering about, weakened by the disease."[16]

As a result of disease and the loss of territory and prey, the number of Japanese wolves declined sharply. In 1905, in the hamlet of Washikaguchi, which was then part of the village of Ogawa (present-day Higashi Yoshino village) in the district of Yoshino, Nara Prefecture, an American named Malcolm Anderson haggled with three local hunters over the price of a wolf carcass. Anderson eventually paid eight yen fifty sen, and the animal was recorded as "the last Japanese wolf." At that moment the species was declared extinct. The skull and pelt of this last animal is presently preserved at the Natural History Museum in London. Anderson had come to Japan as a member of an expedition planned and sponsored by the London Zoological Society and the Natural History Museum to collect specimens of animals from East Asia. A zoologist himself, Anderson was just twenty-five at the time.

Kanai Kiyoshi, a third-year student at the First Higher School who was completing the preparatory course for Tokyo Imperial University, worked as Anderson's interpreter. His account of the transaction eventually appeared in 1939 in the Bulletin of the Manchurian Biological Society. Kanai wrote, "It was hard to conceive then that this wolf would be the last one ever collected in Japan. While Anderson and I were skinning the carcass, the three hunters puffed on their tobacco, watching us. The wolf's belly was tinged a light bluish color and, judging from the decay that had set in, had been killed some days earlier."[17] Kanai also reported that Anderson had purchased a deerskin for four yen forty sen, two head of goat antelope for nine yen fifty sen, a wild boar for three yen fifty sen, as well as tanuki (also known as raccoon dogs), weasels, and various species of squirrels and flying squirrels.

It is possible that an extremely small number of Japanese wolves still existed somewhere after 1905, but theories and accounts presented in articles and newspapers claiming that the species continued to survive were all proven false. In his 1933 article, "A Letter to the People of Yoshino: Concerning the Whereabouts

14. Hiraiwa, p. 248.
15. Hiraiwa, p. 248. Italics are Hiraiwa's.
16. Hiraiwa, p. 248.
17. Cited in Hiraiwa, p. 245.

7

of the Japanese Wolf," Yanagita Kunio discusses the possibility that the species had survived. Hiraiwa subsequently conducted a detailed investigation of each of the twenty-six sightings recorded in a variety of sources—Yanagita's article, Kishida Hideo's *Tales of the Japanese Wolf*, which presents a practical survey of wolf sightings that draws upon Yanagita's work, and a report of a sighting in 1978 in the Ōdai mountains in Mie Prefecture—and concluded that the animals sighted had been wild dogs, foxes, or tanuki, or that they were Korean or Siberian wolves that had once belonged to traveling zoos. In 1935 the naturalist Minamikata Kumagusu wrote a letter to Hiraiwa.

> Wolves probably survived deep in the mountains of the county of Ni-shi-muro (in Wakayama Prefecture) until 1910, but there has been not a single sighting of them in recent years. Still, five years ago (in 1930), a sawyer who was traveling back and forth across the Yamato border claims to have spotted two wolves.[18]

However, this was mere hearsay, not proof that the Japanese wolf survived.

> In the end, there is *not one piece of solid evidence* that, after 1905, any Japanese wolves were still alive.... Regrettably, the fact that not one single animal has been discovered after such a long time must lead us to conclude that the Japanese wolf is extinct.[19]

The Japanese species was a special, small-bodied wolf that ranged across the islands of Honshu, Shikoku, and Kyushu in the Japanese archipelago. Because, as Hiraiwa notes, it did not exist anywhere else, its extinction was a major loss.

The Ezo wolf of Hokkaido, which the Ainu venerated as "the howling deity," was a large-bodied animal similar to wolves on the Asian continent. It appears to have gone extinct earlier than the Japanese wolf, probably around 1889. Hiraiwa blamed the extinction of the Ezo wolf on the intense persecution the species suffered at the hands of humans.

Ethnic Japanese who settled Hokkaido began to hunt deer indiscriminately, robbing the Ezo wolf of its primary source of food. As a result, the wolves began to target horses belonging to livestock farmers. Because of the damage they caused on ranches and stock farms around the town of Niikappu and in the district of Hidaka, the wolves came to be viewed as a major obstacle to the development of Hokkaido. At the suggestion of an American, Edwin Dun, who was working as an instructor and adviser to the Hokkaido Development Agency, ranchers began to use bait laced with powerful poisons. They bought up all the nitrate of strychnine in Japan, and even bought poison from as far away as San Francisco. Simultaneously, a system

18. Hiraiwa, p. 266.
19. Hiraiwa, pp. 282–83. Italics are Hiraiwa's.

was set up to provide bounties for catching wolves. An official total of 1,539 wolves were killed for bounty. Of course, the actual number killed was much greater, and in 1889 the government decided that the Ezo wolf had been largely eradicated and ceased paying bounties.

> Newspaper articles reported that 35 wolves had been taken in the Hakodate region and 4 wolves killed in the Sapporo area; and with those animals the Great Ezo Wolf (*Canis lupus hattai* or *Canis lupus rex*, also known as the Hokkaido Wolf) disappeared forever.... Even so, it was reported as late as 1896 that a fur trader named Matsushita of Hakodate prepared several wolf pelts for export.[20]

According to a report Hiraiwa wrote in 1981, wolves went extinct in Western Europe much earlier than in Japan. For example, they had disappeared in Scotland by 1680 and in Ireland by 1710. Over the course of the nineteenth century wolves went extinct successively in Denmark, Holland, Belgium, France, and Switzerland, and they died out in Germany in 1916. Today a small number of wolves remain in the mountainous region of northwest Spain, in the Apennine range in Italy, and in the mountains of the Balkan Peninsula. Wolf populations began to decrease dramatically in North America following the turn of the twentieth century, and the habitat of the large gray wolf is now limited to central Canada, the Rocky Mountains, Labrador, Baffin Island, the Alexander Archipelago off the southeastern coast of Alaska, and the interior of Alaska. A handful of wolves survive in eastern Minnesota, and the small Red Wolf inhabits a range limited to about sixty miles along the Louisiana coastline. The medium-sized Korean wolf has become extremely rare in the Korean peninsula. In Russia it appears that large numbers of wolves inhabit the Caucasus mountain range in the south, the tundra region of Siberia, and the western shore of Lake Baikal. And in China there are signs of a fairly large population of wolves.

Hiraiwa claims that wolves went extinct so early in Europe because they were always seen as a threat to people who from ancient times had raised livestock such as sheep and cattle. They feared the wolf as man's mortal enemy, and constantly persecuted the animal by every possible means—guns, poisons, traps, and snares, even hand grenades—until they had finally eradicated them. In the fifteenth century a pack of man-eating wolves, led by an alpha wolf named Courtaud (which means "Bobtail") appeared in Paris and attacked and mauled a group of monks in the square in front of Notre Dame Cathedral. Also, in the eighteenth century, in a region of southern France called Gévaudan, there was a monstrous wolf called la Bête ("the Beast"). A huge bounty was offered, the archbishop performed a prayer to exorcise the monster, and the locals carried out a large-scale hunt. It was an age when the fear of wolves was already strong, and so an extraordinary case like this

---

20. Hiraiwa, p. 240.

one magnified that fear and gave birth to a legend. Hiraiwa cites the writings of the French author Pierre Gascar.

> Not a single person could accurately describe the appearance of the ferocious wolf of Gévaudan. The pictures of the beast drawn by the numerous witnesses bore not the slightest resemblance to one another. That hardly mattered, however. Indeed, the lack of agreement about what the wolf looked like did not create doubts, but had just the opposite effect. As the drawings accumulated, they tended to exaggerate the most hideous features of the beast, whose image grew larger and larger until, in the end, it was completely transformed into a monster.[21]

As livestock farming became more industrialized, concerns about economic losses, combined with the fear of wolves as monsters, led to large-scale exterminations, which were carried out mercilessly. For example, during one particular wolf hunt in Lapland in 1949, a light machine gun was placed upon a sleigh and land mines were laid out over the hunting grounds. In order to communicate with one another, hunters used military planes and radio operators. Despite all those efforts, the hunt claimed barely two or three wolves. Hiraiwa presents these examples as proof that stories about wolves are greatly exaggerated, and that in many cases their distant howling intensifies people's fear by creating the illusion that two or three animals are actually a pack of dozens.

Now that the wolf has disappeared from Europe and the Japanese archipelago, only legends about it remain—legends that have become ever more firmly fixed in the imagination. Japanese children, who have never seen a wolf, are familiar with European fairy tales such as Little Red Riding Hood or the Wolf and the Seven Lambs, and they commonly accept the convention that the wolf is always the villain.

The Japanese wolf went extinct in 1905, the year the Russo-Japanese War ended. A little more than thirty years later, the Japanese islands were engulfed first in the war with China and then in the Pacific War, which ended in 1945 with Japan's unconditional surrender. The Japanese wolf was no longer around, but as things turned out, wild dogs who had lost their masters could be spotted running through the smoldering ruins of Japan's cities.

---

21. Cited in Hiraiwa, pp. 4–5.

1. Beginnings

He had memories like this—

Once upon a time there was a child and a father.

They would gather dead leaves in the corner of a patch of ground surrounded by rectangular grey stones. When they covered their bodies with the leaves, the dampness of the earth rose up, permeated with the odor of mold and mud. That stagnant odor was also the scent of the child and the father.

And memories like this—

The child was four years old. Not knowing how to read or write, he gave no thought to the meaning of the Chinese characters carved into the stone markers standing inside the enclosure of rectangular stones. Instead, he would entertain himself by filling up the hollow spaces of those characters with dirt and rotten leaves. He discovered an endless number of stone markers among the trees.

A cluster of trees small and large seemed to be constantly rustling in that space. Whenever the rustling subsided and there was a brief interval of silence, the child could make out the voices of various birds. Night birds. Morning birds. Flocks of crows noisily flying off somewhere in the early morning. The cries of small birds reverberated, as if they were calling to one another. Little birds would descend from the branches of the trees onto the tops of the stones and then onto the ground, sometimes coming so close that the child could almost reach out and touch them. It was impossible, however, for a four-year-old to catch even a single bird. Once his father managed to catch a large-bodied bird with his hands. Had it been a pigeon? The child was awed more by the size of his father's hands than by the bird. The father used those hands to roast the bird over an open fire. He then split the meat and shared it with the child. Only a little bit of meat, hard and gristly. The child chewed on it and sucked on the bones for a long time.

The child was familiar with the pangs of hunger. If he found anything he thought he could eat, he would try stuffing it into his mouth. It was not unusual for him to eat dirt or dead leaves. He would eat the moss covering the stone pillars, or even the bugs that curled up in the shadow of dead leaves. Perhaps that was why both father and child always had diarrhea. Whenever the father dropped his trousers to defecate, it sounded like a trumpet blasting under his butt, followed by white steam rising.

He had other memories as well—

11

Straight dirt paths, some narrow, some wide, stretched out in all directions. Things sparkled keenly here and there along those paths where the rays of morning light filtered through. The child gathered some of them and placed them on the palm of his hand. At once they turned to water. Flustered, he tried sticking them in his mouth. He felt a pain—like something had bitten the tip of his tongue. The child stepped on the ones still sparkling on the ground. A sensation clearer and sharper than withered leaves spread through his body. And he felt happy. Laughing, he tramped on the frost all around him. It was the coldest period of the entire year, but the child never noticed the chill of the night or the depth of the darkness. Was that because a mist-like lethargy always enveloped him, or because he had a blanket to protect his body? Whenever the blanket rubbed against his cheek, he felt a ticklish pain. While the child slept he would constantly stroke the blanket, checking the size and position of the holes as well as the frayed threads on the borders. The scent of the child and the father suffused the blanket too.

Why can't I forget even the smallest detail of my childhood, he wondered. It all seemed so strange to him.

There were times when snow fell. And rain, of course.

He remembered the sound of rain. All at once the murmuring of the trees would grow loud and vibrant, then raindrops would strike the stones and the dead leaves and soak their surfaces. Soon the sound of the rain would merge into a single mass, absorbing the child's ears and eyes into it. Rivers would form on the straight paths, and the sound of splashing water followed after them as the child and the father walked along.

The snow had no sound. But it brought pain. The snow would cover up all sorts of things. It even covered up the short stones. Once he was walking through the snow and stubbed his foot against one of those stones. He started bleeding. When that happened, the child had been merely startled, staring at his gash against the snow.

The child was fascinated by the color of his own pee, which would melt the snow away. It was vivid yellow.

Snow always lingered in the graveyard, unlike in the town. Its hard, frozen surface was like shards of glass that easily slashed the child's red chapped hands.

He could remember such details, but he couldn't recall the appearance of the graveyard completely white under the snow. He had no memory of being surprised by its whiteness. Surely he and his father must have stayed away from the graveyard on evenings when it snowed or rained. They probably sneaked into the town and nestled down somewhere to sleep—in an underground passageway, or a public restroom, or beneath the veranda of someone's house.

In those days it wasn't unusual for people to spend the night in such places.

People who had lost or abandoned their homes settled anywhere they could. The child and the father were part of the homeless population, and the child sensed that his father preferred sleeping in the graveyard to sleeping in the town. Try as he might, the child could never figure out why his father felt that way. Still, whenever they spent the night in one of the underground passages in the town, it always seemed that by the next morning the body of someone who had died in his sleep was discovered. The four-year-old had a memory of seeing corpses carried away.

Why hadn't he and his father died sleeping in the graveyard? Could it be that they were already living as corpses then? When they slept in town, the cops often evicted them. They'd be forced into a truck and taken to a shelter somewhere. There were rumors that the adult men would be sent off to work in the coal mines of Hokkaido. Had the father been afraid he might be sent away? Once separated from their parents, children on their own had to go to a shelter somewhere. As it turned out, the father collapsed six months later, and the child ended up in an orphanage.

The father was extremely thin and wasted. He rarely opened his mouth to speak. He was always sleepy-looking, his back was bent, and he shuffled when he walked.

The child had only memories like that.

The father could not do manual labor, and he had a four-year-old child. The child was quickly nearing the age when he could work shining shoes or collecting cigarette butts. Had the father been counting on that? Perhaps he thought he could hold out until his child started working. So he helped out at a street stall, he begged, he even turned to theft.

Or was the father simply waiting for the two of them to die together in the graveyard? The only thing the father prayed for was a slow, gradual death. Wasn't the graveyard the appropriate place for his prayer to be granted?

Hadn't there been a home somewhere in Tokyo? Wasn't there a time when the child had a mother? The father had a certificate proving they had lost their home during the war, but someone from the orphanage later examined the document and determined it was a fake. Even so, the certificate was important to the child, who used it to conjure up his own home and the family he had when he was born. A moderate-sized house, old but comfortable. A small garden, surrounded by a wooden fence, where his infant self was playing, splashing in a basin. The round face of his mother, who was washing his body. An older brother and sister playing near him. His father holding a white cat, cleaning its ears on the veranda. One day fire came pouring down from the sky. The fence burned, the house burned, his mother, brother, and sister all burned. Even the cat burned. They all vanished from the earth.

"Of course this was all nothing but a fantasy, but because I was always enthralled and comforted by it, it's sweet and dear to me …"

13

The child is now almost an adult. He continues to speak ardently to the twelve-year-old girl, rambling on, doing all the talking. The memories of his childhood slide into her body and vibrantly came alive once more. The girl, wearing her sailor-style school uniform, has pinned up her bangs. The downy hair on her forehead sparkles gold. Her round-cheeked face is still childish. She has placed her heavy leather schoolbag at her side, and from time to time the fingertips of her left hand toy with the metal fittings.

The girl and the young man are sitting in front of a tea stall on the approach to a large shrine near the imperial palace. He buys two bottles of orange soda and hands one to the girl. The young man, who has just turned seventeen, is wearing the frayed black trousers of his school uniform and a wrinkled white shirt. His hair has been closely cropped. A shy smile floats over his sunburned face, and he continues to speak in a low voice. Scraggly whiskers grow around his mouth.

Not many people remain here in the early evening. The large door adorned with the imperial chrysanthemum seal at the front of the main shrine building is closed. Cherry trees line both sides of the approach; small, brightly colored plastic lamps are hanging down amid the fresh new leaves. Neighborhood children run along the gravel road beneath the trees. A young man and woman look up at the bronze statue erected at the side of the approach, which an old man is sweeping clean with a bamboo broom—his final task of the day. A red carpet has been laid out at the tea stall, and the owner is beginning to sprinkle water on the ground around it. A flock of pigeons, startled by the water, rises as one, then just as quickly comes dancing back down. The surface of the bench is covered with gray pigeon droppings.

"… Siberia." The young man says softly.

"Siberia?" The girl asks.

The young man nods, then turns to smile at her. Though she's not quite sure what he's talking about, the girl smiles back.

"There was a time when I was convinced the graveyard was Siberia. Silly, huh?"

The girl frowns slightly and stares at the young man.

It happened when he was in elementary school. Some people who lived near his orphanage had just returned from Siberia. They would go on and on for hours with their stories. To the child's ears what they told him sounded like jokes, their speech studded with Russian words like *kharasho* ("good") or *dawai* ("Let's go, let's go"). They spoke of hunger and cold and sickness, of snow and ice.

As he listened to those stories, he came to think that Siberia referred to the place where he and his father had spent all those nights together. For him, the very sound of the word "Siberia" somehow captured the feel of the stones and dirt that remained in his memory. Because his father had already died, "Siberia" was, for the child, like a posthumous Buddhist name—something to provide a fond memory of his father. He could no longer clearly recall his father's face or voice. He didn't have a single photograph of him. The place where they had slept together wrapped in the moldy smell of the dead leaves and the blanket had for the child been transformed completely into his father.

"Siberia"—the place seemed to spread out limitlessly, wide beyond the comprehension of a four-year-old. Unlike the actual place, there were no Russians speaking Russian in his Siberia, no barbed wire fences, no dog sleds racing along, no reindeer, no wolves running around. His Siberia was far removed from the real thing; it was nothing more than an old, run-down municipal graveyard in the middle of Tokyo. He reluctantly acknowledged that reality only after he had entered middle school. A person could step outside the graveyard and, after walking just a short distance along a boulevard, arrive at the district of Ikebukuro with its absurdly large population.

He visited the graveyard for the first time on his own after he entered middle school. The name of the graveyard had been dryly recorded in a document concerning the father and the child. No fond or nostalgic memories came welling up inside him. Was this really the place? He felt bewildered. And yet he also felt as though he remembered having seen a number of the gravestones. They had all been transformed as well, and were now just small, common markers. Though he had expected to find a much wider space, the narrow graves were tightly cramped, lined up without any warmth or charm. Staring at a slightly larger grave, he tried hard to conjure the image of a small child sleeping there in his father's arms. No matter how many dead leaves they raked together, could they really have slept in such a spot every night with just a blanket wrapped around their bodies? It had been midwinter, after all. The child was shocked, as if the father and child were other people, and then he felt ashamed and left the place as fast as he could.

Yet still this graveyard, which had no name, which could be located on no map, had been more familiar to the four-year-old child than any other place on earth. It was as if the child had been born into the world from there. The child who had grown to be a middle-school student decided that he would forget the municipal graveyard he had visited. He excised that spot and that spot only from the metropolis where he lived, and once he did that, he was able again to treasure the place where his four-year-old self had lived with his father. He carefully protected it, continually sweeping away the dust and polishing it with a delicate cloth. He carried it around inside him wherever he went. When he slept at night, he cradled it in his bosom. The more he polished it, the more radiant it became; and the pleasure it gave revived him, as if the four-year-old child continued to live on, even now, within that radiant light.

The four-year-old child liked that place. A place where there was no odor of the living. He delighted in the cool scent of the stones, each one distinctive in its own way. The scent of black stones. Of white stones. Of stones tinged a green color. Of new stones, smooth and slippery. The scent of stones covered with moss.

There were also stones with strange shapes. Shapes resembling withered leaves. The shape of a towering pagoda. The shape of a cross. A round stone like an egg nestled in the undergrowth. Round stones. Simple flat stones. A stone in the shape of a house with windows.

There was also a stone carved in the shape of a person, his head shaved like a priest's, standing on a single large flower, hands crossed together in front of his chest.

Some stones had fallen over and were covered with dead leaves.

The child was especially fond of an egg-shaped stone. It was just the right height for him to climb up and jump off.

It was rare to see a dog or cat there. Animals don't bother going where there's no food. Crippled dogs, or blind dogs, or mangy dogs would sometimes hide out in the graveyard. Once he almost stepped on a cat that was staggering about.

One night an unfamiliar voice cried out over and over. Like a frog. Like the sound of the wind.

He asked his father about it, but his father said nothing. By the next morning, when the sky brightened, the voice had disappeared. The child walked around among the nearby gravestones. He peeked into the undergrowth. There, in a space between stones, he found a bundle wrapped in newspaper and covered in mud. There was a large rip in the newspaper and a human baby's hands and feet were sticking out. He could only catch a peek of the right side of the face. A white, sleeping face. The child poked the naked, blue-white hands and feet with the tip of his finger. They seemed to tremble. The baby was so small, he couldn't conceive of it as human.

The child announced to his father, "I found a baby over there. But it's not crying anymore."

The father ignored him and, as always, led the child out into the town. When they returned that evening both the baby's body and the newspaper had disappeared. If it had been eaten by a dog, or by the crows, there would have been at least some bones or newspaper left. But no matter how much the child searched, he couldn't find even one tiny finger.

He saw bigger humans, not at all like that baby. An old man seemed to have decided, like the father and the child, to use the graveyard as a place to sleep. Young women came there as well. And middle-school students in uniforms. And men in military clothes. Whenever he and his father walked down those wide straight paths and someone abruptly appeared out of the shadow of the stones, they would all catch their breath in surprise and stare at each other. Then, just as abruptly, they would avert their eyes and walk off in different directions, completely ignoring the other human they had encountered.

Even the four-year-old child had acquired the habit of ignoring people. He knew

16

that others lived in the graveyard, but their existence was a mere shadow to him. It was as if no one else was there—as if the graveyard was always the place with just the child and the father.

One night the child was awakened by the shrill voice of a woman. At first he thought it was the call of a night bird, and he was a little frightened. The voice seemed to echo across the sky, then tumble down sharply as if aiming right for his body. The child opened his eyes and got up from under the dead leaves and the blanket. Everything was brightly lit. The moon must have been out. Like a scene from a dream, the pale white trees and gravestones seemed to hover in the night.

The child was drawn to the shrill voice and began walking through the dim white graveyard. As it turned out, it wasn't just one voice, but two voices clashing together, entwining with one another. They would die away briefly, then rise up again, spiraling round and round, stretching thin until they disappeared. Then he spotted several men and women at the foot of a large tree and realized at last that he was hearing women's voices—though he hadn't been entirely sure earlier if it was a bird or an animal he had heard.

Were there two women? They were lying on the ground, their long, pale legs squirming. The child stood beside a tree. He was sleepy, his eyes half-closed as he cocked his ear toward their voices. Were the women laughing or shrieking? He could make out the dark shadows of men on top of the women. Their white butts were moving. The women's voices rose higher, but the men remained silent. The women laughed, cried out, moaned, and, most curiously, even sang.

The girl is holding an empty bottle of orange soda in both hands, staring at the dry lips of the young man. Her face reddens, but she doesn't look away. The seventeen-year-old boy seems every bit like an adult to the girl, who has just started middle school. There were things about "adult" stories she did not understand very well. Still, she thought she had a vague understanding. She recalled the fingers of a strange man groping her cotton underpants on a crowded trolley. His fingers almost went inside her panties. The girl was still in elementary school at the time. She twisted her body to get away from those fingers. She was crying when she got off the trolley. She also remembered a man standing in the park with the front of his trousers open.

Society tries to suppress such things. But the girl was already noticing signs of their existence, and try as she might, she would never be able to completely avoid them.

No matter what stories the young man tells her, the girl continues to listen without flinching. Though she has doubts about his truthfulness, she decides she will try to believe him. She feels with all her heart that she does not want the young man to dislike her. And she feels, with all her heart, that she does not want to be overwhelmed by fear of him.

Some time after she started elementary school, the toilet on the first floor of her school building was boarded up with plywood. A man had entered another elementary school in the neighborhood and murdered a little girl in a toilet there. She heard that the little girl had been violently murdered, and assumed that meant that the man had beaten and kicked her. However, it was apparent from the way the adults talked about the incident that something else had happened. The secret of the murder was hidden away in a place marked GIRLS—a place where you closed the door and, all alone, pulled down your panties. But she did not understand anything more than that, and so she grew scared of the first-floor toilet boarded up with plywood. A toilet no one was allowed to enter anymore. A place where the lights were left off, dust quickly collected, spiders spun their webs, and countless small insects gathered. The body of the murdered girl was lying somewhere in the darkness there. A little corpse crumbling away. Whenever she listened at the toilet door, she heard the murdered girl's crying voice echo from the other side of the plywood.

She is unable to distinguish between her fear of that toilet and her fear of the young man. The girl is truly convinced that the young man can hear the beating of her own heart. So she smiles at him.

The young man nods slightly back at her and, after finishing his own drink, continues on. He is starting the final, most important memory—

One night he heard mysterious voices.

The graveyard was even more deathly still than usual. It seemed as though each and every leaf on the trees was frozen. At least that was his impression. Maybe that night he had not been awakened by voices. Perhaps the chill had awakened him. A little ways off his father, wrapped in a blanket, huddled in front of a small fire. The child, dragging his own blanket behind him, moved over next to his father. That was when he first noticed. Low voices rumbling gently. Like the howling of wild dogs. Wounded wild dogs feeling pain and sorrow.

The child looked at his father's face. The father's eyes were closed. The child closed his eyes and tried to sleep. After a few moments, he opened his eyes again and stood up. Apparently there were several wounded stray dogs. Wrapping the blanket around his body, the child wandered off. The gravestones and the trees were all transparent, like ice. There were no stray dogs in front of the large gravestone shaped like a house, but he could make out the shadows of three humans. They were lying down, each facing a different direction. The child was a little disappointed. Drunks weren't all that interesting. He started to return to his father, but was drawn back by the sounds coming from those people. They seemed to be dying. Already one of the men had grown quiet, while the other man's breathing rattled faintly like a whistle. The third shadow was a woman. She was moaning softly, her body heaving.

The child cautiously approached the three people. He was poised to run away should one of the shadows get up suddenly and scream at him. In the meantime he

18

could no longer hear the sound of the second man. Something shiny covered the area around them. The child caught a whiff and knew it was blood. The scent of human blood was no different from the scent of animal or bird blood. It did nothing to stimulate the child's appetite, but stray dogs loved the scent of blood and were sensitive to it, no matter how far away they were. Soon they would gather here and begin devouring these people.

The child went back to his father and told him that two men had died and that a woman was on the verge of death. The father, who had been forcibly roused from sleep, groaned and glared at the child. He heaved a sigh, then, pulling a burning dead branch from the open fire, got up.

The child hadn't noticed, but dawn was already approaching.

The father, accompanied by the child, held the burning branch over the two dead men and the woman, protecting them from wild dogs until the sky turned light. When dawn broke, they left the graveyard and informed the cop at the neighborhood police box that a woman was dying in the cemetery. They added that there were two corpses as well. Had it been possible, the father would have preferred to avoid the authorities altogether. If he carelessly showed his face to the police, it could work to his disadvantage, since living in the graveyard was officially prohibited. But as reluctant as the father was to go to the cops, he could not ignore the life of the woman, who might still be saved. On top of that, there were two corpses to deal with. The father had a fond attachment to the graveyard he had chosen as their place to sleep. He believed no other space was as clean. Perhaps he found it distasteful that the corpses might defile it. At least the child sensed that his father felt that way.

After making his report at the police box, the father saw a chance to slip away and, pulling the child by the hand, made his escape. He didn't want to have any further association with the cops. Subsequently the father and child, afraid the police would recognize them, stayed away from the cemetery for a while. Once a sufficient amount of time had passed, however, they began to spend their nights there again. They bundled themselves up in dead leaves and their blankets and slept in front of a gravestone as if nothing had happened. The child had grown accustomed to sleeping in the graveyard.

It was only after the child entered middle school that he came to feel he should try to investigate the story behind those three corpses—though the woman had still been alive when he and his father left. In any case, two corpses would have been discovered, and so the incident must have been reported in the newspapers. He knew the location, and he had a general sense of the period when it had happened—the winter of the year he was four.

He went to the ward library and examined newspaper articles from that period, learning for the first time all that had happened in Japan back then. At last he found the article he was looking for. It was much longer than he had expected. Apparently the person who died first was a painter who was just becoming famous at the time, though the child had no memory of ever having heard the man's name before. His eyes were drawn to a large photograph. Right in front of him was the grave where the child had gone up to the man that night all by himself. His body flushed hot with nostalgia. The scene was just as he remembered it. The photograph was dark and fuzzy, but looking at that dim darkness he had an epiphany. He was able to confirm for the first time that his own memories were real, and the anxiety of being alone in the world, which had tortured him constantly up to that moment, dissipated. He wanted to walk around telling all the people he had ever met in his life that everything he remembered had really happened.

The child secretly cut out that treasured article. It was certainly a naughty thing to do, but under the circumstances it couldn't be helped. That article provided him with his only photograph of the graveyard where he had lived with his father. In his eyes, his father's image seemed to be reproduced in the photograph. Even his four-year-old self appeared there. He could hear the murmuring of the trees and smell the scents of the various stones.

Photographs of the three people who had died were printed next to the photograph of the graveyard. The child had no memory of their faces, but because he had witnessed their deaths, he felt he shared an intimate bond with them—a bond between their bodies, which had just greeted death, and his body, which from that moment on was turned toward death. He recalled the smell of the amazing amount of blood that flowed from the three bodies. The newspaper article gave a fairly detailed account of their lives. The woman was the painter's lover. She was pregnant at the time of her death. The other man was an unemployed veteran who had just returned home from a concentration camp in Siberia. He was the woman's husband, and when he learned that the painter had taken his wife, he began to stalk them. Gradually all three wearied of their relationship; and that night, dead drunk, they strayed into the graveyard and committed suicide together, using a knife the veteran had brought with him. The painter had a wife and two small children.

On seeing the word "Siberia" in the article, the child sighed. He was convinced that was the reason this incident took place, and he could not help feeling a fresh connection with the three people who had died. Staring at their faces in the photographs, he could almost imagine how each of them laughed, talked, cried. The child would sometimes speak to them, tilting his ear to the article to hear the voices that answered.

Is that right? So you were the child who saw us that time? You were just a kid back then, but look how you've grown ...

You had a terrible experience, but you managed to survive and grow up, didn't you. It's wonderful that you didn't end up dying a miserable death like we did. The world changed after that. Now you can get all the butter and eggs you want, can't you? Your father was awfully unlucky.

It's best not to think about why you're still alive. It would have been a lot better if I had died in Siberia. To die the way I did, after going to all the trouble of coming back to Japan ... It just seems so meaningless I can hardly stand it. Well, I guess that's how it goes. It's best to take life easy....

"Look here, this is the newspaper article I was talking about. Of course, you know about this incident already, don't you."

The young man pulls a piece of cardboard, which has been folded over in half, from a cloth bag containing a change of clothes and his lunch box. He had neatly and precisely pasted a piece of gray cloth over the four corners and the fold of the cardboard, and when he opens it up the newspaper article, which is mounted inside, straddles both the left and right sides. The paper has a labyrinthine shape, since he had cut out only that article, carefully following its layout on the page of newsprint. The girl immediately averts her eyes and, her head drooping down, glares sidelong at the young man's face.

"Get rid of that thing—it's just stupid!"

Like the young man, the girl had searched for that same article two or three years earlier. She found it in a reduced-size edition of the newspaper, but as soon as she did, she put it away without reading much of it. The headlines carried the name of her father, and the largest photograph was the one of her father's face. The girl, now filled with regret and fear, starts to leave. She does not want to come back here ever again.

As he slowly puts the newspaper article back in his cloth bag, the young man sighs and mumbles, "How could you say such a thing to me?" He then smiles at the girl and adds, "You shouldn't talk that way, it's not right. He's your father, after all."

The girl doesn't cry. Instead, she smiles at the young man. She can't oppose him; she can no longer run away. The approach is now completely dark, and the lights of the trolleys running along the main thoroughfare momentarily glitter beyond the trees of the shrine and then disappear.

"I guess we should be going soon. I'm starved."

When the young man stands up, the girl gets up too, clutching her schoolbag. A breeze begins to blow and it feels chilly on their skin. She walks beside the young man, who is about four inches taller. She needs to pee much more urgently than she wants to eat, but she has no idea at all how to broach such a matter. She walks cautiously along the gravel path while trying to keep up with the young man, whose stride is longer than hers. Her leather shoes give off sharp taps, while his sneakers hardly make a sound.

2. All Aboard!

If I had wanted to go home that night, I could have. But I didn't.

We were both very hungry, so we went to an inexpensive restaurant near the shrine—the kind of place that serves everyday fare. I had what they call "parent-child rice," that is, chicken and egg over rice, while he had a pork cutlet bowl. We finished eating in the blink of an eye, and were still hungry.

"You want to get something else?" he asked me.

I felt happy and smiled. It was the first time I had ever eaten out. My mother let me eat ice cream at a restaurant in a department store once, but that was it. Ice cream with wafers served in a silver dish. My mother was raised in the home of a provincial teacher and had no idea what it meant to eat out. My father, who perhaps might have given me a chance to eat out, was already long dead. "Parent-child rice"—that was the first time I had ever heard of the dish. I wondered who had come up with such a clever name, and burst into loud laughter in spite of myself. Before that evening everything had seemed so boring to me, but I learned that the world has some very interesting places after all. He also taught me there was a dish called "strangers over rice"—egg with beef instead of chicken.

He ordered *zaru soba*, a simple dish of buckwheat noodles, and we split it. I was quite familiar with *zaru soba*, since my mother occasionally made it at home.

Sipping his tea, his stomach full at last, he quietly asked me, "Well, what should we do now?"

As soon as he spoke, my heart began to race for some strange reason. Wavering, I looked at the clock in the restaurant. It was already past eight o'clock. Then I stared at my wristwatch. My watch was ten minutes fast. I set it ahead because I was always late for school. He didn't have a watch. I suppose no one ever bought one for him, and so I kept mine hidden beneath the cuff of my uniform. My mother gave me the watch as a present when I entered middle school, and, being still quite childish at the time, I was proud of it.

If I had gone back home at that hour, my mother would have scolded me for sure. She'd have interrogated me, demanding to know what I'd been doing out so late. But I would never have been able to answer her, no matter what. I couldn't tell her the truth, and I couldn't lie. Just then I remembered that a *kanji* quiz was scheduled for the following day at school, and my mood turned reckless.

"Where are you going?" I asked.

"I haven't decided yet," he answered, scratching his head. "I'll head over to Ueno and see if there's an overnight train I can catch. I guess I'll just take whatever's available. I've always wanted to ride an overnight train at least once in my life. You want to go with me, Yuki-chan?"

I felt relieved and nodded.

It never occurred to me that boarding an overnight train was the same thing as going on a journey. Still, it seemed as though we would be going somewhere far away—that much I did understand. And that being the case, I thought maybe I should call my mother and let her know. In the end, however, I didn't call her that night—actually, I forgot—and the next day my mother, after contacting my school, went to the police. In short, it was all because of my carelessness that everything became such a big mess. Even now I'm not really sure if he realized at the time what might happen. I never heard anything more about him after it was all over. For a time they called it a kidnapping, and it was written up in all the papers. I moved after that, and changed schools. I didn't change my name, though, so if he had ever considered looking for me, he could have found me. But he didn't, and I never saw him again. Forty years have passed since then, and now we probably wouldn't recognize each other even if he passed me on the street. To tell the truth, that's why I find it hard myself to believe that the whole thing ever really happened.

After Japan lost the war, young girls were kidnapped frequently, and many of those kidnappings ended in murder. Back then, memories of those crimes lingered and hovered menacingly over the whole society. I was always hearing frightening stories. A serial killer who murdered more than ten young girls. A young man who took a little girl on a walk, then murdered her in the mountains. Bodies of girls discovered in department stores, in movie theaters, in rivers. They were left in subways, in parks, and on beaches. Perhaps subconsciously I made up the whole story based on those incidents.

The year I started middle school—the spring of 1959—streetcars, which we called city trolleys, still clanged busily along the main thoroughfares of Tokyo. If I remember correctly, it was around that time that Tokyo Tower was completed, and my mother first showed me the newly issued ten thousand–yen note. Two sled dogs that had been left behind in the frozen wilderness by members of Japan's Antarctic Research Base somehow managed to survive, and they were a major topic of conversation among children. Soldiers who had lost limbs during the war could still be seen in large numbers begging at places that had a lot of pedestrian traffic. And on a night in late May that year, we headed off toward Ueno Station.

I'm sure I needn't mention it, but the day we took off for Ueno wasn't the first time we met. I may have been quite young, but I wasn't so naïve and unguarded to think it was all right to go off on a train with someone I didn't know. And in any case, he wasn't really such a daring young man.

One Sunday in mid-April, more than a month earlier, I was on my way home from a neighborhood bookstore, where I'd bought a magazine. A young man I had never seen before was standing in front of our gate. The peak of cherry-blossom season had passed, and the sun was beating down fiercely. The old threadbare uniform the young man wore was dusty and glistened white. Only his sneakers were brand new. I assumed he had new shoes because it was April and the school year was starting. I had just recently attended the matriculation ceremony at my new middle school, and I had a lot of new clothes and items my mother had either bought or made for me. Back then children throughout Japan all went around dressed the same way. Later I found out that, just as I had guessed, someone had bought his shoes for him as a present. But it wasn't a present for a ceremony to mark his entrance into school. It was a gift from the orphanage that had looked after him for many years celebrating his new independence as a young adult.

If memory serves me right, the young man's build did not strike me at first glance as especially large or powerful, and the expression on his face suggested a shy, introverted childishness. His round eyes, with their long lashes, called to mind the eyes of a dog, and so while he stood there staring blankly at the nameplate on our gate, I spoke to him without a hint of wariness. I assumed he had come to call on my mother. She was a high-school teacher, and her students would occasionally come by for a visit. Also, because my father had been a painter, art students would come barging in on her from time to time.

"Do you want to see my mother?"

He shuddered. He seemed genuinely startled and stared into my face for a few seconds without saying a word. I felt embarrassed.

"Uhhh … are you here for something?" I repeated my question.

"Ahhh …" He finally opened his mouth. "You wouldn't be Yukiko-chan by any chance? I, well, I was thinking your name must be Yukiko-chan for sure, but …"

It felt creepy, but he had my name right, so for the moment I nodded yes.

"Okay, then, it's just as I thought. Your face … it hasn't changed a bit."

He narrowed his long-lashed eyes and smiled at me.

When he said that my face hadn't changed, he meant compared to my face when I was seven years old. At that moment, however, I had no idea what he was talking about. The situation was getting even creepier, and I began to back off a little to the side, positioning myself, just in case, so I could rush past him and get inside our gate. He clearly sensed my fear.

"When we met before, I was only twelve years old, the same age as you are now, Yuki-chan … I don't think I've changed all that much, have I?" he muttered.

He cast his eyes down—his expression seemed a little staged.

Given what he said, I had to ask, "Excuse me, but … have we met before?"

Laughing to hide his embarrassment, he nodded.

"Your mother scolded me at the time, and chased me off. She told me to study hard for my future instead of thinking about the past. Your mother is scary. I never knew my mom, so I was surprised to see that a mother could act like that. She didn't want to hear about the past. She said it served no purpose. That's what she taught me."

24

That sure sounds like my mother, I thought, and so my fear of this young man, whom I had never seen before, began to fade. As my fear left me, I tried to picture his relationship with my mother. Could she have possibly been his *patron*? Wasn't what he told me—that she had opened up his "future" for him—just an old, hackneyed story?

"And did you study hard after that?" I asked

"Are you kidding?" he replied. "I'm not very good at school … I'm good with my hands, though, and I'm good at reading books."

"What do you mean, *reading books*?"

"I read out loud to the little kids at the orphanage. I guess it's a special talent. Of course, I don't read grown-up books to them."

I felt a little disappointed. Once more I studied his face, which was now beaming with pride.

"I see … but what did my mother mean when she said she didn't want to hear about the past?"

My question was naïve. After all, what kind of conversation could my mother have had with a twelve-year-old boy?

He thought deeply, with his head bowed and eyebrows arched. Scratching his head over and over, he stammered at last, "The graveyard …" Then he blurted out, "I was there that time, in the graveyard."

"The graveyard?" I whispered back, shocked. He nodded emphatically, as if he felt relieved.

I was there that time, in the graveyard.

He explained that a few years earlier, when he was twelve, he had gone to my mother and started to tell her about his experience. He felt dizzy as he spoke. He had carefully rehearsed every line—having written and rewritten them many times—and felt confident that, no matter what she might say to him, he'd be able to calmly recite his bizarre tale. When it came time to actually meet my mother, however, he was extremely tense. His mouth stiffened, his cheeks twitched, and he was overcome with the urge to break down and cry on the spot.

That's right. My father and I were living in the Zōshigaya Cemetery at the time. We had no house, and there were just the two of us, and my father was sick. And then, by chance, we found your husband and the other two there, and because there wasn't anything we could do for them, we went to a police box to report it. After that we had to stay away from the graveyard for a while. And then my father went to a hospital and died, and I ended up in an orphanage. So I managed to survive and grow up.

The twelve-year-old boy at first stood stiff as a rod on the concrete floor of our entranceway. My mother was kneeling on the step leading up into the house. She looked prim and straight, her legs folded neatly beneath her. She was staring at the

25

boy's face, checking him up and down. At the time, he was exactly the same age I was when we went on our spring "journey" five years later. He was wearing baggy new school trousers and a school cap so big that his eyes were completely hidden beneath the black bill. It was a hot summer day. Sweat was pouring down his forehead and dripping from the tip of his nose; and his cheap, sweat-soaked polyester white shirt was translucent. My mother was eyeing him with her chilly demeanor, her hair done up in the back in the old-fashioned style. She had on a worn, gray dress—a simple summer shift people back then called an *appappa*. Her arms, sticking out from the sleeveless dress, were extremely thin and white. They must have looked like bones to the boy's eyes, for he seemed a little scared.

In the course of their conversation my mother told the boy to sit down on the step. She disappeared back inside the house, and soon returned with some lukewarm barley tea. Two children peeked out from behind her, and he caught a glimpse of their faces. One was a seven-year-old girl. The other was a boy, fat like a balloon, younger-looking than the girl. Their mother shooed them away with her right hand, and so they came around to the front of the entranceway and squatted down in the shadow outside the sliding glass door, which had been left open. When the young boy turned toward them, they grew flustered, looked down, and pretended to be chasing ants on the ground. They were both dressed in clogs and white underwear. The girl had on a chemise, handmade by her mother and shapeless from repeated washings. Her brother wore a tank top shirt. The boy, who until recently had looked just like those children, gave them a smile filled with as much familiarity as he could possibly muster. At the very least, he thought, they had never known their father.

The branches of a nandina bush glittered above the children's heads. He could hear dogs barking—there were two dogs in the house at the time. As he drank his tea, the boy was so overwhelmed by a sense of contentment that he felt almost on the verge of tears again. He could hardly believe he was actually visiting this house. When he first learned the address, he hesitated, at a loss what to do. Was he entitled to call on them or not? He couldn't make up his mind, and there was no one to turn to for advice. He definitely wanted to visit the house, at least once. He wanted to let them know of the connection they shared with him. He wanted to confirm that connection. He had hoped for nothing more. Thus, he didn't feel sad at all when my mother spoke to him in a cold, indifferent voice.

"You were just four years old, right? It's best to forget about it. I've completely forgotten about it myself. The past is the past. Thank you for taking the trouble to come here. It must be a relief for you to unburden your heart. Now make a clean break and forget it. You understand, don't you?"

She convinced the twelve-year-old boy that only a fool gets obsessed and distracted by stories of the past. The boy himself had not cried, not even once, over the death of his father.

He stayed no more than an hour. I watched him from outside the entranceway, but no trace of him remained in the memory of my seven-year-old self. And of course my older brother, who was born three years before me, wouldn't have remembered anything. When he was a baby he got sick, and the illness affected his mind. My mother, however, almost certainly had not forgotten the incident. Indeed, had the boy, now a young adult of seventeen, been able to see her again that particular day in April, she would have remembered at once and driven him off, her face reddening with anger as she screamed, "In spite of all I told you, you continue this foolishness?"

As things turned out, the seventeen-year-old went home without meeting my mother, and I said nothing to her about running into him. So I missed my chance to see how she would have reacted. Later, when she was informed about the "journey" I had taken with him, she said nothing. She gave me a hard, sidelong stare, as if searching for something. When we unintentionally looked directly at one another, she quickly averted her eyes. Then, without a word, she began to make preparations to move to a new house. Perhaps she really wanted to send me off somewhere, even to a school in a foreign country, in order to distance me from the past once and for all. Back then, of course, it wasn't feasible for an average child to go off to a foreign country on her own. After all—to give just one example of the difficulties involved—the exchange rate was fixed at 360 yen to the dollar.

Now seventeen, the young man understood very well that my mother would lose hope if he visited a second time. And so that day, right after he introduced himself to me, he apologized as he started back home.

"I left the orphanage this spring," he said. "Now that I'm independent and standing on my own, I feel nostalgic about the past. Even so, I should have known better than to come here. I don't have a single relative in the world I can count on, and so I came to your house.... I regret it now. But I'm glad I was able to see you, Yuki-chan. Is your younger brother well?"

"He's dead. And just so you know, he was my older brother. He was sick his whole life, so ..."

He hung his head and mumbled something I couldn't make out. Then he said, "Oh, I see. Well, excuse me, but I'll be leaving now. Please take care of your mother. When she's on her own, she'll be lonely. Oh, I almost forgot. My name is Nishida Mitsuo."

I certainly never believed all the things this young man who called himself Nishida Mitsuo told me. The story of the incident five years earlier, the story about the graveyard twelve years earlier—he may have made it all up. Maybe he learned about my father's suicide and then came to our house just for the hell of it. My father's death was written up in all the major newspapers. Later on his suicide came to be viewed as a symbol of "postwar chaos," and newspapers would send reporters to conduct interviews with "the survivors." Those annoying complications were the reason my

27

mother wanted to cut all ties to the past … and that's why I didn't grow up to be a docile, obedient child.

How credible was this Nishida Mitsuo? Skeptical as I was, I felt an attraction to him precisely because he was such a dubious character. I just couldn't dislike him. I didn't know who he was, after all, and my feelings toward him resembled the feelings I had toward my father's world, which I had never known—I felt afraid but curious, and I wanted to see what that world was like.

Three weeks later I saw him again. I said nothing to my mother about that meeting either.

He was standing at a trolley stop near my house. My classes were finished, and I was on my way home when I got off the trolley and noticed him there. I surprised myself by not feeling surprised to see him.

"Oh, it's you. What's up?"

I was dressed in my school uniform. As soon as I spoke, his face turned red. He was wearing exactly the same clothes as before. "Uhhh, well," he replied, "I had some business to take care of nearby, and … and I was thinking, isn't this maybe the same trolley that Yuki-chan takes to go to school … and then there you were, getting off. Do you always come home from school this late? That's a tough schedule. Is your school far away?"

I nodded, and told him the name and address of my school. Had I been too careless at that moment? If I hadn't said anything, then in all likelihood we would never have had the chance to go off together.

I began telling him about all the trouble I was having adjusting to my new school, even though he hadn't asked about it. From the tone of my voice it must have sounded like I was complaining—about the old, dark school building, about the nuns who taught us, about the mass that all the students had to attend, and the prayers and hymns repeated morning, noon, and night, and those mysterious stories about female saints we had to listen to over the intercom speakers while we ate our box lunches. Even though I harshly criticized the stuffiness of the school, which I hated, perhaps I was actually boasting about it at the same time. It was, after all, a private girls' school. I had gone to the trouble of taking the entrance exams in order to fulfill my mother's hopes for me, and it was now my school. It had most likely never occurred to him that there might be such strange and expensive schools in the world. Did he feel a sense of revulsion or hostility when I told him about it? Perhaps he did, but he betrayed no sign of his feelings as he continued listening to me. Two weeks later, he was waiting for me when I came out of the main gate of my school. His decision to meet me may well have been nothing more than a whim—a turn of events that he himself didn't fully understand.

We stood there talking for about fifteen minutes. Just before I left, I suddenly felt worried.

"Uhhh … were you thinking about dropping by my house?" I asked him.

"No, no, it's nothing like that. It's just a coincidence that I ran into you here." He was flustered and his swarthy face flushed red.

"But today's not Sunday. Are you taking off from work?" My tone was sarcastic, and I was certainly being cheeky. His face turned brighter red.

"I work irregular hours, and was just going back to the company dorm to sleep."

"I see. You know, you told me you lived in a graveyard a long time ago. Weren't you scared at night?"

His face still red, he shook his head side to side and muttered in a low voice, "Afraid or not—listen, one of these days, if we have the chance, we can talk about all that. Today's not the right time. Goodbye."

He left in a rush. I started walking home. I felt a twinge of regret, thinking I should have broached the story of the graveyard more carefully, I also felt relieved. I hadn't made him angry, and I really did want to hear more about the graveyard.

To tell the truth, I couldn't get his story out of my mind. Soon after I first met him, the vague figures of a father and child living in a graveyard began to fade in and out of my dreams. The father looked like the Abominable Snowman of the Himalayas, hair covering his whole body, or like one of those ghosts of the Taira warriors who appear in the story "Earless Hōichi." A small boy, who for some reason was completely naked and pitch-black, walked beside him. Sometimes the boy was crying; other times he was laughing. The father and child would pass silently before me when I was playing at my house, but they never looked my way. They would pass silently before me when I was riding the trolley, or appear in front of me in a classroom. But by the time I noticed and looked at them, their figures had already disappeared. It made me very sad. Tears would run down my cheeks....

"Yukiko-chan! Hey, over here!"

The voice was Mitsuo's.

The sky had been dark and overcast since morning, and it was cold that day, as if suddenly we had gone from May back to March. He was standing in front of a small clinic directly across from the main gate of my school. A cloth bag dangled from his shoulder. He called to me as I came through the gate, exactly as though we had planned our meeting in advance. He raised his right hand a little to show himself, and when he did I forgot my feeling of surprise. I immediately moved away from the crowd of students leaving school, walked over to him, and smiled.

"Have you been waiting long?"

He didn't answer, but just turned his back on the crowd of students and walked into an alley beside the clinic. I followed behind. I don't remember what I was feeling at the time. Perhaps it was a sense of liberation. Any girl would have been elated and grateful if a man—it made no difference who—came to rescue her, and her alone, from that depressing throng of sailor uniforms leaving school. And if her savior were a young male of high school or college age, so much the better. The crowd of sailor uniforms turned its envious gaze on the special individual being greeted by a young man. Fully conscious of that gaze, which seemed to say *if only someone like that would come to meet me as well*, I began to follow "Mitsuo."

I always felt exhausted after spending a quiet, tedious day at my new middle school. I'd nap on the trolley, and when I finally got home I'd doze off at the table during the dinner my mother had prepared, or nap after starting my homework for the next day, or fall asleep in the bath. It was the same monotonous routine every single day. I was always sleepy, and the phrases we had to chant or sing every morning—*Deliver us from evil, and forgive us our sins. Angels we have heard on high, sweetly singing o'er the plains, Gloria in excelsis deo!*—would dance up languidly inside my head along with the English vocabulary I had begun to learn—HOUSE, GIRL, BOY, FLOWER, WHITE. The echo of the Latin songs sung at mass, like the singing voices of birds, would also dance in my head—*Agnus Dei qui tollis peccata mundi, miserere nobis. Tantum ergo Sacramentum* ...

And then, from time to time, the father and child from the graveyard would secretly pass through my head, never turning to face me.

The repetitiveness of my daily routine stopped completely the moment Mitsuo came to meet me that day.

We walked for a while through a residential neighborhood, came out onto a main thoroughfare, and followed a road that ran alongside the inner moat of the imperial palace. He smoked a cigarette—even though he was still a minor—and I got on a swing at a small children's playground. I hadn't been on a swing for a long time, and it felt good. Then the two of us climbed on the jungle gym. He moved quickly and more easily than when he was walking on the ground. When he got to the top he yelled out, "Yo-ho! Akela!"

I didn't understand the meaning of the word "Akela" at that time, and I didn't bother asking him about it. I wasn't very coordinated on the Jungle Gym, and had to focus all my attention on crossing it iron bar by iron bar.

We left the playground and continued walking along the road, finally cutting across a street with a trolley line and arriving at the Yasukuni Shrine in Kudanzaka. My mother and I had had gone for a stroll after my school entrance ceremony, and our walk had taken us past Yasukuni. She had frowned and muttered, "I hate this kind of place. It's disgusting." Even so, she stared inside the shrine grounds, apparently fascinated ... the great *torii* gate, the main hall. Mitsuo and I went around to the back of the main hall without paying our respects to the souls of the war dead enshrined there. We walked through a small garden, took a shortcut through a stand of plum trees, and stroked the bumpy surface of an old cannon that had supposedly been used in the Russo-Japanese War—or perhaps some earlier war. Then we went back to the front of the main hall. Wounded veterans were lined up outside the front gate. One of them had an artificial hand made of iron. He was playing an accordion. Another, who had lost both his legs, kept his head down the whole time. They were begging for money from the visitors who had come here to worship. Some young men wearing school uniforms and headbands emblazoned with the symbol of the Rising Sun were standing next to the veterans. They had a bullhorn and were making speeches. A flock of pigeons flew off in unison, and a breeze swirled around that spot. When the large main gate was closed at evening, the crowds suddenly thinned, and there were very few people left. The gravel approach to the shrine grew quiet, and we decided to rest at a tea stall. After sunset, the air grew cool, and I realized how tired my legs were.

Mitsuo told me he was taking his first vacation since starting his job. I gathered it wasn't a regular vacation, but a substitute for Golden Week that gave him the whole week off. He told me with an innocent smile that he had money he'd been saving up since graduating from middle school, and that he had been planning for some time to go on a trip. He had made sure to put a change of clothing in the bag he was carrying around with him.

"I've hardly ever taken a trip before," he said. "I didn't even go on the class trips in middle school. I was the only kid at the orphanage who was allowed to go to a regular school during the day, but it never occurred to me to go on a school trip or anything like that. The orphanage let me go to school during the day so long as I agreed to help look after the children. I worked in the office there until I graduated from middle school. They paid me a small salary, but I never had time to spend it on anything fun."

I nodded and smiled faintly at Mitsuo's explanation. I had no idea what to say. I found it hard to express even a word of sympathy, and I really didn't feel like praising or admiring him for enduring his troubles—that is, his hard life at the orphanage—because I still harbored doubts about the truthfulness of his story.

So I said, "I have a family, but I haven't been on many trips either. I went to Nikkō when I was in elementary school, but that's about it. That, and I went to my mother's home out in the country. I've only read about travel in books. I've never taken a *real* trip."

Just then the image of Gerda in "The Snow Queen" by Hans Christian Andersen popped into my head. In order to find her friend Kay, who had been locked up in the Ice Palace, Gerda goes on a journey all by herself. Along the way she is captured by bandits, but the daughter of one of the bandits helps her escape on a reindeer. Gerda finally makes her way to a cold, distant land. A real journey.

We got to Ueno Station at about nine o'clock that evening. Inside the station building were old people who had arrived from the countryside, mothers with small children, middle-school students in their uniforms getting ready to go home to the provinces, and high-school students and other young people who were preparing to leave Tokyo. Everyone was crouching down; their faces showed exhaustion. Some people were sound asleep, their heads resting on their luggage. Babies cried, loud voices that sounded like shrieks rose up here and there, and station announcements flowed down from overhead.

I looked up at the ceiling, my mouth agape. The tall dome-shaped vault was white and smoky.

"It's hard to breathe here. And it smells weird," I whispered to Mitsuo. "I just remembered, I've been here before. A long time ago. I came here to take the subway once. For a social studies field trip."

I pointed toward the entrance to a dark stairway that was visible in the interior off to the left. He gazed around silently for a while. When he looked back at me again, his face suddenly seemed drawn.

"Before we buy our tickets," he said, "you'd better get some clothes. You really stick out in that outfit. Some shops may still be open, so let's check them out."

He walked off, heading out of the station. I panicked and chased after him.

"But I've only got thirty yen on me. I can't buy anything. To tell the truth, I can't even buy a ticket. Can't I just go like this?"

Mitsuo glanced back and smiled bitterly.

"You look exactly like a girl who's running away from home. Don't worry about the money—I'm loaded. But just to warn you, the only shops I know sell used clothes. New things are out of the question."

I felt relieved and nodded. Obviously I couldn't go on our journey dressed in a sailor uniform and carrying a schoolbag.

We left the station through one of the side entrances. It was dark out by now, and we couldn't see very well. The peculiar odor wafting inside the station swirled gently, forming a stagnant layer, like smoke left behind by a breeze. Several swarthy-looking men, dimly visible in the shadows, were leaning up against a wall, while another squatted near them, smoking a cigarette. When I passed them in my brand-new uniform, they stared blankly at me—at least it felt that way. A rail line ran overhead, and when a train went by, the shadows of the men and my body and the feeble light from a naked bulb that illuminated the road, all trembled.

I was scared and held onto Mitsuo's belt with my right hand, walking along with my face down to avoid making eye contact with anyone around me. Apparently Mitsuo was no stranger to this place, and he walked at the same leisurely pace he had taken for our daytime stroll. Emerging from the rail overpass, we came upon a row of tiny stalls. The flames of the acetylene lamps in each of the stalls gave off black smoke and an acrid smell that irritated my eyes. Men and women were walking along the front of the stalls, drunk and unkempt, sometimes hugging, sometimes cursing each other. A man was sitting on the ground, crying and vomiting. The vendors were mostly women, but there were some kids there as well. Stalls selling liquor and food, and vendors selling just about everything else—old magazines, used clothing, pens and pencils, bags, underwear, colanders. A baby was sleeping comfortably at a stall that sold underwear—the baby wasn't for sale, of course. I very nearly kicked an old beggar who had wrapped sheets of newspaper all around his body. The street was strewn with garbage, and people were picking things out of it. I don't know what they were scavenging, but they put whatever they found into dented old buckets. Some drunks were singing loudly, and a few old folks, who may have just come in from the country, were standing around looking lost. A group of men wearing Hawaiian shirts passed us—they had on sunglasses, even though it was dark. Their faces were threatening. A little girl was walking about, asking if anyone would buy a flower from her. She may well have been younger than me. Barefoot children dressed in rags were everywhere—I had no idea what they were up to.

I remember my mother warning me that there were still scary places around Shinjuku and Ueno, and that I was not to go to either area, even during the daytime. I knew by the way she talked that she also meant I must never go to places like Shibuya or Ikebukuro either. (She once bought me some ice cream at a department store in Nihonbashi, so I assumed that Nihonbashi was probably safe.)

While my older brother was still alive, my mother hired a succession of girls from her old hometown back in the provinces to come and work as live-in maids. They were all about seventeen or eighteen, and one of them, a girl named Sumi-chan, attended sewing classes at night to learn how to make Western-style clothes. Whenever she went out on the town and came back late wearing a really loud dress, mother would scold her. In the end Sumi-chan was sent back to the country, but she had probably walked along the streets at night, humming a song, wearing a hoop skirt (the new fashion then) and a cute ribbon in her hair. Had suspicious-looking men in sunglasses ever accosted her?

Mitsuo finally stopped in front of a stall—more of a shack, really—that was much bigger than the others. There was a small room inside. Clothes were piled up all over the top of a counter and along the three walls—everything from men's sweaters to brightly colored children's clothes. There were also blue jeans stacked up randomly with no regard to size. Most likely they were originally surplus goods from the American armed forces.

"Hey there!" Mitsuo called out nonchalantly to the woman shopkeeper. He pointed to me and said, "Could you find some clothes that would fit this kid? No girls' clothes. We'd like a shirt and trousers, a jacket and a hat. Also, if you have some sort of bag, we'd like that too. She needs something to put her things in."

I couldn't say anything. And nobody waited for my opinion. The owner was a large woman. Her hair was white, but perhaps because she was plump, her freckled face looked younger than my mother's. She silently stared at me across the flames of the acetylene lamp for about thirty seconds, then, with a single loud click of her tongue quickly fished out a brown pair of trousers from the mountain of clothes. Next, she pulled out a washed-out green shirt, and, from the wall in back, took down a navy blue jacket and a really dirty-looking baseball cap. She worked so swiftly that it looked like magic to my eyes. The woman tossed the bundle of clothes into a small space separated from the rest of the shop by a curtain and, motioning with her jaw, urged me to go inside. I didn't know what was going on, so I glanced over at Mitsuo.

"You can try them on in there. You don't want them to be too big or too small, do you?"

I nodded. Mitsuo seemed to enjoy picking up old clothes one by one and putting them back. Though I was nervous about being separated from him, I resolutely went to the back of the stall. The woman opened the curtain with her right hand and, pointing to my schoolbag with her left, said in a low voice, "Set it down there."

At the raspy sound of her voice, I instinctively glanced up at the woman's large face. I understood what she wanted, and set my schoolbag down at my feet, removed my shoes, and went inside to change. There was no light in there, so I had to wait until my eyes adjusted to the dark. Little by little I was able to make out the clothes she had selected and tossed just beneath the curtain divider. The space was so small that when I stretched out both arms my fingertips touched the cloth walls to my right and left. Mingled smells of mildew and camphor filled the air, and my nose and throat began to itch. Light from the street lamps and acetylene flames outside flickered like fireflies through small holes here and there in the walls and ceiling. Bundles of used clothes, tied up with cords, were piled up around me, and several thin summer robes were hanging down limply from the ceiling. Half groping around, I took off my sailor uniform and, after making sure which side was the front and which was the back, I carefully slipped the trousers on one leg at a time. Next I pulled the shirt on over my slip. The clothes were too big for me, so after fastening the buttons on the shirt, I rolled up the sleeves four times, and the cuffs of the trousers three. I put on a belt, cinched the waist, and stepped out clutching the jacket, the baseball cap, and the blouse and skirt of my school uniform. It was so hard to breathe in that cramped space that I couldn't stand it another minute. When I stepped out, the flame of the acetylene lamp was blinding, and I frowned.

Mitsuo burst out laughing. "That was quick. Hmm … try on your hat. It suits you really well."

The woman stood next to me and took the clothes from my arms. She pulled out the cap and jacket from the bundle and handed them back. She then tossed the two pieces of my uniform into the changing room.

Surprised, I said, "Uh, actually, I want to keep those. I'll take them with me." But when I bent down to retrieve my uniform, the woman grabbed me by the shoulder.

"I'll keep them here for you, Missy." Her smile was unexpectedly kind, and she began to puff on her half-smoked cigarette.

"They're unnecessary baggage, Yuki-chan," Mitsuo chimed in. "You can't take them with you. The lady said she'd keep them here for us, so you can get them later.

The clothes you have on now are way more cool than that depressing old uniform."

Satisfied for now, I moved over to Mitsuo and softly asked him, "Should I leave my schoolbag too?"

"You're kidding, right? Of course you have to leave it. You don't want to have to carry that thing around with you. Okay, then, we're all set. Thanks for your help, ma'am. We'll be back again."

Mitsuo raised his right hand to the side of his head, like a soldier's salute, and strode off.

"You take care, you hear."

The woman's scratchy voice followed after us. I felt like she had spoken kindly for my sake, but her words were probably nothing more than a casual farewell she had tossed off to her regular customer, Mitsuo.

I suppose I was just a foolish child. I should have known I would never be able to go back and retrieve my school uniform and satchel. I suspect that the used clothes Mitsuo bought for me were extremely cheap, and that while I wasn't looking he pocketed the difference between what he paid for them and what he received for selling my things. I have no idea how much he netted—probably about a hundred yen—but once we started out, Mitsuo's money would gradually disappear, so he must have wanted to increase his capital a little. During our journey I began to develop a vague sense about such things—almost like a sense of smell. Yet when we set out I had only thirty yen with me. I felt small and ashamed about that, so I didn't feel I could raise questions about money with Mitsuo, since he couldn't possibly have had all that much.

In spite of my doubts, I continued to believe what Mitsuo told me at the clothing stall. I was grateful he had purchased an outfit for me with what little money he had, even though the clothes were cheap and shabby, and I was thankful to the woman, whose age I couldn't begin to guess, for having placed my uniform and schoolbag in safekeeping. Both of the items were very high quality, and they were still quite new. The school crest on the bag, with its complex design, had a golden luster, and the sailor-style uniform had been specially tailored for me at a Western-style clothing store designated by the school. The white ribbons at the collar and cuffs were made especially thick—really more bands than ribbons. The textbooks and notebooks I had needed for my classes that day, my pencil case, and my *bentō* lunch box were all inside the bag. As it turned out, I bid farewell to all those things that evening without knowing it.

We returned to Ueno Station. Perhaps because I was "in disguise" in my used clothes, I managed not to tremble on the way back whenever I made eye contact with people around me. The station was still crowded. Was everyone waiting for an overnight train? They seemed like people waiting and waiting, day after day, for someone to appear out of thin air and come for them. They spread out their newspapers and slept on them, surrounded by cloth bundles and scraps of food scattered about. Even half the students going on school trips were leaning against their back-packs or Boston bags and napping.

It was past ten. After staring at the timetable posted in the middle of the station, we moved toward the ticket window.

"Shall we try heading north?" Mitsuo asked, as if speaking to himself. I nodded at once, without hesitation. It didn't matter to me where we went. I just wanted to get on a train as soon as I could.

"Third-class to Fukushima. One student, one child."

He was speaking at the ticket window. Obviously I was the "child." I heard a voice from the window asking for his student ID card. Mitsuo produced his ID and paid the fares. Two tickets were tossed out and Mitsuo slid them into his shirt pocket. After we left the ticket window he said proudly, "My old middle-school ID is still useful. You're an elementary-school student, Yuki-chan. Don't forget that. We can decide how far we'll go after we get on the train. I got tickets for Fukushima, but it's no big deal if we want to get off before then. Or even if we want to go as far north as Aomori. This kind of knowledge is important. It's kind of like the law of the jungle. There are lots of laws like this, and they come in handy."

I nodded meekly, not understanding very clearly what he meant. I adjusted the cuffs of my trousers, which were still too long, and my baseball cap. The cap fit per-fectly, but part of the brim was stained with oil, and if I touched it without thinking, the tips of my fingers would turn black and the odor would cling to me. Despite that problem, I convinced myself that in order to maintain my "disguise" I had to wear the cap, no matter what; and so I resigned myself to it. Speaking of odors, the pen-etrating scent of camphor had permeated my clothes, and, though it may have been my imagination, they also reeked of tobacco and acetylene. When I looked more closely, I saw that part of the hem of my jacket had been singed, and the pocket on the right side had been torn off. My trousers were spattered with fine specks of vari-ous colors. No matter how you looked at them, they formed a bizarre combination with my new leather school shoes.

A white board announcing departures was hanging off to the side above the ticket gate. Several long platforms were lined up in front of us, and the tracks that came to a dead end between the platforms seemed to be sinking in the dust. We moved along the very last platform, looking for the place to board the third-class cars. A long line had already formed. The scene here was the same as in the station. People were spreading newspapers on the floor to make a place to sit. Vendors sell-ing *bentō* were walking around with large boxes suspended from their shoulders. Since it was rare for anyone to buy boxed meals at this time of night, however, the vendors looked about ready to call it quits, and had stopped calling out the name of their wares. We squatted down at the end of a long line, imitating the others around us. Less than five minutes later, everyone sitting on the platform stood up as one. A train arrived, accompanied by the smell of coal. The passenger cars pulled in one after another in front of us, giving off a majestic whoosh, like a sigh, until finally the whole train came to a great thudding halt. People began to board immediately, ignoring the order in which they had waited in line. Some people were calling out the names of their companions; others were pushing pieces of luggage in front of them, rushing in a panic to get on the train. Children started crying, baggage was tossed around and dropped, and an argument broke out. The disturbance quickly died down, and before we knew it, the car was completely full.

"Damn, what a bunch of idiots," Mitsuo grumbled. He had a cigarette between his lips, and was striding deliberately, as if he had all the time in the world—or so it looked that way to me. We moved up to the entrance of the car. After standing aside to let me on first, he boarded as well, and we made our way further inside. Of course there wasn't a single seat left, so we passed through that car. Mitsuo tossed his cloth bag into the vestibule of the next car down and sat on it. A group of about ten people, who had staked out their spaces before we got there, was huddled together.

"Hurry up and sit down here, Yuki-chan. Everyone's looking out for himself, so if you stand around waiting, they'll take your spot."

I put my purple hemp knapsack on the floor, just like Mitsuo told me to, and sat down. It looked like it had been made out of an old futon storage bag. There was nothing in it but the handkerchief and tissues that had been in the pocket of my sailor uniform and some newspaper that he had picked up at the station. I studied Mitsuo, pulling my legs up in front of me and hugging my knees with both arms. An old woman sitting right in front of me had assumed the same pose and was already asleep. In addition there was a woman with a small child, and a young woman wearing a pink cardigan over a flowered dress. Four men were laughing and joking in a rural dialect I had trouble understanding. Apparently they had been drinking before they got on the train. Their faces were bright red, and they were passing around a bottle of whiskey. There was also a young man in a school uniform, his head shaved like a priest's, accompanying a short elderly man.

"Are you okay? You can lean up against me if you feel sleepy."

"I'm used to this," I answered, "so it doesn't bother me. Whenever I went to my mother's home in the country, the trains were always crowded."

Actually, my mother and I had been forced to sit on newspaper in the vestibule twice, when the trains we were riding were completely packed.

"Where is it … your mother's hometown?"

"Kōfu. I think we took the Chūō Line, but I'm not sure."

I remember that once I had boarded a train through a window. Some adults lifted me through it. I was probably going to Kōfu then too. I needed to pee at the time, but I couldn't go to the bathroom, and I remember being handed from one person to the next, thrust out through the window, and having my panties removed. It was probably when I was still two years old. But had such a thing really happened? Whenever I think back on it, I relive the sensation of the cool breeze on my buttocks

37

I experienced as my body was lifted through the window. For that reason I believe it happened, even though I have no memory of my mother telling me the story. At that moment I thought, *I should try asking my mother about it when we get back*, but of course, when I finally got back home, I didn't have the presence of mind to ask her. In fact, I had forgotten completely.

"Well, this ain't the Chūō Line," Mitsuo said. "We're heading straight north. I wish we could keep going on and on. We could make it to Siberia. If this train could take us there, I'd ride it all the way, no matter what I had to put up with."

We heard the piercing clang of the departure bell. The steam whistle followed, echoing into the distant skies, and the train gave single great jolt and gradually moved out. No one around us felt any regret over leaving the outside world behind.

Mitsuo took a deep breath and exhaled. It seemed he was nervous after all. "Ahh, we're finally taking off."

"Yeah."

Suddenly and unexpectedly I felt a wave of anxiety and wanted to run back out to the platform. But it was too late. What would happen to us, I wondered. The person next to me wasn't my mother. It was Mitsuo. Just who was he? I felt lonely, and tears filled my eyes and nose. To hide my face from him I drew my knees up to my forehead and closed my eyes.

Mitsuo murmured in my ear, "By the way, you've gone to all this trouble to become a boy, Yuki-chan. So let's think of a name to call you. How about Mowgli? That's perfect for a brand new boy. You know him, right? The human child in *The Jungle Book*? While we're at it, I'll change my name to Akela. I've wanted to be called that for a long time. Pretty cool, huh?"

I held back my tears and raised my head. "I remember Mowgli, but who's Akela?"

"Oh c'mon, don't tell me you don't remember Akela? He's the leader of the wolf pack, the solitary emperor who embodies the law of the jungle. He's the reason the human child Mowgli is allowed to live on the margins of the pack. I'm not all that distinguished, but I'm taking the name because I have responsibility for you. I'm the leader—the father, older brother, and teacher all rolled into one—and you're the apprentice. So I think Akela and Mowgli are perfect for us."

He looked so happy that the feeling was contagious.

I laughed and replied, "In that case, wouldn't it be better if I was the python? You know, the really smart python. His name was Kaa. I think Kaa would be better than Mowgli."

"Yeah, I know what you mean, but that's no good. It won't work if we aren't members of the same pack. Akela and Kaa are companions in the jungle, but they're different species, right? We're … how should I say it … family. To put it another way, I'm the older brother and you're the little brother. That's why you should be Mowgli."

Mitsuo's face turned red with embarrassment. Remembering that he had no living relatives, I blushed as well and gave a big nod.

The night train for Aomori was gaining speed, and the faster it went, the louder the wheels rumbled. I got up and glanced through the window in the door. The cheerful colors of the evening lights flowed by, on and on.

I sat back down next to Mitsuo—I mean Akela. Then I—Mowgli—whispered to him, "It seems strange somehow, but it's all right. This train, it's real, isn't it?" I yawned.

"Ahh, I'm sure it's real." Akela yawned too.

And so from that evening forward—from just a little before eleven, to be precise—we became Akela and Mowgli.

3. The Law of the Jungle

Akela's world was extremely simple. At the same time, it was so complex it made him dizzy. That evening Akela had satisfied a long-held desire to be Akela of *The Jungle Book*. Akela, the Lone Wolf, the majestic gray leader of the pack. Akela, the embodiment of the law of the jungle. The council of wolves always started with Akela's magnificent howl.—*Ye know the Law. Look well, O Wolves!*

The naked human child Mowgli—the little frog—had been brought before Akela to consider recognizing him as a member of the pack. Wretched, hairless, and tailless. His senses of smell and hearing not one–ten thousandth those of the wolf. His toenails and teeth so weak it seemed he had no weapons to fend off enemies. Most pathetic of all was how slowly he grew—how, even after more than six months, he remained a baby and was unable to walk. Blessed with absolutely no powers, ignorant of the dangers around him, he couldn't even be compared to a frog, he was so small and weak. He was more like a baby minnow—a human child that made you feel the urge not to bully him, but to try to protect him as best you could, as though you had no other choice. When there is too great a disparity in strength, the truly heroic cherish the weakest.—*The rights of the pack are the rights of the least member of the pack.*—This too was a principle of the law of the jungle.

Still, a serious problem remained. How long could Akela maintain his dominance over Mowgli? The fact that Mowgli took so much time to grow up meant that by the time he was ten years old—the age when he would begin to display his distinctive human wisdom—Akela would be a doddering, fangless old wolf.

"Come to think of it ..." Akela suddenly recalled the fate of Akela in the story he knew so well. In the end, Akela the Lone Wolf was wounded in a fight with a murderous pack of *dhole*, the Red Dogs. Doing what was expected of a pack leader, he died in Mowgli's arms while loudly singing the "Death Song."

Akela was upset that he had carelessly chosen his name without taking into account the end of the story, and deep in his heart he began to have doubts. However, it would not do to show his uncertainty to Mowgli. After all, this naked little Mowgli was dependent on him; she had entrusted her weak self to him, and was innocently trying to sleep there beside him.

Akela was blessed with a special gift for gaining the affection of little children, which he began to display late in his elementary school years. Although he was terribly awkward at most things, he was surprisingly adept at narrating picture-story shows or reading picture books. He even improvised some interesting stories of his own—the tale of the "Ice Man" who lived in Siberia, the tale of a family of ghosts who haunt a desolate, ruined graveyard, and the story of the father and son

"Birdmen" who could fly freely through the sky. The nurses at the Children's Home quickly noticed his talent and decided to entrust Akela with helping the little ones in the evening. For an hour during the free period between dinner and bedtime, they happily took full advantage of Akela's skills. In exchange for his services, Akela was permitted to attend middle school during the day instead of going to night school like most adolescent orphans who worked or were apprenticed somewhere. In addition, Akela was allowed to continue residing at the Children's Home for a year after he graduated from middle school, and he was kept busy doing various jobs in the office. The orphanage treated him in this exceptional manner because it was an extremely small, privately run institution. Under normal circumstances one might have expected his classmates to bully him, but because most of his peers were gone, Akela passed through this period of his life largely unscathed and unfazed.

As a rule, most orphans didn't remain in an orphanage when they reached adolescence. They would have to find a job, move to a dormitory at their place of work, and begin attending school at night. Indeed, leaving the Children's Home made the orphans feel they were truly grown up. Depending on the situation, some children might be moved to orphanages specifically intended for the care of adolescents, or to provincial temples. In a few cases, however, compassion might be shown, and Akela's case was regarded as deserving compassion. After all, the Children's Home was a world of innocent women and children.

Looking after little children was not a hardship at all for Akela. Even Mowgli, who had already completed elementary school, was still a little child in his eyes. She was still the seven-year-old Mowgli who, with bobbed hair and mouth hanging open, her bottom touching the ground, her slip and panties soiled with mud, her kneecaps grimy, had been squatting in front of the entrance to her home, staring at the twelve-year-old Akela … she was still *that* little Mowgli.

Their bodies were rocking to the motion of the train. Instead of singing a lullaby to her, Akela began telling Mowgli the stories of the jungle that filled his head. At first she was leaning against the wall listening to his stories, her face half-hidden by the baseball cap, but within ten minutes she was sound asleep. Resting her head on Akela's shoulder, she looked cozy, her breathing regular.

Akela pulled a cotton sweater out of his bag and used it to cover the upper half of Mowgli's body. Although it was hot and stuffy inside the passenger car, the vestibule was a little chilly because of the cool outside air passing through.

Akela continued his story for some time, even after Mowgli had fallen asleep. He told of the night Shere Khan, the tiger, abducted Mowgli from the human village. He explained why Shere Khan had become a man-eating tiger and how the two parent wolves adopted Mowgli as one of their own children. He also told of Baloo, the bear who served as tutor to Mowgli, and of Bagheera, the black panther.

Akela continued to softly recite those stories for his own pleasure. Finally he closed his mouth and sighed.

This place is like the Cold Lairs ...

Akela was growing sleepy. He got up early every morning, and was always in bed by ten at night. Yet because he was so excited, his eyelids didn't feel heavy at all. The train stopped at a station about every ten minutes ... Kurihashi ... Koga ... and each time it stopped, the sound of announcements and departure bells would pierce through the drowsiness of his body. The train passed through stations with names he had never heard before. The four men in front of him, drunk on whiskey, apparently had no interest in sleeping quietly. They began playing cards and were speaking crudely at the top of their lungs. But he couldn't understand anything they were saying. Were they from the Yamagata region? To make matters worse, there were more passengers coming and going to the toilet than he had expected, and they all slammed the vestibule door violently, or kicked Akela's feet intentionally. Some creeps who had taken off their trousers to sleep even hurried to the toilet in their underwear, while little kids would come out with their butts exposed, showing no sense of shame as they had their mothers pull their underpants back up for them.

I can't sleep in the Cold Lairs, but Mowgli seems to be sleeping comfortably. I guess she's just an innocent child, so it's nothing to her.

Fed up, Akela closed his eyes. He wished he had plugs for his ears. The train stopped at yet another station. This time there was no announcement. Apparently small stations don't make announcements in the middle of the night.

Cold Lairs was the name given to the ruins of a city abandoned deep in the jungle and occupied by the grey monkeys. Once—Akela carefully searched his memory—it was a city of one hundred elephants and twenty thousand horses, the city of the King of Twenty Kings. For the longest time the White Cobra had continued all alone to guard the underground vault where the King's Treasure was hidden. Of course, the grey monkeys, who were called the *banderlog*, knew nothing about that treasure. With pretensions to being human, they claimed the ruined city as their own territory. Their claim gave them great joy, and they congratulated themselves for being as smart as humans. They would chatter and screech, boasting that no creatures in the jungle were as clever, or strong, or good as they. Still, the monkeys did not know the Law. They neither studied nor protected the essential teachings. They never kept their word. They were shameless liars. Creatures who kept the orthodoxy of the jungle would have absolutely nothing to do with those monkeys. They simply could not associate with creatures who were ignorant of the law of the jungle. It was a matter of pride. To survive in the jungle, there were instances when pride was more important than food.

I didn't mean to bring Mowgli to this Cold Lairs, but ...

Akela scowled, his eyes closed.

All people are selfish, they think only about their own good. That's because they don't know the Law. And because they don't know the Law, they can never live freely. To live freely isn't just doing as one pleases. Shoving people aside to grab a seat—that was proof these people didn't live freely. Only the person who secures a seat and then comes out to the vestibule to see if there's someone who might need it more could be said to be living freely. After all, there were old folks and children out here, right?

> *The law of the jungle is as old and as true as the sky*
> *The Law was like the Giant Creeper, because it dropped on every*
> *one's back and no one could escape.*

Had Baloo the bear taught those lessons to Mowgli? Baloo had also said the following:

> *The jungle is large and the Cub he is small.*

The rocking of the train gradually made Akela drowsy. Next to him a child sleeping in her mother's arms began to sniffle and cry. Was she thirsty? She was only about two or three years old, and her mother looked ill. Where were they going, and what were they going to do? Deserted by a man, unable to survive in Tokyo, was she about to abandon the child somewhere deep in the mountains in the Tōhoku region? Across from them an old man and a middle-school boy were crouching in the opposite corner. They were very suspicious-looking. Just the fact that they looked like simple hicks was suspicious. They might well be a pair of skillful pickpockets—a master criminal and his talented young apprentice—who moved from car to car just as passengers settled down to sleep, and stole purses and valuables with their clever tricks. And the female monkeys with their loud dresses were probably secretly plotting to deceive the honest men of the northeast in order to squeeze money from them. And those drunk monkeys playing cards were, without question, slave traders planning to kidnap children in the northeast and sell them.

The wind blowing in through the cracks in this Cold Lairs was much chillier than he expected for May. In between dream and reality, Akela began to worry. *If it's this cold now, how much colder will it be farther north? If Mowgli gets sick, that would be real trouble.* The warmth from Mowgli's body spread to Akela's right shoulder—little Mowgli, who did not yet know the feeling of wariness. Akela, who was bothered by the smell of the monkeys around him, put his right arm around Mowgli's small shoulders so that her body would not get cold.

The train gave a great lurch and stopped again. Several passengers came out of the car, opened the door, and stepped onto the platform. The rude monkeys didn't bother closing the door. The drunk monkeys followed them outside. Akela opened his eyes a crack to view the scene. Passengers were stretching or getting a drink of water from a spigot. A man, facing away from the train, was taking a piss. Akela could see the sign: *Utsunomiya.* This was a station that even Akela had heard of— and if he'd heard of it, it was probably a big station. Would the train stay here for a while? Akela wanted to go onto the platform to kill time. But he was reluctant to wake Mowgli, who had managed to fall asleep, and he stubbornly refused to act like the monkeys around him. So he continued to crouch there.

A cold late-night wind blew in unceremoniously through the open car door. Some passengers were stepping out onto the platform at the last minute, while others were getting back on the train. Akela again opened his eyes slightly, and when he glanced toward the platform, he was startled to find himself face-to-face with a man directly in front of him, peeking in on the vestibule. A wide strap was dangling from the man's shoulder, supporting a heavy-looking wooden box. Apparently the man was going around selling *bentō*, but since it was late at night he was refraining from shouting "*Bentō ... tea and bentō!*" Ignoring the vendor, Akela closed his eyes and recalled "Night-song in the Jungle."

> *Now Chil the Kite brings home the night*
> *That Mang the Bat sets free—*
> *The herds are shut in byre and hut,*
> *For loosed till dawn are we.*
> *This is the hour of pride and power,*
> *Talon and tush and claw.*
> *Oh, hear the call!—Good hunting all*
> *That keep the Jungle Law!*

However, this did not make Akela feel any happier. Usually, he could change his mood by recalling this song, but not this time. He let out a deep sigh.

> *Through the jungle very softly flits a shadow and a sigh—*
> *He is Fear, O Little Hunter, he is Fear!*
>
> *Comes a breathing hard behind thee—snuffle-snuffle through the nigh*
> *It is Fear, O Little Hunter, it is Fear!*
>
> *But thy throat is shut and dried, and thy heart against thy side*
> *Hammers: Fear, O Little Hunter—this is Fear!*

"The Song of the Little Hunter" echoed gloomily inside Akela's head, and as it did his throat went dry and his chest began to ache. He really couldn't fall asleep in this condition. His hips began to hurt. Quietly shifting Mowgli's head from his right shoulder to his lap, he repositioned his bag and lay down alongside Mowgli's body. As his body became a little more comfortable, he started to count in order to avoid idle thoughts. He couldn't concentrate if he just counted simple numbers, so he decided to count monkeys. There were an endless number just on this train alone. One monkey, two monkeys, three monkeys ...

The number of monkeys continued to increase in Cold Lairs—boastful monkeys imitating the humans who had abandoned the city, ignorant of order, driven to lose control by whatever urges move them in the present moment. Whenever they see something that belongs to someone else, they want to steal it. They forget their obligations; they have no patience. Indeed, they are actually proud of such things. Cold Lairs was overflowing with monkeys, and little by little they were moving closer to Akela and Mowgli. The smirks on their monkey faces. Their stench. The fleas and lice jumping off their monkey bodies. Monkeys in dresses and lipstick. Drunken monkeys with bright red bloodshot eyes. Boss monkeys in white coats, their purplish wrinkled faces aglow. Mother monkeys dragging around infants at their withered breasts. All clicking their yellow teeth like castanets. All determined to take aim at Akela and Mowgli.

Eventually, the monkeys become a single mass and begin to assault Akela and Mowgli. Before Akela can bare his fangs and fight back, Mowgli is quickly carried off. The monkeys hold Mowgli's body in their numberless arms and flee farther and farther upward. Just then the night train leaves its horizontal track and begins following a vertical track headed toward the sky. Akela is a wolf, so he cannot climb trees. He tries following the train, but he can't climb up the tracks either. Left behind, Akela can only curse his own inattentiveness. All he can do is sing a song of anger and lament—all he can do is howl.

Akela had fallen into a light sleep, and his sorrow was so great that he groaned. Why hadn't he taught Mowgli that even a momentary lapse of vigilance was not permitted in Cold Lairs. If the monkeys let go of her on a whim, Mowgli would fall headfirst and die. And the monkeys would in an instant kill the small, weak human child, the only sibling he had ever known in his life. Mowgli, who had put her trust in Akela, would end up dying a miserable death. Even before her life had really begun.

Akela groans, but the train continues to climb upward, and the monkeys are running and clambering up the cars one by one. However much he tries to focus his eyes on them, he cannot make out the figures of either the monkeys or Mowgli.

Come to think of it—Akela at last remembered in his dream—it was the role of Kaa, the large python, to rescue Mowgli when the *banderlog* snatched the boy. Snakes can climb trees, and the very mention of the name Kaa would send a chill up the monkeys' tails and paralyze them. They were weak against normal-sized snakes, and Kaa was huge, a full nine meters long. It takes two hundred years to grow nine meters. Which meant that Kaa also possessed two hundred years worth of wisdom. The appearance of Kaa at Cold Lairs cowed the monkeys, who waited with bated breath, and Mowgli was safely rescued. Then the python began his "Dance of the Hunger of Kaa" before the monkeys. Swaying his head back and forth, making great circles with his body, becoming a figure eight, a triangle, a square, hissing all the while, he slowly but relentlessly coiled himself up. The monkeys, as if under a magic spell, came walking one by one into Kaa's enormous open mouth, and ended up inside the python's stomach.

45

As the figures of the monkeys disappeared in Akela's dream, Kaa's long body slowly stretched out heavily to the side and dissolved in the shadows of the train running along the tracks. Then the little human Mowgli, wearing her baggy clothes, came running up to Akela. She was laughing. She clung to the deep coat of fur on Akela's neck and whispered, half-sobbing, "Forgive me. I didn't mean to make you worry. Next time I'll be careful around monkeys."

If only I could do the things Kaa can do.

Akela's body puffed out with a sense of relief, but he also felt envious of Kaa's powers. The only way to defeat all the various kinds of monkeys—male and female, big ones and little ones—was to become Kaa. After all, monkeys were everywhere in this world. It seemed better to give up being Akela and become Kaa instead.

Akela began to regret all over again that he had chosen to become Akela. Why had he selected that name? In *The Jungle Book*, Akela eventually fails during a hunt and has to cede his position as leader of the pack; and when he grows old, he meets the fate that all must suffer. Kaa, on the other hand, is immune to that fate and goes on living for hundreds of years. The problem for Akela was that he was actually afraid of snakes. One time a striped snake cut across the garden of the Children's Home—it probably came from a gutter that flowed at the back of the garden. One of the little kids found snake eggs in a clump of grass. Akela didn't scream or anything—he was a boy, after all—but he felt paralyzed, unable to move, just like those monkeys in the jungle when they saw Kaa. He didn't mind being in the company of a snake in a story, but choosing to be a snake felt creepy, even if it meant being a two-hundred-year–old python.

Besides, Akela continued thinking in his sleep, it wouldn't be right to be a member of a species completely different from Mowgli. After all, the two of them were "family." If he didn't really care so much about family, then it might have been more appropriate for him, given his personality, to be Baloo the bear. Indeed, at the beginning, Akela had considered it. Old Baloo—good-natured and fond of naps, living on nothing but honey. Tender-hearted and quick to shed tears. Sincere, honest Baloo, who cherished the human child Mowgli more than anyone else and worked faithfully as a tutor to teach him the law of the jungle. Baloo, with his large body, was an idler who loved flowers; and in reality, Akela was just like him—though physically smaller, of course. Baloo reminded Akela of the nurses at the Children's Home, and so in the end he rejected the idea of taking the bear's name. After all, the qualities that made Akela Baloo-esque weren't much for a seventeen-year-old adolescent to brag about. He wondered if, at some point, Mowgli might not discover his inner Baloo? And when she did, wouldn't she laugh and make fun of him, calling him a blockhead bear?

The night train continued north through the darkness, making a station stop about every ten minutes. From time to time the cold air would wake him from his slumber. He would let out a deep breath through his nose, then fall back to sleep.

As soon as he confirmed that Mowgli was asleep, feeling her rhythmic breathing, his anxiety would gently melt and flow away. Sleeping fitfully like that, thoughts continued to race through his mind until morning. Thoughts about Cold Lairs. About the relative merits of Akela and Kaa and Baloo. About the meaning of "The Song of the Little Hunter." About what he ought to teach Mowgli.

A loud racket awakened him. A station announcement … *Kōriyama, Kōriyama*! … the voices of vendors selling *bentō* … "*Bentō! Tea and bentō!*" The doors on the cars were open, and passengers were getting off one after another. Some people were carrying large suitcases. Perhaps they had reached their destination. Dawn was breaking in the sky visible beyond the roof of the platform, and the electric lights under that roof seemed to grow dimmer as morning approached. Akela, his head now clear, raised his upper body in a panic and looked around for Mowgli, who should have been asleep beside him. She was awake already and sitting there, small, hugging her knees, staring eagerly at the platform. Noticing that Akela was stirring, Mowgli spoke to him, her mouth in an embarrassed-looking pout.

"Is it okay if I go out? I want to get a drink of water."

Rubbing his eyes, Akela nodded and stood up. At some point the young woman in the dress, the woman with the child, and the old man and the middle-school student had all disappeared. Had they gotten off the train, or had they gone inside the coach to get away from the cold? After letting Mowgli off ahead of him, Akela glanced inside the car. Although it was growing light outside, most of the passengers were still in a deep sleep. Filthy hands and feet sprawled out from the seats. Ugly, sallow faces, mouths agape, stuck out into the aisle, some hanging nearly upside down. Passengers were crammed together on top of one another in the aisle. Trash was scattered everywhere, and all types of jackets and trousers dangled from the mesh luggage racks. Shocked by the mess inside the car, Akela clicked his tongue in disgust. Just then he noticed the woman with the child who had been on the vestibule earlier shrewdly sleeping on one of the seats. The old man was sitting a little farther away, and his travel companion, the middle-school student, was asleep, crouching down in the aisle next to him.

Akela hopped onto the platform and looked around for Mowgli. She was standing in line waiting for the water fountain. She was so much the image of a street urchin that he wanted to laugh in spite of himself. She was dressed neatly, the complexion of her face was white, and she was wearing high-quality leather shoes. None of those things exactly matched the image of a homeless child, but even a real street urchin might have worn leather shoes she had found somewhere, and she might well properly wash her face. The little street urchin Mowgli was hugging herself, her body drawn in. She looked cold standing there, staring blankly across the other tracks, where no trains were waiting.

"Listen, if we move inside the car, we just might be able to find a seat. I'd given

47

up on getting one, but obviously we'd be better off if we could sit down."

Mowgli's face looked pale. She took a little breath and whispered, "But I'm okay where we are. The inside of the car is packed. I'd hate it if people around me thought I was strange."

"Yeah, you may be right …" Akela was also whispering. "But if you're worried about that, you need to stop talking like a girl. You're dressed like a boy, so use the right pronoun for yourself, for goodness sake. Boys say '*boku*,' not '*watashi*.' And try talking in a deeper voice."

"Oh, that's right," Mowgli answered meekly. She smiled at Akela for the first time that morning. And when she did, he felt more at ease and a smile broke over his face, which until then had been stiff from sleep.

"I'm Akela and you're Mowgli," he continued. "Remember?"

"Yeah, I remember." Mowgli nodded childishly, then looked across the platform. "Wow, this is Kōriyama. We've sure come a long way."

"We haven't come all that far," Akela replied, a little flustered. "We haven't even reached Fukushima yet. When I bought the tickets, they told me we'd get to Fukushima at around six in the morning."

"Hmm." Mowgli looked up at the station clock and then peeked at her wristwatch. "You're right. It's still only 4:30. Fukushima's in Fukushima Prefecture. That's the southernmost part of the Tōhoku region, right?"

Mowgli seemed to be trying to call up the geography of Japan she had studied in school.

"Yeah, that's right," Akela said. "Are you hungry, Mowgli? You want to eat a *bentō*?"

Mowgli's expression suddenly changed. "You'll buy a *bentō* for me? I'm starving, which is strange. I mean, I really ate a lot last night."

"To tell the truth, I'm really hungry myself. Okay, then, let's forget about getting water. We'll buy some tea as well, so let's go back to the train."

Akela urged Mowgli to go back while he hurried to find a vendor.

"But I don't care. Oops, that's not the right pronoun." Mowgli lowered the pitch of her voice and said, "*I* don't care about getting a drink, but *I* want to wash my face. And *I* want to rinse my mouth. It feels really gross like this."

"Really? … So you like things clean and tidy?" Akela had a puzzled look on his face. He left Mowgli there and, tucking his own shirt into his trousers, went over to a vendor.

The departure bell rang. Akela and Mowgli hurried back to the train. Sitting back down in the same spots in the vestibule, Akela handed tea and a *bentō* box to Mowgli.

"No one else is eating right now," Mowgli muttered. "Is it okay?" She glanced into the car through the open door. Akela, who already had the lid off his box and his disposable chopsticks in his hand, answered offhandedly.

"It's okay, don't pay any attention to what others think. They're selling them, aren't they? There must be some people who eat at this hour."

Just then the train let out a shrill whistle and started to move.

"Okay then I—no, no, *I*—You know, it's easier for me to say '*oira*' than '*boku*.' It's okay to use '*oira*,' isn't it? It sounds more vulgar ... and masculine too. Okay then, this is *my* first time eating a station *bentō*. Mother is so stingy that she always makes her own rice balls when we travel."

"To be honest, this is the first time for me as well. I've always wanted to get one."

They looked at each other and laughed. Then they silently began eating their boxed meals while the food was still warm. The boxes contained a small piece of salted salmon, some Japanese-style omelet, a red wiener sausage, and slices of pickled *daikon* radish. The two of them ate and ate with gusto, savoring every bite. They had never had tea from a little brown earthenware teapot, and so they couldn't help laughing.

"Thank you for the meal. It sure didn't take long to finish it. But now that we've eaten, we'll probably be hungry again at nine or ten o'clock."

Akela answered magnanimously, "In that case, we'll just have to get another *bentō* then. I don't care how many times a day we eat."

"Really? Do you mean it?"

Akela squinted and nodded, grandly striking the pose of a rich man.

"But in that case, what if I end up eating and eating and eating. Is that okay?"

"You bet it is! You may still be a child, Mowgli, but you sure eat a lot."

Akela's answer made her happy.

"Yes, I've got an enormous appetite. When my mother first made curry over rice for me it tasted so good I asked for seconds *twelve* times. Have you ever eaten curry over rice?"

Akela smiled. "I've eaten it until I couldn't stand to eat anymore. But you've got to be exaggerating when you say you had seconds twelve times. The best I've ever done is three times."

"It's the truth. I counted. I remember being really surprised at myself. It was when I was in third grade."

Mowgli glared at Akela. The whites of her eyes were bloodshot from lack of sleep.

"You must have dreamed it, right?"

"It's the truth! Why don't you believe me?"

Akela, at a loss, scratched his head. Flakes of white dandruff drifted down.

"Well, you can say 'believe me' all you like, but it's a little hard to believe."

Mowgli pulled her knees up. Wrapping her arms around her knees, she rested her chin on top of them and muttered, "It's the truth ... it really is!"

The train stopped frequently at small stations, and the slowly turning wheels continued to rumble on and on. Morning light streamed into the car, and the passengers began to stir noisily. A line of people going to the toilet formed, and people getting off and on the train gathered in the vestibule with their bags slung over their shoulders. Each time they passed, Akela and Mowgli had to pull their legs in to avoid being kicked. By then the four drunken monkeys were curled up on top of one another, sound asleep. Their unpleasant snoring was deafening. One of them was drooling. Because the four monkeys were sprawled out as they slept, Akela and Mowgli felt cramped for space. A little old woman was sitting properly on some newspaper in the corner opposite them holding a bundle wrapped in a *furoshiki* cloth and smoking a cigarette. She seemed accustomed to traveling. From inside the car sleepy children, who were just waking up, could be heard crying. Somebody remarked that mountains had come into view, while another voice could be heard exclaiming how beautiful they looked in the morning sun.

Hearing them, Akela stood up and looked outside. He could make out what looked like a line of mountains, but it wasn't a tall, especially impressive range, and it was obscured by the blue-black darkness of the sky. He could, however, clearly make out a large river, shining white, flowing alongside the tracks. Akela moved over to the car door on the other side, and when he looked out he gasped instinctively. The fresh light of a new dawn was turning gold, creating a divide in the light-blue sky and revealing the shapes of mountains. Light and shade were clearly separated, like beautifully crafted origami paper. A little bit of snow remained at the summits, and the green color of the trees was not yet distinguishable in the blinding morning light. He had never seen a proper mountain until that moment. Akela's body trembled. He had trouble catching his breath, and he felt like he was going to cry. These mountains were completely different from the ones he had seen in movies.

Enraptured for several moments by the mountains, which were a glittering gold color, it occurred to him that he ought to show them to Mowgli, so he turned toward her. She still had her face pressed against her knees, looking as if she were fast asleep. Glancing down at his feet at the old woman, who was casually puffing on her cigarette, he moved over to Mowgli and poked her shoulder.

"Hey, you can see the mountains from here. Come and take a look."

Mowgli lifted her face. Apparently she hadn't been asleep after all. The bulge in her forehead, where it had been resting on her knees, was red. She was indifferent to Akela's excitement, and muttered as if talking to herself.

"I'm—no, no," she said, deepening her voice. "*I'm* going back to Tokyo right away."

Akela had no immediate response. He just sat down beside Mowgli. She was staring at her knees as she continued to speak.

"If I go back right now, I can make it to school around noon. I'll be tardy, but at least it won't count as an absence.

"So you're going home, just like that?"

Mowgli nodded expressionlessly.

"If I don't go to school, everyone will think it's strange. It's not right to be the only one playing when everyone else is studying."

Mowgli's nose and ears were not yet fully developed. They were small and soft and supple. Akela wanted to pull one of her ears. Instead he gave such a powerful tug on his own right earlobe he hurt himself. Akela was proud of his plump, moderately generous ears.

"That's so stupid," he said.

Mowgli turned toward him, her own underdeveloped nose turning red.

"I'm not stupid!" she countered. "Compared to Ton-chan, I could do anything. But mother would get really mad at me about that, and say it was only natural that I wasn't as stupid as Ton-chan. And even though he's dead, she still gets angry and says I'm stupid and have to study harder."

The area around Mowgli's eyes flushed crimson, and it looked like tears were welling up. Akela kept pulling on his earlobe.

"I take it 'Ton-chan' was your older brother? Was his head … uh, did it not work right, or something?"

A small teardrop ran down the side of Mowgli's nose. She nodded.

"I see … You know, we haven't gone anywhere, and yet you want to turn around and go back. Wouldn't that be a complete waste? Don't forget, I'm the one who bought your ticket. Do you really like school all that much?"

Rubbing her eyes violently with both hands, Mowgli shook her head sideways. When she did, her hair lightly tapped the downy fuzz glowing on her cheeks.

"*We be of one blood, ye and I.* Those are the Master Words of the Jungle. They're good words, right? Don't you think we started this journey so that we could truly say those words together? That's way more important than going to school. Isn't it?"

Uncertain, Akela put his arm around Mowgli's shoulder. He could feel her sharp bones. He grew worried, wondering how much of their conversation the old woman sitting on the opposite side of the vestibule had heard. He looked over at her. She looked half-asleep, a bright yellow nylon neckerchief wrapped around her collar. Finishing her cigarette, she pulled out a dried rice cake and started nibbling on it.

"If we go far enough north," Akela whispered into Mowgli's ear, "the cherry trees will probably be blooming. They say the cherry trees in the north have a deeper color, and when they all bloom together they're so wonderful they make your head swim. The rape blossoms will be out, and even the *genge* will be in purple flower along the rice fields. And when they bloom, there'll be swarms of butterflies, and marvelous birds we've never seen before will be singing in the sky. There'll be cattle and horses, and mountain goats, and rabbits and foxes, and bears. Everything. We might see an elephant. I'll bet there's even a black panther."

Mowgli giggled as though she were being tickled.

"There are no elephants or black panthers in Japan!"

"I don't know about that. I wonder. In ancient times there were Naumann elephants."

"But they're extinct. And there are *no* black panthers. I've never heard any such stories about them."

"That may be, but how can you be so sure there's not a single elephant or black panther in all of Japan? Do you have any proof? Oh, I just remembered … the mountains! You can see the mountains from the window on that side. Look, stand up! From now on we'll be able to see a lot of tremendous mountains. I thought it was really amazing."

Akela stood up and, lightly taking Mowgli's arm, tried to pull her up too. Mowgli, who was already in better spirits, quickly got up on her own and hurried over to the door on the opposite side of the vestibule.

During the short time they had been talking, the shape of the mountains visible from the window had changed. One peak was more or less right in front of them now; looming large, it seemed radiant. The light was white and bright. The sky had also turned white. The mountain caught the morning sun and glowed with such majesty that it looked like a true living god staring down at Akela and Mowgli.

"Even if this is all we see, I think we did the right thing leaving Tokyo. It may be disrespectful to my old man to say this, but I'm glad I survived." Akela seemed spellbound as he spoke to Mowgli.

"There're no mountains like that one in Tokyo. What's it called? Is it famous?" she asked.

"I don't know, but it must be famous. The only mountain I know of is Fuji."

Suddenly a low but distinct voice could be heard rising up from below.

"It's Mount Adatara!"

Startled, they stepped back from the door and looked down. The old woman holding the dried rice cake in her hand was angrily glaring up at them.

"You really are ignorant, aren't you!"

"Ohh, you mean that's … oh, I see," Akela answered as affably as possible. Pushing Mowgli in the back, they quickly returned to their spots in the vestibule.

"Let's move inside the car," he whispered to Mowgli.

They picked up their bags, and he opened the door into the car. Mowgli went in first. He followed, closing the door behind him.

"What gives with that old lady?" he burst out laughing.

Mowgli broke down laughing behind the door. "*It's Mount Adatara!* I'll bet that mountain is the old lady's pride and joy. She was irritated that we didn't know its name."

"How the hell would I know anything about Mount Adatara?"

"Shhh! She'll hear you!" Mowgli was still laughing.

The train stopped again. Though it was not yet six o'clock, the sky was brightening and people began moving around the interior of the car just as if it were midday. At each stop the number of passengers getting off and on grew larger. Some of the women who boarded the train were dressed in boots and loose work trousers and were carrying large baskets on their backs. Several men were carrying two or three tin cases, which were stacked up on their backs as well. When the tin cases passed by them, Akela and Mowgli caught a whiff of the odor of fish, but neither had the faintest idea where the men were taking their catch. They saw that some of the seats were being vacated, and, knowing that other people would quickly claim them, wanted to find spaces for themselves before they missed their chance.

"Let's move further in," Akela suggested. "It looks like we can sit here. After all, we paid the same price for our tickets as everyone else, so let's sit down when we can."

He proceeded down the aisle. The women and men "peddlers" who had just boarded the train were now seated next to their bundles in the aisle. Some passengers were still asleep, apparently without a care. The old man and the middle-school student who had been together in the vestibule were fast asleep in their seats, and the woman with the child was curled up, sleeping with the child on top of her.

Akela stopped midway down the car.

"I'll keep an eye out, Mowgli, so you sit here and sleep. We'll get to Fukushima soon, right? And when we do, a lot of passengers will probably get off there."

Mowgli looked at her wristwatch. "It won't be six o'clock for another forty minutes. Of course, we got up awfully early. Now that you mention it, I ... *I* am a little sleepy."

"So sleep here. Like I said, if a seat opens up, I'll let you know."

Akela was eagerly glancing over an arts magazine that a young girl in the next seat had spread open to read. Mowgli sat down and quietly settled in, resting her head against Akela's leg. On the floor next to Akela's leg was a bundle someone had tossed there. It was wrapped in newspapers and bound with string. There were brown spots all over the newspaper. Right in front of Mowgli was a basket that could be strapped on a person's back and used to carry a load of vegetables. To her right, a bald, middle-aged man was scrunched up, asleep.

Akela had guessed right. When they arrived at Fukushima, he got Mowgli up and, prodding her, had her plop down on an empty seat. Immediately Akela sat down next to her.

"Oh, this seat is so comfortable," he said.

Mowgli, still half-asleep, looked out the window. Her eyes fell on the word *Fukushima*. She looked at her watch. Not yet six. With a sudden realization, she took off the watch and, concerned that the people around her might hear, whispered to him, "I think you should keep this for me, Akela. That'd be best."

"Doesn't matter to me either way, but I'll keep it for you."

Akela knit his eyebrows and stared at the little wristwatch with its red leather strap. It was obviously made for a young girl. He dropped it into his shirt pocket and whispered in Mowgli's ear, "Most of those peddlers got off here. I figured they'd be going much farther."

"Really?"

Mowgli rubbed her eyes, placed her hand over her mouth and gave a great yawn. Her eyes teared up, so she rubbed them again. Outside her window people were bustling about, coming and going. The echo of the station announcements, the voices of the *bentō* vendors and the newspaper and magazine sellers all mingled together. Akela bent over and, using an empty *bentō* box, fussily gathered up the newsprint, candy wrappers, mandarin orange peels, and chestnut hulls scattered around his feet. He then pushed them in under his seat. There was no way to block the cloudy, fishy-smelling liquid flowing in a thread down the aisle.

"Monkeys are such a nuisance," he muttered.

"Monkeys?" Mowgli muttered in reply, and glanced toward the floor at her feet.

"Be clean, for the strength of the hunter is known by the gloss of his hide." Akela was still muttering.

"What's that you're saying?"

"Filthy monkeys who leave a mess behind aren't qualified to be hunters. The world is full of monkeys, so you need to be on guard, Mowgli."

She chuckled. "Over there and over here, they're *alllll* monkeys … but *we're* not monkeys."

"You're right. Like they say, *Good hunting all, that keep the Law!*"

At that moment the train gave a tremendous lurch, and they could hear what sounded like heavy things colliding. They looked at each other, then looked around. No one seemed to have paid any attention to the noise. Akela shrugged his shoulders. "Now that we've managed to get seats," he whispered, "is it all right with you if we ride a little bit farther? Even if we hurry and get off, there won't be any place open to eat at this hour."

Mowgli nodded and turned back toward the window. The sign said that the next station after Fukushima was Sasakino. She could see people on the platform eating *soba* noodles. She also heard voices hawking something they were calling *radium manjū*. Mowgli assumed they must be those steamed buns filled with red-bean jam that vendors sold at hot springs. Of course, she didn't really know what kind of *manjū* they were, and she figured it wouldn't help to ask Akela, since he probably wouldn't know either. So she stopped listening to the voices. A station attendant in his red cap went running busily past them. An old man with a cloth knapsack on his back was bowing his head over and over to a middle-aged woman, who was holding a child by the hand. The red-cheeked child was licking the head of a Kewpie doll. The paint on the doll was flaking off. *Monkeys. All monkeys.* The moment that thought occurred to her, everyone really did start to look like monkeys. Mowgli couldn't help but laugh again.

The departure bell gave a piercing clang. The people on the platform began to move as one.

Good hunting all, that keep the Law!

Mowgli tried silently mouthing those words. She turned back toward Akela. He was already dozing, his arms crossed. She was going to ask him if "the Law" meant "the law of the jungle," but she let it pass.

The steam whistle gave a shrill blast, and the train started moving. The voices of women standing and talking in the aisle grated on her ears. A young woman wearing loose work trousers and carrying a baby on her back was laughing on and on with two slightly older women. They were evidently gossiping maliciously about someone they knew. Still, it was difficult to make out what they were saying. A man wearing a thick winter-style coat and a middle-aged woman wearing a plain kimono were sitting in front of Mowgli and Akela. The man was holding a leather bag on his lap, intently inspecting what looked like an accounts ledger. He may have been a schoolteacher. Mowgli felt a little uneasy. The woman began knitting some navy blue yarn, as if she begrudged wasting a moment of time. She was apparently making a sweater. Her ball of yarn was hidden inside a handbag on her lap, and from time to time she would stick her hand inside and pull on the yarn to unwind it. Mowgli began to recall her own mother. Upset by that thought, she closed her eyes. She pulled her baseball cap down to cover her face, leaned her head against the window, and tried to go to sleep.

In a few minutes a line of elephants slowly moved across the inside of Mowgli's head. A black panther ran along beside them. And then she heard the sound of Akela's voice—*Many are the laws of the jungle. Good hunting all, that keep the Law!*—Mowgli could hear her own voice murmuring, like an insect, words she had just learned at school.—*Give us this day our daily bread. And forgive us our trespasses.*—Vividly colored birds fluttered through the sky, crying noisily. A great python was lying among the trees.—*Be clean, for the strength of the hunter is known by the gloss of his hide.*—The fur of the monkeys was poor and shabby. A grey wolf came up close to Mowgli. Blue and yellow and red and green butterflies were flitting around her. Mowgli stretched out her arm to touch the fur of the grey wolf with her fingertips. It felt nice and soft.—*Deliver us from evil.*—Mowgli touched her own body, to make sure of her own fur. The fur on her neck, on her throat, and her arms and legs. The sheen and the length weren't fully developed yet. She supposed that when she became an adult, she'd have a full coat of fur then.

The whistle blared. The train stopped, but soon started moving again. Mowgli, her eyes still closed, saw off the line of elephants. All of them flashed their white tusks and swung their long noses around. Their trumpeting cries overlapped the sound of the whistle, which shrilly beat against her ears. A peacock spreading its tail feathers strutted beside the elephants. A pack of wolves came running up and, raising their faces to the sky, began to howl. Their well-groomed fur was tinted a shining silver. A small naked boy was crouching amid the wolf pack. The instant Mowgli noticed him, the pack disappeared, the peacock and elephants disappeared, and the shadow of a man wrapped in a blanket full of holes came drifting up. The shadow went over to the naked boy. Laughing, the boy stood up and clasped the man's hand. The man, whose long hair was tangled like straw, was the boy's father. They may have resembled one another, but it was impossible to tell since the man's face was obscured by his hair. The father and child walked off without a word. Their surroundings looked like the grounds of a shrine at twilight with small pink lamps in a row. Mowgli's mother was calling her children.—*Yukiko! Ton-chan! Deliver us from evil.*—Before she knew it, the figures of the father and son had completely disappeared. She continued to hear her mother's voice.—*We be of one blood.*—Ton-chan, still a small child, appeared at the top of a cherry tree, waving his hand to his mother. But she didn't notice him. The place where mother was walking was now a garden with red canna and salvia flowers in full bloom. Mother sat down on a veranda and, sighing, began to knit. From three knitting needles she produced, little by little, a sweater for Ton-chan. Of green wool. The ball of yarn rolled and fell into the garden. Still, the mother didn't notice. A python was crawling among the red flowers in the garden, and gray wolves were silently circling around. Still, her mother didn't notice. Ton-chan got tired of waving and fell from the cherry tree, hitting the ground and splitting his head in two. Still, her mother didn't notice.—*Yukiko, I'm going to wind a ball of yarn, so give me a hand.*—Her mother picked up a bundle of yarn that had just been re-dyed a dark red, and called to Mowgli.—*Many are the laws of the jungle. Good hunting all, that keep the Law! Angels we have heard on high. Gloria in excelsis Deo!*—The wolves howled in the garden. The python's eyes glittered.—*We be of one blood. Tantum ergo Sacramentum*—

"Tickets, please."

A voice woke Mowgli. Next to her, Akela was handing the two tickets he had pulled out of his breast pocket to the conductor. It was dark outside, and all she could see was her own face in the window. She began to think it was still night, then realized that the train was passing through a tunnel. The train was wrapped in smoke and the smell of soot seeped into the car.

She heard Akela's voice.

"You see, we planned to get off in Fukushima, but my little brother was tired, and he didn't want to get off, so we decided to go straight on to Yamagata. Our grandma is waiting there. Grandma broke her leg. Our mom's busy with work … Ohh, a switchback. Sure, I know. I've been to Yamagata lots of times…. Okay, I'll tell my brother. When the train goes over the pass, we'll switch to an electric engine…. Yes, thank you. My little brother's crazy about trains. He's always saying

56

how he wants to become an engineer."

After the conductor moved on to the next seat, Mowgli glanced at Akela's face and quickly stuck her tongue out at him. Conscious of the people around them, Akela paid no attention to her and began to speak with an earnest look on his face. The train emerged from the tunnel, but almost immediately entered a second.

"I see you're up. I bought tickets to Yamagata, so you don't have to worry. Did you understand our conversation just now? The train has to make steep climbs in this region. Earlier they attached three steam engines to the train to make the climb, but now they've attached an electric engine especially for this mountain, and we're climbing by way of switchbacks. That's what the conductor told me. A switchback is when a train zigzags little by little back and forth to get over a mountain. Understand?"

Now that she was the little brother in elementary school, Mowgli intentionally answered like a child.

"*I* think *I* get it. Is it like the little engine that could? Climbing the mountain with all his might, saying *I think I can, I think I can, I think I can.*"

"Here comes another tunnel. We're hitting a lot of them all of a sudden."

"Well, we're in the mountains, after all."

Mowgli muttered as she yawned. Akela also gave a great yawn and roughly wiped his moist eyes with his left hand.

They heard a woman's voice above their heads.

"Your mama's from Yamagata?"

They looked around, and there was the woman carrying a baby on her back, laughing at them, flashing a gold tooth.

Akela glanced over at Mowgli before answering cautiously.

"No ... Our mother and ... well, our own family's from Tokyo. Grandma was in Tokyo a long time too, but some things came up, and now she's living with our uncle in Yamagata."

"Well, I'll be. It's an awful long way. Isn't it hard on you?"

Wary of continuing the conversation, Akela intentionally made a show of yawning. Imitating him, Mowgli also yawned, but in a more reserved manner. The train entered yet another tunnel.

"Yeah, I'm so sleepy, I can barely keep my eyes open...."

As if to drive the point home, Akela yawned again, adjusted the position of his body, then rubbed and closed his eyes. Mowgli leaned her head on his shoulder and quickly tried to go to sleep. The women in the aisle gave up trying to pass the time with these kids, and started talking among themselves again, only much faster, which made it difficult to follow what they were saying. Apparently they worked at a nearby hot springs inn, for they were chatting about customers from Tokyo, remarking on how people from the capital didn't drink all that much liquor, and how so many of them were gloomy and reserved. Hearing them talk like that, Akela and

Mowgli felt relieved, and sleep came over them for real. Because they felt drowsy, they were able to fall asleep as soon as they closed their eyes.

Monkeys cause trouble because *they are curious*. Akela was in the midst of another dream. He clicked his tongue and twisted up his face. Mowgli's hair was tickling his neck. Monkeys can never tell when they're bothering others. It's because they're simple … or insensitive. Monkeys are everywhere, but those that live further out in the provinces exhibit the worst characteristics. They like to pry into your business, and before you know it they start harboring suspicions about you for no reason at all and eventually go running off to tell the cops.—*Those kids are acting real funny. They don't look a bit like brothers. On top of that, the younger one's a girl!*—How can we slip out of Cold Lairs? "The Song of the Little Hunter" was again ringing in his head.—*Very softly down the glade runs a waiting, watching shade and the whisper spreads and widens far and near … He is Fear, O Little Hunter, he is Fear!*

Akela's thoughts moved back to the familiar world of the graveyard. During that period of his life he had never felt fear. Had he been too young to feel it? The graveyard … a place where the bones of dead people were gathered. People even killed themselves there. People like Mowgli's father. Some loitered there, experiencing death in life. Akela and his father belonged to that group. Still, "fear" had never passed through the place, and he had never noticed a fretful murmur or whispering voices. What he heard was the murmuring of the trees, the cries of birds, the sounds of babies and dogs. The Law had been alive there. That's probably why the shadow of "fear" never drew near. People who were fated to die, died. Those fated to live, lived. It was a simple and quiet world. If his father hadn't collapsed before him, Akela would probably have collapsed and died. But because Akela survived, he could never go back there again. Akela's blanket, so full of holes, had been thrown away. In its place the orphanage gave him a blanket, army surplus from the Occupation forces. The smell of his new blanket was unpleasant to him, and when they wrapped him in it, his stomach began to hurt and he groaned. Still, he couldn't explain to the children around him why he felt that way. If he had said anything, they would have taken his valuable blanket away for sure.

The faces of those children floated up before him. Kids he got along with and those he didn't, no matter how hard he tried. They were all being raised together, so maybe they were a kind of family. *A family.* No matter what he did, he couldn't help thinking about his own real family. Was that because his mind was deficient somehow?

There was Law at the Children's Home as well. But it was different from the Law at the graveyard. Up at six, breakfast at seven, putting away the bedding when you got up, taking turns serving meals, helping with the cleaning, exercising to the radio … You couldn't stop anywhere on your own on the way to and from school. Books belonged to everyone, so you couldn't secretly stash them away. Everyone had to eat their meals without saying what they liked or disliked. They were all told to wash their bottoms and behind their ears really well.... "It doesn't matter where you're raised, there's always some rule you have to follow when there's an adult around," a classmate who knew a real family told him once. And it must have been true. After all, if being with her mother was really so much fun, then surely Mowgli wouldn't have followed Akela so eagerly.

So why did you follow me?

Akela wanted to ask Mowgli, but, of course, he couldn't.

Even after moving from the vestibule into the car, even after leaning against Mowgli, Cold Lairs didn't warm up one bit. The Children's Home never warmed up either. Why was that? Akela was still asleep. The familiar faces of three of the five nurses at his orphanage appeared before him—faces that were becoming noticeably wrinkled. Akela hadn't been especially dissatisfied living there, and he had full trust in the old couple who ran the place—he called them "Mom" and "Pop." Evidently they had lost their own children in an air raid, and their decision to operate the orphanage was so conscientious that they were even interviewed about it by a newspaper reporter. When Akela was still very young, he had slept in the bed of his "Mom." Even though his body was weak, Akela was in the habit of getting up in the middle of the night and trying to go outside. When he was older, he helped out with the accounts, and so Akela understood very well the struggles of operating such a home. "Pop" and "Mom" and the nurses spent their days in poverty and fatigue in order to look after little children, and they experienced pure, genuine joy, worry, and sorrow. In spite of all their love, why was it then that the orphanage never became a Warm Lairs?

Akela recalled the house where Mowgli was raised, which he had visited that one time five years ago. A small, nondescript house down an alley, with cracks in the glass of the door at the entranceway, children who looked slightly dirty, and a mother who was skin and bones, who never smiled, who had deep furrows between her eyebrows and a face that had never known a single happy thought. Akela's "Mom" seemed to be a far gentler mother. And then there was Akela's father in the graveyard. Of course, Akela had no memory of his father ever smiling. His father, who was already only half-lingering in the world, never once tried talking directly to the four-year-old Akela. And yet he did not forget Akela. Whenever he caught a bird, he always, without fail, fed his son.

Mowgli's mother and Akela's father. Their two real parents had not been kind in the least. Always putting their children second, lamenting their loneliness, cursing something or the other, hating the monkeys around them.

I see now. In other words, Cold Lairs did not hate the monkeys, and so it always remained the same ... Cold Lairs.

Akela exhaled deeply through his nose. When he did, his mood changed completely, and he began pleasantly to draw an image in his mind based on the words "our own family," which he had used so casually when questioned by the local woman a few minutes ago. Naturally the house where his family lived in Tokyo was Mowgli's house. A dreary place, but it was a convenient size, and it had a garden. There was even a dog. Originally the grandmother lived with them, but now she lives in Yamagata. There's an uncle in Yamagata too. Was he the older brother of Mowgli's mother? What does he do? Mowgli's mother was a schoolteacher, so maybe they should make the uncle a schoolteacher as well. A history teacher, or a science teacher. Sometimes he comes to stay at the house in Tokyo. Bringing lots of souvenirs from Yamagata. But what kind of souvenirs do they have in Yamagata anyway? He couldn't think of any. When the uncle comes to the house in Tokyo, he sleeps in the tatami room on the second floor. There's a staircase next to the dark entryway. He had definitely spotted those stairs five years ago. If you go straight in through the hall that leads from the entrance, you come to the room where the mother and children sleep. At least that's the likely layout, since that kind of house is a standard design. The mother sleeps in the middle, with Mowgli and Akela to her left and right. But now that Akela was grown up, perhaps it would be strange for him to sleep in the same room with Mowgli's mother. It would be more appropriate for the seventeen-year-old Akela to sleep in the second-floor room with his uncle. Akela would thus go up the stairs. At the landing is a small window. Looking down from there, he can see a muddy stream. In the evening the stream seems to shine white. A hall continues off to his right. There are four doors. Pictures drawn by little children are hanging on the wall. Pale blue curtains on the hall windows. Faded and bleak, but clean curtains …

Akela had returned to the second floor of the Children's Home where he used to live. He found his own room and went in. Akela occupied one of the four bunk beds there. He threw himself onto the bottom bunk. He breathed in the nostalgic smell. A smell different from the graveyard, but one that resembled it in certain ways.

The scent of the graveyard. The scent of the stone markers. The scent of withered leaves. Akela conjured up memories of the graveyard in his dozing dream. Trees murmuring above his head, stone markers lined up in rows. Dead leaves piling up, the wind blowing. Birds crying, stray dogs groaning and running past. His father, wrapped in a blanket, crouching in a corner of the graveyard, waiting for the four-year-old Akela. The father is fast asleep, paying no heed to his son. The blanket is full of holes, a thin, worn blanket that roughly scratches his skin.

The four-year-old Akela laughs at the call of the birds, is enchanted by the smell of the stones. His laughter rings out as he scatters the dead leaves and savors to his heart's content a wide, cold graveyard possessing not one single thing that would bring comfort to a small human child.

4. Outsiders

Akela woke up moaning. Someone was tapping on his shoulder and whispering in his ear.

"It's Yamagata. You're getting off here, aren't you?"

The man sitting across from him and clutching a leather satchel was peering into Akela's face. After making sure Akela's eyes were open, the man hurried off the train. White letters spelling "Yamagata" were visible on a pillar on the platform. Akela caught an announcement—something about transfers. In his muddled state, he wondered what business he had in a place like Yamagata, but then remembered his story about "Grandma." Having told a lie, they had no choice but to get off here for the time being. Otherwise they might arouse the suspicions of the other passengers and the conductor. Why had he blurted out Yamagata? It was a stupid lie. Cursing himself, he stood up, roughly pulling on Mowgli's arm. She was still fast asleep beside him.

"This is Yamagata. We've got to hurry and get off."

He spoke in an unnaturally loud voice so that the passengers around him could hear. He grabbed Mowgli's arm and started toward the exit on the vestibule, even though she was still asleep. After being practically dragged out onto the platform by Akela, Mowgli was finally wakened by the cold air.

"This is Yamagata?" she mumbled.

Akela stopped and nodded.

"I guess so. I was asleep too and didn't realize we'd arrived. The man across from us woke me up, so we had to get off, but, well, it's okay. Since we've gone to all this trouble, let's go into town and get something to eat."

"So this is Yamagata? Unbelievable. It seemed so far away."

Mowgli was rubbing her face and speaking in a nasal, fawning voice. After having slept, she completely reverted back to being a girl. It wasn't just her voice, it was the expression on her face, the way she gestured with her hands—all the icky-sweet girlish habits of a young child. Was it because Akela was still drowsy himself that he sensed that about her?

They started walking in the same direction everyone else was headed. Akela whispered in Mowgli's ear, "Now listen up, you're still Mowgli, got it? *We be of one blood*, and all that."

Mowgli adjusted her baseball cap, snickered and replied in a deeper voice.

"Uh-huh, and our grandma is in Yamagata. She broke her leg. We were worried about her, so we've come from Tokyo to see her."

"Right, that's the story."

Akela stared into Mowgli's face to be sure. Her soft round cheeks were flushed pink. Little kids who had just gotten up in the morning naturally had faces like this. It was probably her cheeks that were making her look like a girl. Her right cheek was redder than the left, and there was a vertical line on it. No doubt that had come from resting her head against Akela's shoulder. The two of them had been fast asleep.

Akela wanted to know the time, and began to look for the station clock. Then he remembered Mowgli's wristwatch in his shirt pocket. He pulled it out.

"Let's see, it's already nine o'clock. It was six when we got to Fukushima, so we must have slept for close to three hours."

"We ate the *bentō* at 4:30." Mowgli added. "I'm hungry now. I'd like some hot milk."

Mowgli's voice sounded excited. At least it seemed she was no longer thinking about wanting to return to Tokyo. For the moment, Akela felt relieved.

The two mingled with the crowd, climbed the stairs, and walked across the pedestrian bridge spanning the tracks. No one paid any attention to these two kids from Tokyo. People were carrying luggage—some speaking loudly in the region's dialect, others busily hurrying ahead without a word. There was no need to be afraid. Akela nodded to himself, then spoke.

"If it's hot milk you want, they probably sell it at the station. But let's go to the toilet first. I can't hold it anymore."

Mowgli laughed. "Me … I mean, *me* too. Gotta wash my face and rinse my mouth. It feels all gritty from the soot, and I bet for sure my nostrils are all black. We've come so far north, it's a little cold. Sure wish I had a sweater. The farther north we go, the colder it'll get."

Akela silently nodded in reply. Names he had never heard before—the Senzan Line, the Aterazawa Line—were posted above some of the exits leading down to the platforms from both sides of the pedestrian bridge. One of the windows on the bridge had been flung open and they could see an ad balloon drifting in the cloudy sky. The weather had definitely been clear around Fukushima, but by the time they reached Yamagata it had changed. Akela was a little concerned, wondering if it would rain. If they got soaked, then this little one with him might catch a cold.

"Oh, look at that poster!" Mowgli read excitedly. "'Risshakuji, the mountain temple that inspired Bashō's famous poem: *Such stillness! / The shrill screech of cicadas / seeps into the craggy rocks.*' Wow, Bashō came here. Back in the old days, when they didn't have trains or anything. You know that haiku, don't you, Akela?"

They started down the stairs.

"I've heard of it, but that's about all. I sure don't know why it's so great." Akela cautiously answered in a low voice. Soon they would be nearing the ticket gate.

"*I sure don't know why* either." Mowgli thought it was fun to imitate Akela's manner of speaking, and she laughed out loud. Then, keeping time with her footsteps as she traipsed down the stairs, she recited a silly patter in a small singsong voice.

"I don't know, I don't know … someone gave my head a blow! Now I'm foolish, now I'm slow, now my stupid hair won't grow … all because I just don't know!"

The rhythm of Mowgli's footsteps sped up to keep time with her voice. She reached the bottom of the steps ahead of Akela and walked on toward the ticket gate, continuing her patter. Akela hurried to catch up with her. Before he knew it, he was also muttering *now my stupid hair won't grow, now I'm foolish, now I'm slow …*

They got in line at the ticket gate. Mowgli was quiet now, staring up in curious wonder at the people around her. An old man was standing in front of them. On his back he had a large bundle wrapped in a *furoshiki*. Since that large square bulging bundle kept other people from observing them, Akela found it reassuring. He took the two tickets he had bought on the train out of his breast pocket, then turned to Mowgli and whispered, "Don't say anything until we get outside."

Mowgli nodded.

Their turn came and, in spite of Akela's anxiety, they were able to pass through the ticket gate without incident. Once they had exited the magnificent wooden structure, Akela let out a big sigh. Glancing quickly left and right, he found a public toilet.

"Okay then, I'll probably come out before you do, so I'll wait right here," he told her, pointing to a wooden bench in front of the public toilet. "All right? Take as much time as you like. Wash your face, wash your hair…."

Mowgli immediately replied, "I can't wash my hair in a place like this."

"Then do what you like." Akela casually tossed off his words and went into the men's toilet. After relieving himself, which felt good, he turned on the water full force in the sink. First he washed his face, and then he poured water over his head and washed away the soot from the train. Because his mouth was dry and scratchy, he gargled and rinsed. He pulled out the only towel he had from his knapsack and, wiping his head and face, went back outside. Mowgli was nowhere to be seen. Surely she hadn't come out ahead of him and wandered off somewhere on her own, had she? It wouldn't do at all to try yelling Mowgli's name from outside the toilet, so he pulled out his cigarettes and began to smoke. Akela brooded over how inconvenient it was, when you thought about it, to have separate toilets for men and women. It didn't seem right to have to worry about her every time they used a toilet. If he told her to use the men's toilet from now on, would Mowgli be willing? If she just used one of the stalls instead of the urinals, it wouldn't make much difference for her, would it? But then he considered how he might feel if he were asked to use the women's toilet, and he knew he would regret it if he forced Mowgli to do that. Why was it that, once they decided to separate toilets for men and women, people became afraid to violate that distinction? If you could choose, whenever possible, a toilet that made no distinction between men and women, like the ones on a train, then the kind of problem Akela was facing wouldn't arise.

He glanced up at the dark sky. It looked like it was about to rain. He glanced at a bus standing in the plaza in front of the station. It occurred to him that they might try taking a bus. He wondered, *Where could the bus take us—the sea, the mountains?* In elementary school, he rode a bus when they went on excursions, even when they went as far as Nagatoro. Just as he was recalling that trip, Mowgli finally came out of the women's toilet. She came over to him, a damp handkerchief spread out in both her hands. When she saw Akela with a towel draped over his shoulder, Mowgli pouted and said, "Oh, so you have a towel? This handkerchief's completely useless. Let me borrow your towel."

Akela quickly handed it to her.

"So you washed your hair after all?" he asked.

She wiped her face, then briskly rubbed her hair with the towel.

"I didn't wash it. I just rinsed it with water. It felt so gritty."

"You can keep that towel, Mowgli. I'm sorry it's dirty."

Mowgli laughed mischievously. "Hmm, now that you mention it, it does have a weird smell. It hasn't been washed for a long time, I bet."

Staring at her damp hair, Akela smiled and said, "You should cut it short. Your school cut isn't very Mowgli-like. And cutting it short would be a lot better for us."

"Should we go to a barber?"

Mowgli lowered her hands with the towel and searched Akela's face.

"I'll cut it for you. When I was at "The Children's Home" I cut the little kids' hair, so I'm pretty good at it. We'll have to buy a pair of scissors, but let's do that after we go into town and eat something."

The plaza in front of the station was as broad as an athletic field. For the time being they decided to proceed down the road running from the front of the station. The area around the plaza seemed to them to lack the busy atmosphere of a city. But Yamagata was a famous place that even the uneducated Akela had heard of, so there had to be spots that were livelier than this. Walking along the deserted street, he thought about the many bustling districts in Tokyo he knew like the back of his hand—Ikebukuro, Sugamo, Takadanobaba, Nerima. And Higashi Jūjō, though he really had only a passing familiarity with that place. There was a popular shopping area around Higashi Jūjō, which even had a theater.

"You know, a cheap pair of scissors won't cut very well and that'll hurt. I won't like that at all," Mowgli said as she strolled beside Akela.

"Are you still going on about that?" Akela laughed through his nose, then looked at Mowgli. The baseball cap was again pulled down over her pale face.

"But I don't want it to hurt. Please buy a decent pair of scissors."

"I wonder how much they cost? If it's more than the cost of a haircut, what we should do?"

Mowgli looked worried; her brows knitted.

"They can't be all that expensive, can they?"

"Probably not ... and we might get in trouble if we go to a barbershop and they start asking a lot of questions. Listen, it'll be all right. And in any case, you know that everyone has something they can't stand."

"Is that also the law of the jungle?"

Mowgli raised the bill of her baseball cap slightly with her left hand and stared into Akela's swarthy face. Uneven, scraggly whiskers were growing around his chin and mouth. Especially long whiskers were growing on both cheeks, making him look like a raccoon dog. Mowgli wanted to laugh. He didn't look a bit like a wolf.

"Is it the Law? Nah, it's more like a proverb. There are others, like *A monkey's hand and a person's eye are never satisfied.* Another one goes, *The rights of all are the rights of the least.*"

"And there's *Comfort us in sorrow and in woe, Jesus, Mary, Joseph, and grant us your strength in pain and suffering,*" Mowgli responded with a smirk.

"What are you talking about, what's that?"

"And then there's *To Thee all the Angels, the Heavens and the Powers, all the Cherubim and Seraphim unceasingly sing.*" Mowgli was speaking with more and more pride.

"That's just gibberish to me. It's really annoying," Akela mumbled. He sounded irritated.

"It's a hymn we have to sing at school. Every morning we have to sing things like that."

"What are Cherubim and Seraphim?" Akela asked. His face showed that he was now in a bad mood.

Mowgli cocked her head and answered, "I'm not really sure, but … they use a lot of hard words at my new school. Like *Tantum ergo Sacramentum*, or *Calvary*, or *Helpless children of Eve, lost in darkness.*"

"What a weird school. When you say 'helpless children,' does that mean 'hopeless children'? Or since they're lost in darkness, does it mean 'homeless children'?"

The mention of homeless children reminded Akela of a novel he knew really well, *Nobody's Boy.*

"Is that what it means?" Mowgli asked. "I never understood it before. I thought it was just creepy."

Judging from her face, she didn't seem to be all that concerned about it. Akela, on the other hand, felt embarrassed and awkward, and he couldn't help stammering in reply, "I don't know. I may be wrong, since Jesus has absolutely nothing to do with me."

They were standing at an intersection. Looking both ways, they decided to turn left where most of the people were heading. They spotted a dignified-looking tile-roofed building. In the distance they could see a block of buildings. There were three ad balloons drifting in the overcast sky. Apparently they had not gone the wrong direction after all. Just off to the right they saw a white sign painted with the word *Soba.*

Akela, who was feeling hungry, said, "You want to go into that shop there? The menu says they have *ramen* and milk, so you can get what you want. We may have come a long way, but it isn't too different from Tokyo, is it? The buildings all look splendid, and they have buses here too."

"But they don't have traffic lights. And there aren't as many people," Mowgli muttered.

"Everyone's probably at school, or at work."

As soon as he said that, Akela glanced at her face, worried about her reaction.

But Mowgli was staring eagerly at the bill of fare dangling down beside the entrance to the *soba* shop, and didn't seem to have heard him.

"Let's see … they've got *zaru soba, mori soba, nabeyaki udon, wonton, ramen*. What should I order?"

"Let's just go on in."

Akela slid the glass door open.

The interior was dark, and there wasn't a customer in sight. They hesitated, wondering if the shop owner was still preparing to open, when a woman wearing a Japanese-style apron flipped on the light switch. Then, without so much as a word, she went back inside. Since she had turned the lights on, they figured she must be open for business. Akela sat down at a table near the entrance. Mowgli sat down across from him and began staring again at the menu items posted along the wall.

"I think I'll have curry over rice," said Akela.

"I'll … oops … I mean, *I'll* have *ramen*. I've never eaten it before."

"You must be kidding. Never?"

Just then the woman who had appeared from the back a few seconds earlier brought out a tray with glasses of water, and the two of them clammed up.

"Whatcha'll wanna eat?" The shop woman snarled at them, sizing up their faces with a menacing look.

"Curry over rice and *ramen*," Akela answered curtly, looking away from the woman. As soon as she heard his accent she'd know they were outsiders, so he didn't want to give her an opening to ask where they'd come from and why they were here. It was best to remain silent. As long as they kept quiet, no one could tell they weren't locals.

Fortunately, the woman let them be and went into the back room again.

"Now listen, we shouldn't talk in a loud voice up here. If they know we're from Tokyo, people will get nosy. There's a lot of meddlesome monkeys out here in the sticks."

Mowgli nodded, then glanced up at him reproachfully and said, "But … I wanted a cup of hot milk."

"Oh, I forgot. Can you get some later?"

"I'd rather have it now," Mowgli muttered, puffing her cheeks out in a pout. Akela was a little flustered, and so he clapped his hands. The woman in the back must have been deaf, because no matter how many times he clapped, she didn't come out. Akela stood up, clicking his tongue, and went toward the back of the shop.

"Hey!" he yelled.

"Yeah?" Finally a voice answered him. He looked toward the kitchen, which was so dark he couldn't make out anything, and yelled again.

"Bring us some hot milk. Right away!"

"Yeah, okay!"

It was the exact same voice. Reassured, Akela went back to his seat and began smoking a cigarette.

"Thanks. Sorry for being demanding."

Mowgli bowed her head slightly to him across the table.

"It's okay, never mind ..."

Akela's face reddened as he glanced over at Mowgli's face. Her appearance and demeanor made her look like a boy who had stopped growing. As a boy, she seemed to be lacking something. A boy not fully developed, faithfully following Akela. At least she had stopped saying she wanted to go back to Tokyo. Akela felt the urge to stretch out his hand and stroke Mowgli's soft cheeks. Instead, he blew a puff of smoke from his mouth, and began speaking in a low voice.

"Say, Mowgli, since you're pretending to be a boy anyway, would it be all right if you tried acting like you were ... a little slow? That would be safest. Because no matter what anyone says to you, you could just stare blankly at them. Since your older brother was like that, it won't be too hard for you to fake, will it? It should be a snap for you. I mean ... the two of us are outsiders here, so we have to be really careful."

For an instant Mowgli glared at Akela with her narrow eyes, then hung her head. Akela patiently, silently waited for an answer. "The Song of the Little Hunter" echoed in his ears.

But thy throat is shut and dried, and thy heart against thy side, Hammers ...

Overlapping the echo of that song was another—a childlike, innocent voice singing one of Mowgli's weird chants.

Comfort us in sorrow and in woe, Jesus, Mary ... I don't know, I don't know, someone gave my head a blow!...

"I can't *fake* it, and I hate the way you put it. *A little slow*," Mowgli mumbled, her head still hanging down.

They heard bicycle bells and other random noises outside the shop—the sound of feet running, someone shouting like a squawking bird, and, in the distance, something like a car horn. Then rain began to fall.

"His mind was just turned in a different direction, that's all. He always understood perfectly what he had to understand. He would never get distracted like me. He was weak, he got sick a lot, and in the end he died, but when he was having fun he'd sing and make squealing noises with his tongue. I could never, ever imitate

67

that. His way of laughing was special, his way of walking … it's scary, and it's not right to imitate him."

Mowgli's face was drained of color.

"I'm sorry, I shouldn't have said that. When I think about it, I'd be too scared to be able to imitate someone who's dead. I could never imitate my father. I mean my father from the time we were in the graveyard, and … still, I couldn't do it either." Akela's apology was interspersed with sighs. Just then the woman came out from the back of the shop bringing the curry over rice and the hot milk.

"It's rainin' cats and dogs, an' y'all don't have a umberella I'm guessin'."

Akela nodded right away, and just smiled back at the woman. He wanted to speak as little as possible. Mowgli was still hanging her head, sunk in silence.

"Ya got no umberella, ya got trouble. Well, it'll stop soon, so ya can stay here a spell till it passes."

Akela again flashed a bright, friendly smile and nodded. The woman wasn't expecting a response anyway. She quickly moved over to the glass door and glanced outside before returning to the back of the shop, mumbling to herself all the while. Apparently she hadn't noticed yet that the two of them were outsiders.

Akela exhaled, his shoulders slumping, then he began laughing and said to Mowgli, "Whew! If you smile and stay quiet like I did just now, that'll do. What I said before, that's really what I meant. What do you say? If that's all you have to do, you can manage that, can't you?"

"I guess …"

Mowgli raised her head and began to drink the hot milk in the cup. She gulped it down without taking a breath. Her white throat moved rhythmically with each swallow. Akela watched her throat in fascination, wondering if the milk was really as delicious as all that. Having drained the cup in a flash, she looked over at the glass door, a white moustache on her lip.

"Will the rain really stop soon? It's getting darker outside."

"If it doesn't stop, there's not much we can do about it. We could buy an umbrella, I suppose, but that'll only become extra baggage, so I don't really want to, but …"

He pulled the plate of curry in front of him and began to shovel it in.

"And it's a waste of money. Every time we eat, I fear, Akela's yen will disappear."

Mowgli once more gave her words a singsong rhythm. Perhaps she was poking fun at him as payback for what he had said earlier.

The woman came out again, this time bringing the *ramen*. Because the air inside the shop was cold, white steam was rising visibly from the large bowl.

"Ya eat up slow, ya' hear! Anyhow, it's rainin', so no need to go rushin' off. Say, ain't ya a girl? Dressed up jes' like yer older brother, now, ain't ya!"

The woman laughed, her face revealing her simple surprise. Mowgli stared blankly at the woman, and a faint, weird smile crossed her lips. When the woman saw Mowgli's face, a look of comprehension came over her and, after a quick glance at Akela, she nodded slightly and hurried back into the kitchen.

Immediately Akela whispered to Mowgli, "You're really good. You caught it just right. Still, she saw right through the clothes and knew you were a girl. We'll be in a real fix if we don't cut your hair soon."

"I didn't do anything. I just gave a blank stare. Does that make me look like an idiot?"

It seemed a mystery to Mowgli. Evidently she hadn't been acting dumb on purpose.

"I don't know, whatever. Maybe it's best this way. Hurry up and eat. If you don't eat it while it's hot—"

"Oooh, it smells so good."

Mowgli picked up a pair of disposable chopsticks and put her face close to the large bowl of *ramen*.

The glass door opened, and three men rushed into the shop. Their heads and shoulders were soaked. They weren't carrying anything, and they were dressed properly in suits. Talking hurriedly among themselves, they wiped their faces and heads with white handkerchiefs and sat down at the table next to Akela and Mowgli.

Akela and Mowgli kept quiet and focused their attention on their curry and *ramen*. There was nothing but potato in the curry, but it didn't taste too bad. He wondered if the noodles were only so-so. When Mowgli told him this was her first time to eat *ramen*, Akela had been completely flummoxed. Was it possible that a child raised *normally*, unlike his upbringing, never ate *ramen*? He was also puzzled by how the woman had figured out Mowgli was a girl. It wasn't just a problem of her hair. It was her white hands. Tiny hands that were too soft, and thin fingernails that had a pink glow. Her ears, her neck, everything was too clean and smooth. Were men and women different, even as little kids? If she lived for several days without taking a bath, would she lose her girliness? The pert, doughy little nose sat snugly under her slender eyebrows. No doubt, it was still a child's face. Yet there was something about it that was a little different from a boy's face. He recalled Mowgli's idiot face a few moments earlier. Her head had looked utterly vacant. Although she seemed quite grown-up and sassy for a little girl when they first met, there were times she came across as a child without much in the way of smarts. Apparently her older brother had some sort of brain disease, and that kind of disease was probably contagious. Was she smart, or stupid, or was it that she simply didn't know anything of the world? Whatever the case, if he didn't protect this little one really well, she'd have all sorts of terrible things happen to her for sure. Akela reminded himself that regardless of what might happen, he alone was Mowgli's support—this pitiful little frog, fangless, weak of claw, with a poor sense of smell.

They drank up the *bancha* tea the woman had brought to them after they finished eating, but the rain showed no sign of letting up. The shop was now bustling. In addition to the three men, four young women had come in seeking shelter a few minutes earlier. An hour had already passed, and though they could continue to wait there, the rain showed no sign of stopping anytime soon. And so, after drinking a second cup of tea, Akela left money on the table, winked at Mowgli, and stood up.

They opened the glass door and were assaulted by the sound of a fierce rain. They couldn't very well go back inside now, so they took a breath, and for better or worse leapt out into the avenue in the middle of a rainstorm. They ran about two hundred meters and ducked under the eaves at the front of a sweets shop. Mowgli came running in after Akela. She was painfully out of breath.

"Aw man, this is terrible. There's an arcade a little farther ahead. Let's try to make it there, if you can. Are you okay?"

Wiping the rain off her face, Mowgli panted as she answered.

"I'm all right … we just ate a while ago … and I ate too much."

"Listen up. Can you see it? The clock tower over there? It sure is strange. And that building is really splendid, like some castle. And even that bookstore, and the inn next to it? They're not half-bad designs either. This town has an awful lot of impressive buildings."

Mowgli looked up and gazed at the shops lining the road. In the heavy rain everything was misty, even just a meter in front of them. Buildings and objects just across the street were faint shadows hard to make out. If she hadn't been told, she would never have guessed what they were. She looked at what Akela said was a clock tower, a pointed shadow floating in the air, flickering above a second-story roof. She wanted to get a clearer view of it with her own eyes, but just then it was obscured by a torrent of rain and disappeared altogether. *Was Akela's eyesight especially acute?* Mowgli wondered, but then somehow she was able to make out a bookstore and an inn standing very close by to her right. Certainly their appearance was different from the shops Mowgli was used to in Tokyo. Each of the buildings was solemn-looking, and made her feel they had returned to a time in the distant past. Because of the rain, they couldn't make out any details, and so the place felt all the more old-fashioned.

"Yamagata must be a rich town. You don't see any shanties here like you do in Tokyo."

Akela nodded as if he had special knowledge about the subject and replied, "Tokyo was flattened by the fire bombings, so that's why there are so many shanties around. There are even Quonset huts—you know, those buildings shaped like *kamaboko* fish cake. Some plots of land have been left vacant, and people are still living there in storehouses that escaped the fire bombings. It's terrible."

"There are three of those *kamaboko* things on the roof of my school. I guess they use them for storage, though."

"I'll bet people lived in them once. The Occupation army distributed them as

70

relief aid. I don't know firsthand about what happened around that time, and I don't remember anything about the air raids. Whenever I heard people talk about it, I'd get a feeling like, wasn't I surrounded by fire from an air raid, wasn't I crying and wailing, looking for my mother? But I really don't know. This place was never fire-bombed. That's why there aren't any delinquents like me around."

"Or like me," Mowgli added quietly. "I was born after the war, but—if I had been a kid in Yamagata, I think my father and Ton-chan would still be alive, and my mother would smile more often, and, uh ... I wouldn't be taking this trip with you."

"Yeah, I suppose you're right."

He deliberately scowled and turned away from Mowgli.

"Okay, let's make a dash for that arcade. There's probably a shop that sells scissors in there, and maybe a coffeehouse. We've been out here in the rain, and I can't stand the cold anymore. Ready ... go!"

Hunching his back, Akela dashed out first, with Mowgli following right behind him. They couldn't keep their eyes fully open, so their field of vision grew narrower and narrower, until it came to feel like they were running at the bottom of a pool. They heard nothing but the sound of water. Of course their heads and feet were completely soaked. The water in their shoes was squishing around, making a disagreeable sound.

As soon as they reached the arcade, they realized they were in front of a department store.

"Wow! There are department stores all over the place."

Akela spoke excitedly as he shook his drenched head. Mowgli took off her baseball cap, shook her head in the same way, and wiped her face off with her hand.

"You're right, they really are department stores! They'll definitely have scissors. I'm sure they sell anything we could want."

"This seems to be the busiest place in town, for sure. My intuition is amazing. We're right in the heart of the town, I'd say."

Akela looked up, as if admiring the building that towered above them on the opposite side of the intersection. Because the arcade obstructed the upper part of the department store right in front of them, they couldn't see all of the building or tell what it was like.

"We're going inside, aren't we? Which one is best? I didn't think they'd have department stores here," said Mowgli.

After hesitating for a moment, Akela replied, "We'd be fools to get soaked all over again. Let's just go in here. I mean, the stores all look alike. We shouldn't get wet like this, it's not good for us. By the way, you've gone back to talking like a girl. If you keep using women's speech and a high voice, you'll never be able to pass as a boy. That's no good."

Mowgli looked confused. She stared at Akela, gave a reluctant nod, and in a deeper voice said, "Okay, but once we go in, I won't say a thing. Just as I promised."

She set off ahead of him and moved over to the entrance of the department store in front of them. A crowd of people had gathered around the entrance. Some were standing there to get out of the rain, while others, who seemed to have business there, continued inside. A large brown dog was lying by the entrance, asleep—probably a pet that belonged to someone shopping inside. Bicycles were lined up and buses ran along the street in front of them.

She pushed open the glass door and stepped in. Violin music flowed around her, and the interior was bright. The counters where they sold cosmetics and bags were identical to those in the department stores in Tokyo. The store was decorated with artificial pink flowers.

Akela followed after Mowgli and began to whisper in her ear. "Let's find a toilet first. If we don't wring our clothes out, they'll feel terrible. And we can't very well take them off here."

Mowgli smiled and nodded. She was still holding her wet baseball cap in her hand.

"I wonder where the toilets are? I really don't want to ask anyone … let's just get on the elevator and go up. There's usually a food court on the upper floors. There are probably toilets there, too."

Mowgli nodded again and said nothing. Her silence was making Akela uneasy. He felt he was being mocked, having told her not to speak in front of people. However, he couldn't very well back down now. He glanced around the store and looked for an elevator. A woman wearing thick makeup, a small hat perched on her head, was standing off to the side striking an affected pose. That seemed to be the elevator.

"Oh, man, I despise monkeys who wear so much makeup. And there's another made-up monkey keeping an eye on the escalator as well. Let's walk up."

They passed the cosmetics counters and headed toward the stairs. There was no one around except for three old men taking a break, sitting on the wide staircase. Akela took large strides, two steps at a time; Mowgli took one step at a time, all the while staring up at Akela's back. They climbed up to the third floor without even glancing to see what goods were sold on the second floor. An old person and a woman with a baby on her back were sitting there. The flowing tones of the violin pursued Akela and Mowgli throughout the store. Announcements would occasionally interrupt the music, pursuing them even more insistently. *Thank you for shopping at* … Those were the only words spoken in the Tokyo dialect. When they got to the fourth floor they were out of breath. They rested on the way up for a moment, and then went on climbing.

The stairs ended at the fifth floor, which looked like a hall used for wedding ceremonies. They found the toilets they were looking for, but they still didn't know where the restaurants were. He had Mowgli go ahead to the women's toilet. He wasn't sure if he should have her go to the men's toilet, but since no one was likely to see them there, he decided it was best not to ask too much of her. Akela went into the men's toilet and, after relieving himself, took off his shoes and socks at the sink area. He wrung out his socks and dumped the water out of his sneakers. He got some toilet paper from one of the stalls and wiped the inside of his shoes. Next he dried his hair. Then he pulled off his sweater and wrung it out as well. His shirt was wet too, but not enough to wring it out. He didn't bother pulling off his trousers, but he did wring out the cuffs with both hands. He felt warm from having climbed all those stairs, and a smell just like steam from an old, murky bath began to rise from his clothes. It didn't feel all that good, but by doing this, his clothes would probably dry out. He had a change of undershirt and shirt in his cloth knapsack, but he didn't think he was at the point yet where he should use them. If he just changed clothes as he pleased, he'd then be faced with having to do a laundry. His knapsack was damp, but the things inside weren't all that wet, probably because the bag was made of thick cloth. His handmade folder, where he kept his important newspaper clippings, was unharmed. Just to be safe, he covered it with the oilpaper that had been wrapped around his empty *bentō* box. He then put all of that inside the clean undershirt as well.

When he came out of the men's toilet, Mowgli was already standing and leaning against a window at the side of the toilet doors. She hadn't put the cap back on her head yet.

"Whoa, that was fast."

Mowgli nodded.

"Did you wring out your socks?"

Mowgli nodded, her expression serious.

"And your jacket?"

Mowgli shook her head from side to side.

"You didn't wring out the cuffs of your trousers either, did you? If you don't at least squeeze them a little, they'll never dry out."

Akela squatted down at Mowgli's feet and began to wring out the cuffs of her trousers. Beginning with the right pant leg, he pulled up the cuffs, squeezing them little by little. He then went around behind her and continued squeezing. Rainwater dribbled drop by drop onto the floor. When he was finished, he felt Mowgli's socks.

"Look at this, they're still soaked! I'll wring them out for you, so take them off. Don't you even know how to wring things out, Mowgli? Haven't you ever cleaned up anything with a cloth?"

Mowgli hurriedly took off her white socks, which were stained by mud and the leather of her shoes. Hanging her head, she handed them to Akela. At once Akela bundled them together and thoroughly wrung them out. Water fell to the floor.

"Wait a second. If you put the socks back on while they're still damp, it won't feel very nice."

He handed her the socks, then dashed back into the men's toilet and brought out a roll of toilet paper he had taken off the spindle. He wiped out the inside of

Mowgli's shoes and spread fresh pieces of paper inside.

"This should do. You can change the paper again in a little while."

Mowgli, who already had her socks on, cautiously put her feet into her shoes. Akela had stuffed tissue inside her socks.

"We have lots of paper. And if we run out, we can always get more from the toilet," he muttered.

Akela began wiping down Mowgli's hair with the tissue paper.

"Your hair is still really wet."

Akela liberally tore off one piece of paper after another, each about a meter long, and repeatedly wiped Mowgli's hair strand by strand, tossing away the used pieces of paper at her feet.

Mowgli burst out laughing, as though she couldn't stand it anymore.

"So you think it's funny, do you? Even though you can't do anything for yourself? Look, take off your jacket. Isn't your shirt wet too? … Well, it's not that wet, so I suppose you don't have to wring it out."

Mowgli was still laughing. Her laugh was contagious, and Akela, grinning now, began to wring out Mowgli's jacket with all his strength. The material was thick cotton, so if he didn't put a lot of force into it, it would be impossible to get the water out.

After returning the jacket to Mowgli, Akela intentionally spoke as though he were giving orders.

"Gather up the used paper and wipe the water off the floor. Then throw it away in the women's toilet."

Although Mowgli continued laughing as before, she carried out his orders faithfully.

Feeling like he had finished a job, Akela pulled the cigarettes and matches out of his pocket and tried to have a smoke, but the matches were damp, and some of his cigarettes were soaked. He muttered to himself that he had to buy scissors and cigarettes. He somehow wanted to manage without buying an umbrella. In the meantime, wouldn't he also have to buy underwear for Mowgli? He immediately erased that thought from his mind. His own underwear would be good enough for her, he figured. He had two pairs each of socks and underwear in his sack. They were clean, since he had just washed them. Cleanliness took priority over everything. *Be clean, for the strength of the hunter is known by the gloss of his hide.* Mere looks meant nothing.

Because he had helped out with the little kids at the Children's Home, Akela's old habits took over whenever he looked at Mowgli. She had almost no skills, which played on his instincts to help. And when he helped her, it calmed his own heart. To Akela there was no difference between little boys and little girls. At the Children's Home they weren't allowed to look different. Same haircut. Same clothes. Same way of talking. Boys and girls used the same children's toilet. Little kids, nothing

74

more. They were really noisy, but then again they were also cute. When they were old enough to go to school … but then, by that time, they weren't little kids anymore. The boys were separated from the girls. The girls began to use strange words. Akela had not liked that change. Akela was a boy, to be sure, but he wanted to be something other than human—something cleaner, prouder, more beautiful. And he wanted Mowgli to become something other than human as well. He didn't want her to grow up to be just another tedious monkey.

Mowgli returned from the women's toilet and sat down on a vinyl-covered bench near the window. Akela sat down beside her and gave a great yawn.

"If your body gets soaked, it makes you sleepy. Come to think of it, we haven't had enough sleep … you know, it's all right to talk a little when there's no one around."

Mowgli nodded, then spoke up at last. "I'm … I'm sleepy. We won't get in trouble if we take a nap here?" She yawned and rubbed her watery eyes as she spoke.

"You know, I've been thinking. Was that really the first time you ate *ramen*?" Akela asked, yawning again.

"Yeah, it was. And it was good. Probably better than your curry … you're kind, Akela. I mean, just now, I was embarrassed and laughed, but you're like a mother to me. Or maybe you're more like a grandmother. I've never known a grandmother, so … Akela, it seems like I've known you for a long time."

Her voice sounded drowsy. She had already closed her eyes. Akela put his hand on her shoulder and said, "Go ahead and put your head on my lap and lie down. You'll be a lot more comfortable that way."

Doing as she was told, Mowgli slipped her head onto his lap, her hair still damp, raised her legs onto the bench, and curled up. Akela took off his sweater and spread it over her back, then closed his eyes. With his right hand on her shoulder, he placed his left hand around the outside to support her so that her head would not droop. Mowgli's small, fragile body—he could feel its warmth seep into both his hands. Unexpectedly, Akela's heart started beating faster. He took a deep breath. In order to bring on his own quiet sleepiness, he conjured in his mind the sound of the wind in the graveyard and the scent of dead leaves and stones. The murmuring of the trees and the cries of the birds. The scent of cold, hard stones. The dry rustling of dead leaves dancing over the surface of the ground. Yellow leaves. Brown leaves. A few red leaves. And under the leaves, columns of glittering frost spreading over the ground.

Soon, Akela's heart began to beat more gently, and he and Mowgli fell into a deep slumber. Their regular breathing mingled together in dreamless sleep.

The shrieking of monkeys and the piercing sounds of construction suddenly came pouring down on them. Akela and Mowgli jumped up at the same time. A small kid had tumbled onto the floor right in front of them and was screaming and crying. Next to him an older child was brandishing a toy machine gun that fired with a crackling rattle. Another child was quietly pushing a bus along the floor. Four female monkeys were sitting next to the wall in the opposite corner, laughing and chattering. One of them was breastfeeding a baby wrapped up in a blanket.

Seeing that Akela and Mowgli were awake, the four mother monkeys turned their smiling faces toward them. Their pushy, smiling expressions seemed to be saying, *My, you've slept well, haven't you? But we'd like to use that bench now.* Akela didn't want to give the mother monkeys any cause to celebrate, but he also didn't want to stay in a place like this, which was now permeated with the stench of monkeys. So he made a great show of raising his arms high overhead and slowly stretching, then leisurely picking up his bag and standing up. Mowgli also got up, clutching at Akela's sweater, a sleepy look on her face. He was of a mind to say something to the mother monkeys in their cheap Western-style clothes, and to their little monkeys, but he restrained himself, figuring that it wouldn't do for someone as noble as Akela to make such trivial comments. He headed for the stairs, Mowgli in tow.

As soon as they were out of sight of the mother monkeys, Akela pulled the wristwatch out of his shirt pocket and checked the time. It was past noon.

"So how long were we asleep? I don't think it was all that long, but I slept really soundly. How about you?"

Still sleepy, Mowgli rubbed her eyes and nodded.

"If those monkeys hadn't gotten us up, we'd have slept for hours for sure. Damn, my shoes aren't dry yet. My feet feel all weird and itchy. Wait a sec. I'm going to put some paper in my shoes. You'd better change the paper in yours as well. We've got a lot of toilet paper left, but before we go we'd better take two or three more rolls. After all, the department store won't miss them. And if there's anything else we can use, we should take that too."

Akela sat down on the stairs and removed his sneakers. Mowgli sat down beside him and took off her leather shoes. The paper she had spread inside was wet and brown. She pulled out the paper she had stuffed inside her socks and, wadding it up, slipped it into her jacket pocket. There was no one else around. Piece by piece, Mowgli took the toilet paper Akela handed her and put it inside her shoes.

"Do you think we can find some soap somewhere?" she asked in a low voice.

"We can get soap anywhere."

Akela rested his sneakers on his lap and began to stuff paper inside them.

"What about a toothbrush?"

Akela hesitated for a moment. "A toothbrush? That's out of the question. If you want one, use mine."

"A used toothbrush? That's gross." Mowgli's face turned red.

"C'mon, you. You really are a brat. I'll buy you one if it's that important. Not here, though. At another store. The scissors come first. Let's find a stationery counter, then get out of here. I wonder if it's still raining. If we head back to the station, we'll get soaked again. Should we get an umbrella?"

They got up and started back down the stairs.

"Are we heading back to the station?" Mowgli muttered.

"We've been hanging around here so long, what else are we going to do?"

"So how far will we go? Somewhere where the flowers are blooming?"

Mowgli sounded angry. Akela laughed at her.

"Now look, we've come all this way, and you want to go somewhere where flowers are in bloom? They haven't even bloomed here yet."

"Let's see… the flowers aren't in bloom, there aren't any exotic birds … and there sure aren't any elephants."

Mowgli gave a sigh that did not sound like a child's.

They went down to the fourth floor. The various toys there gave off high-pitched squeaks and sparkled brightly. They saw children with their mothers. Was that a stationery counter next to the toy section? Having only limited experience at department stores in Tokyo, Akela proceeded into the fourth floor and moved slowly along the wall. It wasn't all that big, and so it wouldn't take them much time to make one circuit. And if it wasn't on the fourth floor, then they could go around the third floor once as well. Having decided on a plan of action, it was thus an anticlimax for him when they came to the stationery department right away. Akela gave a little whistle and tapped Mowgli on the shoulder.

"Just like I thought. It seems to be giving us a big welcome. Okay, scissors, scissors …"

There were fountain pens, document cases, notebooks, rulers and compasses, and scissors gleaming brightly in front of them.

"All right, I'll go buy a pair. You wait here."

Mowgli stood in front of a pillar near the stationer's department while Akela went over by himself to the shelf where the scissors were lined up. There weren't all that many kinds. Most of them were the small scissors kids use in elementary school, but there were scissors for household use, and expensive-looking scissors apparently designed for draftsmen or artists. There were also high-quality foreign-made scissors arranged in a glass case together with some large Japanese sewing scissors. After looking over all of them once, Akela, with no hesitation, picked out a pair of household scissors of middling size and price.

Mowgli was anxiously taking in the scene. Observing Akela from a short distance, she couldn't help fretting that people around him were glancing over as well, wondering who he was. It seemed as though they were about to raise a big stink about him, and there was nothing she could do about it. *Where are you from? Why are you here? Can't answer? You certainly smell strange! Seize him! Seize him and lock him up somewhere!* Such voices were buzzing around like the wings of insects inside Mowgli's head. There was something about Akela's body, about his face, that put the people around him on their guard. Mowgli couldn't help thinking he looked peculiar. His body violated the atmosphere of the department store, and the friction created by his presence here was giving off sparks. Akela had come to this town with no particular aim in mind, and so the more people questioned him or made a fuss about him, the more suspicious-looking he would become. Eventually, the police would take him in. If that happened, what would become of Mowgli? She had no money, and if she were left on her own, how would she manage to get food? Would she collapse on the road? Would she have no choice but to become a beggar? If things were going to turn out like that, it would be better to go with Akela to the police station. Then she would try to maintain her silence. She would cling to Akela and refuse to let other people come near her, so that they would believe she really was his younger sister—after all, it would be out of the question to try to make them think she was his younger brother. Would Akela repeat the story about their "grandma"? Where would "grandma" be living this time? Someplace farther away than Yamagata? Akita, maybe, or perhaps Aomori?

Mowgli was praying with all her heart that somehow Akela would finish his shopping without incident. *Deliver us from evil. Forgive us our trespasses. We be of one blood. Protect us....*

At last Akela came trotting back. Mowgli felt the strength leave her shoulders, and she instinctively teared up. She headed for the empty stairs ahead of him. Her anxiety disappeared with the tears in her eyes, and she told herself that she had to become more younger brother-like for Akela's sake. Since they had come this far, she made up her mind once and for all. *We be of one blood.* They had to look out for one another.

Running down to the landing on the stairway and waiting there for Akela, Mowgli asked him in a quiet voice, "So tell me, was it *good hunting all, that keep the Law*?"

"Of course, what else? But it wasn't cheap. A hundred and fifty yen. For now, let's just get out of here."

Seeing Akela's self-satisfied face, Mowgli smiled and nodded. Again, she felt the inside of her nose grow hot.

The third floor held the menswear and the kimono departments. Hardly anyone was there. Akela figured that the toilets on this floor would almost certainly be empty, and so, following his hunch, they decided to first use them, and then get whatever they could while they were at it. If they went to the first-floor toilets, it would be more difficult. Doing exactly as Akela told her, Mowgli first went into a stall and took the roll of paper off the spindle and stuffed it into her bag. She then moved to the next stall and took another roll of paper. No one else was using the women's toilet, but because there was always the danger that someone might come in suddenly, she quickly searched around the sink area. Unhooking a dented tin cup from its chain, she jammed that into her bag, and then, seeing some bars of soap, she selected the newest one, wrapped it in her handkerchief, and stuck it in her trousers pocket. She really wanted a box to put the soap in, but she couldn't be choosy. Finally, she opened the supplies locker, where she found cleaning cloths and a bucket. More than ten new rolls of toilet paper were piled up there. She took one of those, as well as a slightly soiled blue towel that had been left there, and put them into her bag.

"Mission accomplished!" Mowgli muttered, feeling happy. She winked to herself in front of the mirror over the sink. Or she tried to wink, that is. No matter how much she practiced, she still couldn't do it very well.

She ran up to Akela, who was standing near the entrance, and whispered to him excitedly, "*Good hunting all, that keep the Law*! I got several things. I feel really great now."

"Don't look so happy. If you attract suspicion, we'll be in for it. We got what we came for, so let's go," Akela said, affecting a solemn voice. He briskly walked off. Mowgli put her baseball cap on and followed him. She kept her face down and was trying to suppress her laughter. Their bags were now fairly bulging.

They proceeded straight down ... second floor ... first floor ... and out the front entrance. The rain hadn't stopped, though it had slowed to a drizzle. Akela looked at Mowgli's face and then stared out at the rain, lost in thought for a few moments. More than two dozen shoppers were standing around, yapping noisily. Children were shouting as well. Cars and bicycles moved along the street. The bicycle riders wore black waterproof hats and raincoats and didn't seem to mind the rain. Whenever people coming and going along the street left the arcade, they would open up their black, or red, or navy blue umbrellas one after another. Some people in the crowd walked along without umbrellas, seemingly indifferent to the rain.

"It doesn't look like we need an umbrella. Let's just go as we are. We'll stay under the eaves as much as possible," Akela whispered to Mowgli. He dashed out in the direction they'd come from. Mowgli took off right behind him. In order to get back to the station, they would simply follow the road they had taken earlier. Certainly that was the best way to make sure they didn't get lost. As they took off running, they discovered the rain wasn't really a concern. Their clothes, which had not completely dried at the department store, had made them itchy, so the coolness of the rain actually felt good.

Akela tried to run in a manner befitting his namesake, Akela the Lone Wolf, kicking the ground in long, powerful strides. His body was gracefully supple, as though it could easily fly through space, bounding upward so the raindrops had no time to soak his body. Akela and Mowgli ran silently along the thoroughfare, where there were now many more cars and pedestrians than there had been that morning. The two of them probably looked like shadows to the people moving along that noisy street. Two shadows dashing headlong, silent, leaving behind only a breeze. Actually, Akela couldn't have cared less how they looked to others. The more precious something was, the less visible it was. Akela calmly proceeded through the monkeys, his rich silver coat streaming in the breeze. And after him followed little Mowgli, trying with all her might to imitate Akela's way of running. Mowgli, the little human cub, had neither claws nor fangs. She had no beautiful fur like his. A wretched, naked little one. When he considered that Mowgli was doing all she could to learn from him, it made his heart ache. Was this how fathers think about their own flawed, inferior children? Akela and Mowgli were outsiders in this territory, and as outsiders they had to observe the Law. It was an unfamiliar jungle. They didn't know the roads well, and the language was different. For that reason, outsiders had to maintain silence; they had to pass through stealthily. Like a shadow, like a scent.

Kicking up the drizzling rain, Akela felt good as he ran along with great strides.

For the rush through the mist, and the quarry blind-started!
For the cry of our mates when the sambhur has wheeled and is standing at bay,
For the risk and the riot of night!
For the sleep at the lair-mouth by day,
It is met, and we go to the light.
Bay! O bay!

Entranced, he was humming "The Song of the Hunt of the Red Dogs." The Red Dogs were wild dogs called *dhole*, cruel murderers who, unlike wolves, did not obey the Law. Wolves traveled in small packs only, but the *dhole* formed large groups of a hundred or more, and it didn't matter to them if their prey was a tiger or an elephant; they would attack and kill all the same. Whenever a pack of *dhole* passed, only white bones would be left in their wake. Like a landslide, a flood, a great whirlwind, the *dhole* pushed forward in any direction they wanted, fearing nothing. Even wolves fled before the *dhole* hordes, for if they fought them head-on, they would be slaughtered. Nonetheless, Akela and Mowgli, in order to protect the hunting grounds of the wolves, defeated the *dhole*. Mowgli came up with the idea of using swarms of bees to weaken them. Then, after enticing the *dhole*, a daytime animal, to a riverbank at night, they began to fight. It went down in wolf history as an unprecedented, tragic battle. Mowgli fought using a knife as a substitute for fangs and claws. Female wolves and even wolf pups just a year old joined in the fight. One of them was sacrificed, and the mother wolf raised a howl of grief. Come to think of it, Akela also died in this battle.

Suddenly remembering that part of the story, Akela wanted to come to a halt. He would soon be gasping painfully for breath, but he decided not to stop. He ran past the *soba* shop where they had eaten when they first arrived, and they closed in on the corner of a large intersection. Once they turned there, they would be on the street leading straight to the station.

That's right. Akela was first bitten by three *dhole* before being attacked by six *dhole* in the terrible battle with the Red Dogs. Somehow he managed to kill all nine of those dogs, but he was mortally wounded in the course of the fight and breathed his last with his wounded head nestled on the lap of his beloved Mowgli.

> *"Even so. I die, and I would ... I would die by thee, Little Brother. It is long since the old days of Shere Khan, and a Man-cub that rolled naked in the dust."*

Akela, breathing painfully, spoke to Mowgli.
> *"Thou art a man, Little Brother, wolfling of my watching. Thou art a man, or else the Pack had fled before the* dhole. *My life I owe to thee, and today thou hast saved the Pack even as once I saved thee. Hast thou forgotten? All debts are paid now. Go to thine own people. I tell thee again, eye of my eye, this hunting is ended. Go to thine own people."*

Mowgli shouted, *"Nay, nay, I am a wolf. I am of one skin with the Free People. It is no will of mine that I am a man."*

And Akela said, *"After the summer come the Rains, and after the Rains comes the spring. Go back before thou art driven ... Mowgli will drive Mowgli. Go back to thy people. Go to Man."*

Mowgli answered, *"When Mowgli drives Mowgli I will go."*

And Akela said, *"There is no more to say. Little Brother, canst thou raise me to my feet? I also was a leader of the Free People."*

Then Akela, in a strong, lifting voice, sang the "Death Song," which a leader of the pack must sing when he dies. The song reverberated far into the night jungle, and all the animals and birds listened in rapt attention. When he finished singing, Akela shook himself clear of Mowgli's arms and, leaping into the air, died, collapsing on top of a *dhole* carcass.

Akela would always cry at this scene when he was a child. It was a fitting, noble end for the majestic Akela, was it not? The "Death Song" echoed inside Akela's head like the note from a single flute. Now, as he ran along, Akela was again on the verge of tears. Mowgli sat beside the dead Akela until daybreak. Later, Mowgli, doing as Baloo the bear and Kaa the python had told him, would leave the jungle, weeping.

> Baloo said, *Little Frog, take thine own trail; make thy lair with thine own blood and pack and people; but when there is need of foot or tooth or eye or word carried swiftly by night, remember, Master of the Jungle, the Jungle is thine at call.... Go now, but first come to me. O wise Little Frog, come to me!*

Akela wiped his face, wet from tears, or raindrops, or sweat, he couldn't tell which, then stopped all at once under the eaves of a shop at the corner. Mowgli, who had fallen behind, came running up and immediately crouched down. Her back was rising and falling, and she was panting audibly. Akela was also having trouble catching his breath. Silent, they stayed under the eaves for about ten minutes. The station lay just a little ahead of them. Realizing where they were, Akela wanted to get to the station in one more burst. Waiting for Mowgli to catch her breath, he began to run through the rain again, only more slowly this time. It was difficult to recover that feeling of sprinting like Akela, which he had experienced moments before. In reality, his body had grown heavy. Still, they would soon be at the station. This kind of ordeal didn't really qualify as an ordeal. He expected that Mowgli, who was running behind him, would understand that well enough. Akela continued to run, while turning his thoughts back to that terrible battle with the Red Dogs.

Brave, old, valiant Akela died in the end after the battle with the *dhole*. Then the human child Mowgli returned to the home of the human mother who had given birth to him. As a story, that's how things turned out. However, I am not really a wolf. Mowgli isn't a boy. Time in real life doesn't progress as fast as it does in a book. Mowgli is a little child, and she'll still be a little child after a week passes, and I'll still be a youthful hero brimming with strength. The Mowgli and Akela who appeared at the beginning of *The Jungle Book* couldn't have imagined what might become of them fifteen or twenty years later, and they wouldn't have been concerned about it in any case. Akela and Mowgli were similar in that regard. Akela wasn't old yet, and there was no need to think that the fate that befell the old Akela foreshadowed his own. Unlike the world of books, people in the real world exist in the "present." Thus, because Akela was still just seventeen, he was interested only in the young valiant Akela. This was even truer for Mowgli, who was only a girl of twelve. Even five years from now, her voice would not change, it would not become masculine, and she would not grow a beard. She would probably never participate in a battle with the Red Dogs. Poor little Mowgli. But because she *is* poor little Mowgli, she'll manage to avoid having to return to the human world after the battle with the *dhole*. And Akela will not die.

Feeling relieved at last, Akela turned to look at Mowgli behind him.

"It's just a little farther. If you're tired, it's okay to walk. I'll be at the station entrance," he said and, without waiting for an answer, began running faster again.

> It is met, and we go to the light.
> Bay! O bay!

Singing loudly in his heart, Akela was staring at the round clock on the roof of the station building, which had come into sight. Soaked by the rain, he felt flushed and hot, and sweat poured from his body.

5. Lost in Darkness

At two o'clock that afternoon they boarded another train. Sitting in a corner of their largely empty car, they immediately scarfed down the *bentō* and the six dried persimmons they had purchased in the station.

This time they had tickets to Akita. Because they wanted to go as far north as possible—maybe far enough to see Siberia—it might have been better to have bought tickets for Aomori. However, the station attendant told them that neither the train they were on now nor the next scheduled departure went as far as Aomori; and in any case, Akela wanted to save his money. If they went beyond their station stop, all they would have to do is pay a fare adjustment.

They were able to grab a spot with four empty seats. They took off their shoes and, sitting side by side, stretched their legs out, propping them on the two seats opposite. Although they had only been traveling together since the previous night, they felt a sense of relief when they got on the train, as if somehow they had returned safely to their own abode. It was warm inside, and there was a toilet nearby. And people would come by selling food. There was no need to hide the fact that they were outsiders. Even so, Mowgli had to be quiet when other people were around. She had promised to do that. Though she had cut her hair and was now more boyish-looking, there was the real possibility that her girlish voice might carelessly slip out. Akela had no idea when or where her girliness might show, and even Mowgli wasn't sure.

When she reached the front of the station, where Akela was waiting for her, Mowgli was convinced her heart would stop that very instant and that she would leave this world. But after ten minutes she realized her heart was still pumping. Standing up again on her own feet, she took a deep breath and was amazed that people didn't die from this sort of exertion. Running had been that painful. She absolutely did not want to be abandoned in a strange land, and so she chased after Akela with all her might. But over the final hundred meters a gap had opened up between them. Mowgli was not very good at sports or exercise, and she was a slow runner. She hated the sports days at her school. Who wouldn't hate them if it meant every year having to wear a green ribbon on her chest showing she had finished last? She wondered how far they had run just now. Maybe more than three kilometers? They did rest once along the way, but even so, running that distance was quite a feat for Mowgli. Being with Akela, she came to feel she could do all sorts of things. And now she had learned one more thing from him. Out of the blue, Mowgli thought of the words "older brother." Her real older brother had been clumsier at running than she, and he didn't know how to speak—he didn't even know what to do when it rained. And of course he had never given her *ramen*, or a *bentō* at a railway station.

They checked the timetable and found out they had fifty minutes before the next train arrived. Soaked a second time by the rain, they went to the toilet, wrung the water out of their clothes, wiped their heads with a towel, and put fresh toilet paper inside their shoes. Because a third or so of the toilet paper they had managed to get at the department store downtown was ruined, they decided, with some regret, to throw it away. The only place they could possibly get a high-quality product like toilet paper was at a department store. They went into the waiting room for a few minutes. The air was stagnant, and they felt uneasy being near other passengers, so they immediately headed back outside. Having nothing else to do, they wandered around to the right side of the station building, where they found a small storage shed covered in zinc siding. The back of the shed directly abutted the end of the railroad tracks, and on a long, narrow strip of empty land alongside those tracks was a flowerbed filled with trumpet-shaped daffodils.

"Flowers blooming in a place like this?" Mowgli exclaimed in surprise.

In the rain the dark yellow daffodils looked like gold birds with trembling wings. Primroses and hyacinths, also in bloom, were mingled in among them. *As they went farther north, they'd find even more flowers blooming in wild profusion, as well as butterflies and beautiful birds flitting about.* Akela's claims came rising back to Mowgli's ears. It really was true. It was spring now in the northern provinces. Still, just because it was spring and flowers were blooming, it certainly didn't mean they'd encounter any black panthers or elephants.

Crouching under the eaves of the shed, Mowgli was entranced by the yellow of the daffodils while Akela was cutting her hair with the new scissors. He handled the scissors more professionally than her mother. The sound of his scissors was different. Mowgli didn't request anything special. She left the style of cut to Akela. She wasn't at all particular about her hair. When she and her brother were little, her mother would cut it for her. Now she went to a barber in the neighborhood. It hadn't yet occurred to Mowgli or to her mother that she should go to a beauty parlor.

Akela quickly finished the haircut. Gathering the clipped hair up in a newspaper and throwing it into a trash can, Mowgli hurried off to a toilet in the station to examine her new do in the mirror. Her ears were visible now, but her bangs hid her forehead. She turned around and, bending her neck, inspected the back of her head. The bluish-white nape of her neck was also visible now, and looked rather cold. Her hair was not cut straight all over, but zigzagged a little, like the head of a longhaired dog. She had not expected it would suit her so well, and so she felt satisfied. She even thought she looked cuter than with her hair cut in a bob.

Pulling her baseball cap way down over her head, Mowgli set out with Akela for the platform and waited for the train to arrive. The scruff of her neck and her earlobes were exposed, and that felt refreshing to her. Even so, if they went further north, she would probably get chilled and catch a cold. Because her clothes were damp, her body slowly began to get cold, and she had to stamp her feet and rub her arms and legs with the palms of her hands to stay warm.

Once they had finally boarded the two-o'clock train and enjoyed their *bentō*, hot tea, and dried persimmons, a feeling of warmth and drowsiness swept over their bodies. The monotonous rumbling of the train wheels made Mowgli sleepy. The prickly hair that had fallen on her back and chest during her haircut was making her itchy, but she leaned against Akela's shoulder and soon dozed off.

Akela smoked one of the fresh cigarettes he'd bought at the station, yawning repeatedly. He felt a sense of annoyance, wondering why they had ever gotten off the train in Yamagata. It seemed now that it was simply to get rained on. He had been able to buy a pair of scissors and cut Mowgli's hair, but that wasn't anything they had to go out of their way to do in Yamagata. Certainly it didn't merit getting soaked.

Akela gently rubbed Mowgli's back for a few minutes to warm her a bit. Akela's body had not yet warmed up, and the area around his waist in particular felt chilled. Picking up a dirty newspaper that had been dropped on the floor, he tried wrapping it around their waists. There was cleaner newspaper in his cloth knapsack, but that had gotten wet in the rain, and for now it looked to be of no use.

The train proceeded slowly through the rain, constantly stopping at small stations. Akela closed his eyes and listened to Mowgli breathe as she slept. There is nothing as calming as the breathing of a sleeping child. Come to think of it, his own father may well have had the same calm feeling when he slept snuggled up with the four-year-old Akela in the graveyard. Perhaps that feeling is also the affection one feels for a small child. Had the four-year-old Akela, by his regular breathing and by the warmth of his body, sustained his father when he was asleep? As he grew more and more drowsy, Akela continued to follow the train of his own thoughts. He knew for certain that Mowgli had her own worries. Even small children had to put up with various sufferings and sorrows. Whenever he was convinced that the little ones at the Children's Home were attached to him, their hackles would suddenly rise, they would bare their fangs, and turn their backs on him. They would growl and glare from a corner of the room, and when he asked what was wrong, they'd say, "Go away!" When he asked them why they said such a thing, they'd cry and say that even though he was a child in the home too, he acted more like a teacher or a father. But from Akela's point of view they were just little children; the smallness of their bodies was adorable; their soft round heads and their childish way of talking were endearing; and holding them brought him a sense of calm and peace. Perhaps "Mom" and "Pop" and the nurses at the home had felt the same affection for Akela when he was little. Akela had constantly bared his fangs and sharp claws at them.

The dying emperor Akela closed the curtain on his life while Mowgli held him in his lap. *That* Akela felt peace in the warm, soft existence of the Little Frog, and so was able to accept his own death in a calm a state of mind.

It was the same for Akela's father, who had held him, constantly staring at his own death amid the withered leaves in the graveyard.—That's right, the old Lone Wolf who went to his death was Akela's father. The father had admonished the four-year-old Akela, telling him he was human, that he had to go back to the place of the humans. The father was committed to a hospital, and Akela, having been left behind, was taken into a foster home, then was moved to a different place, and finally was brought to the Children's Home. Akela had been made to go back to the Man Pack. And his father, as emperor of the jungle, sang the "Death Song" in the hospital, his voice ringing out to every corner of Tokyo. Like a whistle in the depths of night …

In her dream, swaying to the motion of the train, Mowgli was walking with her older brother down the alley in front of their house. They came out onto the main street, where the city trolleys ran. A temple stretched out on their left side, and the street there began to slope downward precipitously, as though it was leading them to the bottom of the ocean. Her brother continued walking straight ahead down that street, and Mowgli followed him. Neither of them had any money. They were carrying nothing. They had been playing inside the house, and had gone outside just as they were, and started walking. They were familiar with their neighborhood up to the place where the street sloped sharply down, but they had never gone beyond that point by themselves. They remembered their mother taking them to the trolley once. They rode along the sloping street until they eventually arrived at a zoo. The stone fences along one side became taller and taller, plunging the street into shadow. Mowgli was frightened by those shadows, but her brother didn't seem to mind that sort of thing. They descended the slope and then climbed the street as it continued on up the next hill. There were rows of shops they had never seen before, and the unfamiliar temples frightened them. People they didn't know were coming and going, glaring at them. They made quite a pair, with their noses running, their chins chapped red from drooling, their mouths agape, their thick tongues hanging out. Their way of walking made them look like two sick baby monkeys who couldn't understand human speech, and who had no one to watch over them. It was very odd that they would be wandering around. Had they escaped from somewhere? Were they accompanying one another in a bid for freedom?

The unfamiliar slope continued on and on, and as adults and children stared at Mowgli and her brother with flashing white eyes, the two began to walk faster. They didn't want to be taken into custody by the police before they reached the zoo. At last the road leveled out. They were tired, they were sweaty, they were drooling more and more, and they began groaning. They kept following the trolley line. That earlier time, when they took the trolley, they'd arrived at the zoo quickly, but now, no matter how long they walked, the zoo still was nowhere in sight. Their groaning grew louder. They held hands and pressed forward, their bodies swaying as if they were walking through heavy water. The street widened out, there were more trees, and suddenly the back gate of the zoo appeared before them. Surprised, they moved closer to it. A man in uniform was standing there. They peeked in and could see large black animals. They caught the familiar odors of the zoo. They stopped groaning, sucked in their drool, and tried to go inside. The man in the uniform called out and stopped them. *You can't go in without tickets. Tickets? You can buy them at the window over there.*

They didn't understand what was going on. Shaking free of the man, who was restraining them, they tried to force their way inside. The man's eyes opened wide. He grabbed their arms in his powerful grip and dragged them outside. A spiteful man who had great strength, like one of the guardian Deva gods. The two of them clung to the outside of the iron fence, screaming and crying. But the man wouldn't look their way. As they were screaming, they peed their pants. But the man didn't even notice the smell of urine.

Eventually they ventured off again, dragging their legs, which were wet from their pee. Thirsty, hungry, their eyes bleary, they didn't know the way home. Their faces were streaked with snot and spittle and tears. Their wailing rose as loud as the trumpeting of the elephants in the zoo. They crouched by the side of the road with their shoulders huddled together. A concrete wall ran on for a considerable distance behind them, and they could see a bridge off to their right. Crowds of people were coming and going along the street. Some noticed the two children, some didn't. Some even fished around in a pocket and tossed one-yen coins to them. A chipped teacup was sitting in front of them. In the blink of an eye several days passed, then several weeks, and the children, who continued to crouch there, began to resemble a clump of rags. Whenever a coin was thrown into the cup, they would drool and lower their heads. When they did so, their hair, which was now matted with mud and a nest for lice, would tremble, and an odor like the scent one smells in the zoo would drift up. A clean little girl, accompanied by her mother, nervously approached the two of them, placed some money in the cup, and then ran away as fast as she could. Mowgli suddenly realized that she was that little girl. Once, when she had gone out with her mother and brother to some place much farther than the zoo, she had discovered a clump of rags near a temple gate. Puzzled, she wondered what it could be, and had the feeling that maybe there was a mangy, starving dog there.

The girl and her older brother had turned into rags—because they had left home without telling their mother and without bringing any money, because they had gone walking along a street that stretched out, flowing uninterrupted, forever.

A dog's barking came pressing in on her—a stray dog pursued by a dogcatcher from the public health center. Mowgli's family once had a pet dog, but when it strayed outside, it was caught and disposed of. She went with her mother to the dog pound to look for it, and they walked around looking at more than a hundred dogs, one by one. Big dogs, little dogs, black dogs, white dogs, even shepherds and bulldogs that seemed to have been carefully looked after were mingling together in the cage there. When Mowgli and her mother passed in front of the cage, the dogs put their front paws up on the wire mesh, pressed their noses against it, and barked as if they were screaming. Because the dogs were all barking that same way, it got so noisy she had to cover her ears. A dogcatcher might try to wrap a loop of wire attached to a stick around the necks of Mowgli and her older brother, just like he did with these dogs, and force them into a vehicle. The loop was frightening, but the stray dogs were frightening too. The diseased dogs were especially scary.

Crying, the two of them tried to crawl away. It felt like the sounds of barking were pursuing them, and they moved out onto a bridge. A flat-bottom boat was drifting on the river below. Children were playing and laundry was fluttering on the boat. The two of them held hands and jumped from the bridge, hoping to land in the boat. But they missed their target and ended up falling into the water. The water was lukewarm and smelled of rotting fish. They drifted about, clinging to one another. Something white came bobbing along on the surface. It looked like the body of a dead baby. A little further away the body of a woman, her long hair fanning out, floated by as well.

Overwhelmed by fear, Mowgli began thrashing her arms and legs, trying to get out of the water. Her brother's body was sinking to the bottom, and the corpse of the infant drifted over Mowgli's head.

The train continued heading north. Akela was asleep next to Mowgli, his mouth hanging open. He didn't look at all like her older brother. She recalled her brother's runny nose, his drooling, the times when he peed his pants, or even sometimes pooped himself. Suddenly feeling as though she was about to pee her own pants, she became flustered and tried shifting her bottom a little on the seat. She also tried rubbing her lips. Her nose wasn't running and she wasn't drooling. Relieved, Mowgli sighed. Then, she noticed a pain in her stomach. It was the kind of pain she had when her stomach was upset. Gazing out the window, she focused on the condition of her stomach. Rain was still falling. Rice paddies spread out all around, and, perhaps because of the rain, the color of the water in the paddies looked fresh and vivid, like the color of a baby tree frog. Nothing else particularly caught her eye. Then, just as she had a moment ago, she experienced a sharp pain deep in her belly. She stood up quietly, so as not to wake Akela, only to find she couldn't get out to the aisle if she didn't step over his legs. She tried to be careful, but the tip of her trailing foot caught his knee. Akela opened his eyes with a terrified expression.

"What the ... oh, it's you! What're you doing?"

"I'm just going to the toilet," Mowgli answered as she hurried down the aisle.

When she moved her body, the pain suddenly worsened, and it felt like poop would come shooting out her butt. Holding herself, a cold sweat broke out on her forehead. If she crapped her panties at a time like this, Akela would utterly abandon her. Preoccupied by that thought, she went out into the vestibule. Luckily, no one was using the toilet. Fumbling with the handle, she opened the door and went in.

At the very least, she wanted to get rid of as much of her diarrhea as she could, so she stayed in the toilet a full twenty minutes. During that time, apart from the pain in her stomach, she also felt dizzy. She finally gave up and went back into the car dragging her legs, which had fallen asleep. Akela stood up and greeted Mowgli. Her face was pale.

"I thought you might have tumbled off the train. Do you have motion sickness?"

"My stomach hurts. I think it'll be all right soon."

No sooner had she spoken than her stomach started to hurt again.

"We'll be in for it if you've caught a cold. Children's colds easily affect the stomach. I feel a little chilled myself. What a fine place Cold Lairs is. We've got no blankets, no sweaters...."

Listening to Akela, she felt a new attack of diarrhea come on, and she broke out in a cold sweat again. "I've got to go back to the toilet," she said. She had no choice but to stand up and, holding her stomach, hurry once more to the toilet in the vestibule.

This time she was there for ten minutes before returning to her seat. Her face was becoming more and more pale. While waiting for her, Akela gathered up some newspapers that had been left behind by other passengers.

"It may not look very nice, but newspaper is warm, so use this in place of a blanket."

Akela brushed the dirt off the newspapers sheet by sheet, spread them out, and began to wrap Mowgli's upper body and hips in them. Next he wrapped his own body in newspaper.

"Dammit, this is pretty shabby. But we'll warm up, so we can't worry about how we look."

Mowgli laughed at being wrapped up inside her newspaper blanket. But when she did, her stomach hurt again. She felt a pushing sensation on her butt. If she weren't careful, poop would squirt out. She sighed, and, pulling aside the newspaper that Akela had gone to the trouble of wrapping her in, she stood up.

"I'm going to the toilet."

"Again? Is it that bad? Do you have some strange disease?" Akela's voice sounded alarmed.

"Strange disease?" Mowgli asked, holding her stomach.

"You know, dysentery, or typhus ..."

"Don't be ridiculous!"

She wanted to laugh at Akela for being such a worrywart, but she didn't really have time for that and hurried down the aisle to the toilet.

While Mowgli was in the toilet, the train gave a violent jolt, then went quiet. She could hear the station announcement. *Shinjō. Now arriving at Shinjō* ... She still had the runs, but only a little was coming out now. She was through the worst of it, and, feeling relieved, washed her hands thoroughly. She knew nothing at all about dysentery and typhus, but they were probably much more painful and serious. Her mother had often frightened Mowgli with her talk of dysentery and typhus. Whenever they went to a festival, her mother would tell her that cotton candy, popsicles, and candy-coated apricots on a stick all caused dysentery. That's why her mother never bought them for her.

She walked down the aisle, thinking that when she got back to her seat she would tell Akela that she was okay, that her diarrhea had subsided. The train was still at Shinjō, and passengers were getting on after another. Middle-school and high-school students had gathered on their way home in groups of four or five and were chattering loudly in a dialect that Mowgli had a hard time understanding. Some of the girls wore sailor-style outfits. Some of the boys had school uniforms, some didn't. One girl had on loose work trousers and a sweater full of holes, while a boy was wearing trousers and a loose garment that looked like an undershirt. Almost all their clothes were patched and the colors thoroughly faded. Some were wearing worn-out sneakers, others clogs or floppy old rubber boots. Each student's shirt had a white cloth tag attached to the front that listed both name and blood type. No one was carrying a leather school bag. They had exhausted-looking cloth satchels and rucksacks instead. Many were holding umbrellas repaired with cotton patches, clutching them as though they were valuable. Some had old-fashioned parasols made of bamboo ribs and oiled paper, while others held things that looked like straw mats. It was hard to imagine that people still used such items in this day and age.

Scrawny-looking men with sickly complexions also got on the train. There were about ten of them, all wearing dirty military hats and uniforms with gaiters on their legs. They were a sullen lot, their hair and whiskers long and unkempt, their mouths hanging open. They moved sluggishly down the aisle; rucksacks and canteens hung together from their shoulders. Several young boys, who were about the same age as Mowgli, had congregated at the other end of the car. Like the men, their complexions were swarthy and sickly, and their clothes looked like rags. Apparently they had no luggage. One young man, who was wearing better clothes than the others, was handing out *bentō* boxes that he had bought at the station. Other people got on the train as well. Their exhaustion was apparent in their faces. Most of them had slung worn knapsacks over their backs, and many were wearing faded military uniforms and hats. Women in dirty work trousers and clogs were leading children along by the hand. The faces of the children and the women were dusky, as if they hadn't had a bath in a long time. Of course, the crowd of people included women with tightly curled perms and Western-style dresses with large shoulder pads, and men in fedoras who looked like company employees. But even those nicer clothes looked out of date. Mowgli had the impression that people dressed like that in the old days.

When she returned to her seat, Akela was looking down, and it was clear from his face that he was in a bad mood. Already new passengers were occupying the seats directly across from them, and he had just barely been able to save Mowgli's seat by placing the newspapers and their two bags on it. Mowgli sat down and held her cloth bag and the newspapers on her lap. Akela leaned toward Mowgli.

"It was a real struggle holding onto this seat," he whispered. "So how's your stomach?"

The departure bell sounded, and a high-pitched whistle rang out. The heavy body of the train shook, the whistle rang out once more, and they began to move. The bodies of all the passengers lurched in unison. A murmur rose up, and then quickly dissipated. Only the cheerful voices of the local middle- and high-school students floated around the car.

"It doesn't hurt much anymore," Mowgli whispered back. "It's really crowded now. What happened?"

"I suppose it's the time of day. Early evening commute."

"There sure are a lot of weirdly dressed people."

"Because we're in the sticks. It's like time has stopped here. It's just like when I was a little kid. Nothing has changed. It almost makes me feel nostalgic. Anyway, thanks to them our newspaper won't look so conspicuous. And with so many people, the car will warm up too."

Mowgli nodded, spread the newspaper out and wrapped herself up in it. Akela had already wrapped himself up so that he looked liked an Egyptian mummy. The old man and the middle-aged woman sitting directly across from them seemed not to give any notice to Akela's appearance. They looked tired and had closed their eyes. The old man wore a black deerstalker cap and boots; the woman had tossed a woolen shawl around her kimono and was holding a fairly large bundle wrapped in a *furoshiki* cloth. She was cradling it carefully on her lap, as if it contained something valuable. Mowgli couldn't tell if the two were traveling together, because they hadn't exchanged a single word between them.

The car was crammed full of people standing or squatting in the aisle. One man was perched on the armrest of the seat across from Mowgli. Before long, someone would probably sit on the armrest of her seat as well, and someone else might even try to squeeze into the space at her feet. It had been terribly crowded all the way from Ueno to around Fukushima, but that was an overnight train. It was daytime now, and no one was sleeping. This train was only going as far as Noshiro, so it really couldn't be called a long-distance train. So why was it so crowded? Because it was early evening and raining? Because it was some special day in this region she knew nothing about?

Mowgli wrapped herself up in the newspaper, taking special care to cover her stomach, and closed her eyes. Her clothes had pretty much dried out, and it felt warm and comfy inside the paper. The dusty smell of the newspaper tickled her nose. She figured that she'd need to go to the toilet again in a little while. Because she had the runs, she was extremely tired. Still, it wasn't dysentery, and so she wasn't all that worried about it.

The train stopped at a small station, and then started up again. A baby was crying at the end of the car. Somewhere a baby had died of children's dysentery. She had heard that story from her mother, but couldn't remember when it happened, or where the baby was from. She couldn't really distinguish between children's dysentery and dysentery. But it was certain that at least one baby had died because of it. The time her brother Ton-chan had the runs, he had to wear a diaper, even though he was in middle school; and when her mother took that diaper off, his poop shot out like a water pistol. It hit her mother in the face, and she was furious and screamed at Ton-chan. The tatami mats and shoji doors all around were covered with yellowish shit. Oddly, it didn't stink at all. Apparently it was just plain old diarrhea, not dysentery or children's dysentery. However, Ton-chan died after his illness, so maybe it wasn't just diarrhea.

The face of her dead brother rose up in Mowgli's mind. A stagnant, yellowish face. He wasn't drooling, and the area under his nose was perfectly clean. He wasn't trying to open his eyes in a disagreeable manner, or to move the tips of his fingers, or his eyelids, or his mouth. There wasn't one thing about him that was like her brother. Just a yellowish lump that was the spitting image of him. His nostrils were stuffed with cotton. The acrid smell of the crematorium had irritated Mowgli's nose.

It became hard for her to breathe, and Mowgli quickly opened her eyes. She breathed in through her mouth, and stared out the window. She mustn't remember that sort of thing. Mowgli tried pushing her memories back deep inside her body and out of sight. It was like using her hands to try, in a panic, to push glue that was oozing out back into its container.

The rain was still falling. Wondering if they would have to run through it again when they reached Akita, she felt discouraged. Or would they transfer to a different train? Now that she thought about it, they were still in Tokyo at about this time yesterday. The thought made it hard for Mowgli to catch her breath, and her heart started pounding violently. She had been wearing her sailor-style uniform and carrying her school satchel. It all seemed like something from the distant past. A terrible mistake had been made, but there was no turning back now, for they had come to a far distant place. What's more, she wasn't even clear what kind of mistake she had made. There was no use thinking about it. In any case, she was now on a train, and that train was moving along the tracks for the sake of the passengers.

The train stopped at yet another station, and waves of people surged in the aisle. The students who had made the car so lively got off the train a few at a time, and their numbers gradually dwindled. The car, which had been full of passengers, grew quiet, and Mowgli could make out voices a little distance away. The dissatisfied voices of the young boys—and a man's voice trying to calm them. She couldn't make out the words, but the voices brought to mind sounds familiar to her in Tokyo. Perhaps they had come from Tokyo. The women's voices she heard were complaining about the hardships of their lives—they were undoubtedly the voices of people from this region. From time to time laughing male voices would bubble up.

Mowgli's stomach began to hurt again. This time she woke Akela first before standing up. It was so crowded, there was bound to be someone who would try to take her seat, regardless.

"Again? But your complexion is a lot better. I don't feel very good myself. When you run through the rain feeling good, you end up like this. I'm no longer young, you know. All right, then, hurry up and go. This place is swarming with people, so watch your step."

The aisle was more crowded than she had imagined. All sorts of baggage—rucksacks, *furoshiki* bundles, bamboo baskets—had been placed on the floor, and as she went along step by step, searching for places to walk, she had to lift her feet carefully, left and right. When she bumped into someone, she bowed her head and apologized. Mowgli was a child, so no one got angry, but they all clearly looked displeased. A little girl dressed in baggy work trousers was asleep on the floor. Crouching beside her was a woman with a large belly—apparently her mother. Though Mowgli did her best to watch where she was stepping, the heel of her leather shoe clipped the little girl's head. The girl started crying in a remarkably florid way. Her mother glared at Mowgli, scolding her in a low voice.

"Don't be so high and mighty in your leather shoes!"

Mumbling that she was so, so sorry, Mowgli cut through the crowd and pushed ahead. Then she realized that the woman had spoken to her in a Tokyo dialect, even though it wasn't a night train. Mowgli also realized that when she apologized, she had instinctively spoken the words she always used. She had to be more careful.

She reached the vestibule at last. It was overflowing with people, and three old men were squatting in front of the toilet. Mowgli stared at the door, and then stared at the old men. They moved their backs away from the door and signaled with their eyes for her to go in. She bowed her head, and stepped inside. She came to a halt, as if paralyzed. A baby wrapped up in rags was asleep on the lower part of the floor. Her first thought was, had it been abandoned? But if that were the case, surely the old men in front of the door would have noticed. Perhaps the baby's mother was nearby and had intentionally put the baby here so that it could sleep. But why would she put it in the toilet? It seemed weird.

Mowgli wavered for a moment, but went in and, pulling on the ragged cloth, dragged it near the door. She then tapped one of the old men on the shoulder and pointed at the cloth. He apparently didn't understand what she meant, and made no effort to move. Mowgli forcibly pushed the old man's body and, as the old man grunted, she moved the bundled baby outside the door into the space that had opened up when he shifted his hips. She then very quickly shut the door. She pulled down her trousers and pants and straddled the toilet. It was a narrow escape, but she managed to not soil herself. When she was finished, she felt a momentary sense of relief, and tears suddenly came to her eyes. She didn't want to leave the toilet. That baby. Those old men. The people in the aisle. She had no idea what kind of terrible things were waiting for her once she opened the door. Still, if she didn't go back, Akela would be worried. It would be nice if Akela would come to get her. Was the baby still asleep? Should she put the baby back in here? Surely it had not been abandoned. No one would intentionally abandon a baby in a toilet on a train. Yet maybe that wasn't true. What would Akela make of it? Certainly he wouldn't be all that surprised. She was hoping that Akela would come for her, but would he?

About thirty minutes had passed by the time Mowgli returned to her seat next to Akela. She sat down with a deep sigh. Her cheeks were pale, and her mouth was puckered as if she were going to cry.

"Is your stomach really bad? You were gone so long, I was thinking about going to the toilet to check on you. But I thought if I went to see we'd probably not get our seats back, and so I wanted to go but couldn't, and I was really worried about you."

Hearing Akela say this, tears came to Mowgli's eyes.

"I'm not going to the toilet on my own anymore. I'll just have to put up with it somehow. And if I can't put up with it … well, it's OK. I don't care if we lose our seats."

"Tell me what's wrong? Did something happen?" Akela whispered, peering into Mowgli's face. Mowgli made no effort to answer.

"Well, all right then. I'm going to the toilet myself, so watch my seat. And keep your stomach warm."

Mowgli nodded, and watched Akela's back as he proceeded down the aisle, cutting through the crowd of people. When he got to the toilet, Akela would find the baby. When he did, what would he do? He'll probably call the conductor. Or maybe, like Mowgli, he'll leave the baby and come back to his seat. Either way, he would understand why she was upset.

Akela's bag and newspapers had been placed on the seat beside her. Covering those with her right hand, Mowgli looked around her seat again. The men with sickly faces dressed in old military clothes had, at some point, moved closer up the aisle. They were all sitting on the floor, stretching out their gaitered legs. Emaciated, their mouths agape, they seemed to have no energy. Some wore hospital masks. Some were still young. Two men, one in front of the group and one in back, would alternately stand and crouch, occasionally calling out to the scrawny men, or writing something down on papers that looked like some kind of documents. These two weren't as emaciated and their complexions were much better. They had on clean work clothes and white shirts. Perhaps they had gathered the scrawny men together and were taking them somewhere.

Mowgli could hear a husky woman's voice chattering on and on close by. It seemed that out of curiosity she had struck up a conversation with one of the emaciated-looking men. The woman's unreserved voice echoed through the car, but Mowgli couldn't hear the man's voice.

"All this pain and suffering, it feels like the gods and Buddha have deserted us.... It's the times we're living in.... It's nothing compared to what you've suffered, but even in this region of the country we had so many young men die in battle.... How did things get so terrible?... Yeah, but, the survivors can't do a thing except go on living.... Things can't get much worse than what they've been. The deal you've got, it's not so bad, is it?... It'll be summer soon in Hokkaido, and then it'll be easier to get along for sure.... After all, it's for the sake of the country, right? If there's no coal, we won't be able to do anything.... Really, even the trains are in terrible shape, and yet at least we're better off out here in the country. We've got food and can be a little more easy-going. I hear Tokyo and Osaka are living hells.... Well, you'll be serving your country, working in the coal mines, but I'm sure it'll be tough on you.... You take care of yourself...."

Akela came back to his seat. Mowgli studied his face.

"What's up? You look surprised to see me. I had no reason to be in the toilet as long as you," Akela said casually.

"Was there a baby in there?" Mowgli whispered in his ear.

"In where?"

"What do you mean, *in where*?"

"There're babies practically everywhere, but I sure didn't bother to look at each one. Why are you concerned about a baby?"

"Oh, nothing. Never mind."

Mowgli frowned and fell silent. Where did that baby go? Was it an illusion? She started to doubt herself.

"Damn, you sure are moody all of a sudden. I'm not feeling all that great myself, so don't bother me with such stuff. If I don't sleep now when I have the chance, I'm really going to be in for it."

"Do you have a fever?"

Suddenly worried, Mowgli tried placing her hand on Akela's forehead. He seemed to be a little feverish, but it wasn't clear. Taking off her baseball cap, she pushed up her bangs with her hand and pressed her forehead up against Akela's. For an instant Akela was confused and pulled back, then he lightly closed his eyes as if he were embarrassed.

"Hmm ... it feels like you have a slight fever," Mowgli whispered solemnly, moving her forehead away from his face.

"You've got diarrhea and I've got a fever. What a fine mess." Akela laughed sarcastically, then drew close to Mowgli's ear and whispered, "You've gone back to speaking like a girl. Watch yourself."

95

Mowgli glared at Akela and muttered, "You know, those men near us are going to Hokkaido. They're going to work in the coal mines. There are all kinds of people here, aren't there."

Glancing sideways, Akela looked over at the men in the aisle, and nodded. "If my old man hadn't been careful, he probably would have ended up like those guys."

Startled by Akela's whispered words, Mowgli now looked at the men in the aisle in a different light. Were they and Akela's father, who had made his bed in a graveyard, similar kinds of men? In her mind, she pictured a man, his back turned toward her, accompanied by a four-year-old child, disappearing silently into the darkness—his head down, a blanket full of holes dragging behind him, passing through the graveyard, passing through the streets as though sliding over the surface of water. He passes through Mowgli's mind as well. The pitch-black shadow of the child follows him. The man, though still walking, is already dead. And so he says nothing, his footsteps make no sound. His back bent, he continues searching for a place where he can die for real. Though he is already dead, he has a four-year-old child, and so it isn't all that easy for him to become a real corpse. The child and the man are wrapped in the murmuring of trees as they wander through the graveyard, moving past Mowgli's body, heading toward Hokkaido from Akita, walking over the ash-gray sea.

The train came to a stop, but almost no one got off. Akela and Mowgli fell silent and stared out the window. The train took off again. The rain continued to fall, and the raindrops struck the glass windows with a hard rapping sound, flowing down in glimmering white streaks.

One of the sickly-looking men in the aisle stood up. The train lurched, and the man suddenly fell right across Akela and Mowgli. Mowgli instinctively let out a small cry. Akela had quickly raised both hands to break the man's fall, and slowly began to push him back up. Meanwhile, the man stared into Mowgli's face with bloodshot eyes. Utterly expressionless, he kept peering into her eyes. A soft sound escaped his throat. It sounded like a groan, but also like a belch. A rank stench assaulted Mowgli's nose. He was escorted away by one of the men in the work clothes, staggering as he went down the aisle. Apparently he went to the toilet. Akela sighed and looked at Mowgli's face. The pale, pain-ridden expression he'd seen there earlier was back. It looked like she was tearing up, that her stomach was hurting again. But she made no effort to go to the toilet. Did she plan to go to the toilet after the man who had fallen onto them got back? With these thoughts racing through his mind, Akela gathered up the newspapers on his lap, stuffed them into his cloth bag, and began to smoke a cigarette. Perhaps it was his imagination, but he felt like the men in the aisle were stealing envious glances at his cigarettes. He sensed the other passengers looking at him in the same way, and he wanted to say to all of them, *It's just a cigarette. If you want one, why don't you go buy your own at the station! I suppose a seventeen-year-old like me could give cigarettes to you adults if you wanted them. But if I did, you'd all look pathetic, now, wouldn't you?*

Akela frowned and continued to puff away. Perhaps because he had a fever, his throat felt scratchy, and he wanted to throw the cigarette on the floor. If he did, would these men come scrambling over one another saying *it's mine, it's mine* like a bunch of starving monkeys? He felt like giving it a try, but he wasn't that brave, so he stuck it out and continued puffing away. It was enough to simply let them smell the aroma of the tobacco.

These men didn't really resemble Akela's father all that much. Some of them were smaller framed, some had rounder faces, some were younger, some had glasses. Of course, Akela could no longer clearly remember what his father looked like. He simply concluded that his father bore no resemblance to these men. But then he started to doubt himself, and as he pondered the matter, he began to look for the image of his father in the figures of those men. Were his father's hands dark like theirs? Did his only set of ragged clothes have the same kind of sweaty sheen? Did he stink like them? Akela stubbornly persisted in thinking it was unlikely that these men resembled his father. Even to the eyes of someone like Akela, these men were extremely wretched and filthy. The lowest of the monkeys—defeated monkeys no one wanted anything to do with. Yet hadn't Akela's father also been just another defeated monkey? Hadn't he been just another of the dead who had fallen by the wayside?

He started feeling worse and worse and was becoming nauseous. Akela stamped his cigarette out on the floor, put the butt in a pocket of his trousers, then closed his eyes. If he had a fever, it would be best not to think useless thoughts. Since he had gone to the trouble of taking the name Akela, it was best to sing, Akela-like, the "Night-Song in the Jungle."—*This is the hour of pride and power, Talon and tush and claw. Oh hear the call! ... Bay! Oh Bay!*

"All right, men, we'll be arriving at Yokote in a little bit. You're all probably tired, right? After we get to Yokote, we'll eat right away. You'll get your fill of white rice. Then we'll go to Kurosawa. The people who are coming to meet you will be waiting there."

Akela could hear the unpleasantly unctuous voice of some obsequious monkey behind him. Several shabby-looking young men had congregated near the door. Apparently the man had been talking to them. Akela had never realized before that the Tokyo dialect could sound so vulgar.

Off to the side he heard a woman's voice—it was like earthworms crawling stealthily through Cold Lairs.

"But you know, I think it's good you were able to get back to Japan like this. I've heard there's still twenty or thirty thousand people who want to come back from the continent but can't. And even if they struggle and do manage to get back to Japan, if they've got no house or family to go to, then they'll just be a nuisance ... but you know, in the countryside we've got our own problems, and we're always

97

being told to hand over our rice and vegetables, and that's not right...."

"Listen up, everyone. I know you may be anxious, but there's no need to worry. The work is easy, and you're free in the evenings.... Oh yeah, they have movie theaters there. Not as many as Tokyo, mind you, but it's a real nice town, so you won't be bored. And remember, food will not be a problem. So if you think about how it was in Tokyo, wandering around dying of starvation, you guys are pretty lucky...."

Bay! Oh Bay!
This is the hour of pride and power
Talon and tush and claw.
Through the Jungle very softly flits a shadow and a sigh
And thy heart against thy side hammers:
Fear, O Little Hunter—this is Fear!

"Please."

Akela felt his arm being pulled hard and heard Mowgli's whimpering voice in his ear. "Listen, I can't stand it anymore. I'm getting off at the next station. Whatever happens, I'm getting off. It feels like I'm going to throw up."

All at once Mowgli gathered up her bag and newspapers and stepped out into the aisle. Surprised and bewildered, Akela followed after her in a rush. For whatever reason, Mowgli wanted to get off the train, so there was nothing he could do but get off. They were under no obligation to stay on this train, and it was vital that the two of them always stay near each other.

While they were moving down the aisle, the train came to a stop. It was a small station, which meant the train would start moving again very quickly. Akela went ahead and, holding Mowgli's hand, they roughly shoved and elbowed their way through the passengers in the aisle and went out into the vestibule. Just as they opened the door, the train started to move. There had been no departure bell or whistle. Grasping Mowgli's hand, Akela jumped down onto the platform.

The train left the two of them behind with unexpected speed, disappearing in a flash. Crouching down on the dark platform, they were left staring at the shining, rain-soaked tracks, panting and trying to calm their throbbing hearts. Then, noticing the white breath puffing out of their mouths, they shivered.

"It's cold," Mowgli muttered.

"It's just like winter."

The few other passengers who had gotten off here were nowhere to be seen. On the opposite platform about ten people were standing, waiting for the next train, not moving a muscle in the rain. Large bundles wrapped in *furoshiki*, suitcases, and wooden boxes wound around with cords were lined up in a row, looking like the shadows of those people. The name of the station, *Daigo*, was written on a pillar.

A lone man carrying an umbrella came walking toward them. Akela and Mowgli stood up, holding hands, and started walking with relaxed, cheerful faces. The man passed by them without saying a word. They continued on, crossing over the tracks and moving to the opposite platform. For the time being they sat down on a bench covered with a roof. A woman with a large belly and an old woman who seemed to be her companion were also sitting on the bench and looking off absentmindedly. People waiting for the next train had gathered around them—some holding up umbrellas, others standing in the rain with rubber rain caps on their heads. A few people had placed straw mats over their heads. For some reason, a muddy cat was sprawled under the bench. After taking extra care to position their feet so they wouldn't kick the cat's nose, Akela whispered to Mowgli, "Didn't you want to go to the toilet?"

Worrying about the cat under the bench, Mowgli whispered back, "Yeah, but there doesn't seem to be one here."

Akela glanced around again. There was a signal light just beyond the platform where they got off a few minutes ago, and he could see a fence that looked like the ticket turnstile. However, there were no station attendants, and he couldn't see any building with a roof or lights. Bluish-green rice paddies spread out all around the platform. In the rain, in the twilight darkness, he had the sensation that they were in the middle of a lake.

"There's nothing here. They may have a toilet, but that's about it.... All of a sudden you said you wanted to get off, so we leapt off the train, but now what do we do? We can't go anywhere like this. I have no idea where people live around here. It's pouring rain, and to top it off it's getting cold as hell."

Hearing Akela speak to her that way, Mowgli shrugged her shoulders and muttered, "But I wasn't feeling well, and I felt like I was going to throw up ... the train was full of weird people, and I was afraid. The longer I was around them, the more I felt like they were going to drag me to the bottom of the ocean ... and then there was that baby in the toilet."

Akela sighed. "Really? A baby in the toilet? There *were* some pretty suspicious-looking people, that's for sure. Maybe even slave traders."

A whistle sounded, and the women on the bench stood up. The cat feigned ignorance, sprawled out, and continued to nap. One person hunched down to slip his luggage over his shoulder. Another person lifted up a trunk and headed for the front edge of the platform.

"Listen up. A train's coming. We can't very well stay in a place like this, so let's just get on board. We have to. If we stick around here, we'll end up dying in a ditch somewhere."

Mowgli nodded. She had wanted to get away from the previous train, but once they got off, she wanted to go back to a bright, warm train car.

Soon a black locomotive spouting smoke appeared, moving in the opposite direction of their previous train. Steam was leaking from under the body of the engine, and it lumbered heavily and noisily to a stop at the platform. Confused, wondering if the earlier train had come back for them, Akela once again took Mowgli's cold hand and ran from the bench. He caught sight of a sign on the side of the door that indicated the train's destination: *Aomori → Ueno*. Unfortunately, it looked like a night train heading back to Ueno. After stepping up into the vestibule, Akela put his arm around Mowgli's shoulder and laughed.

"Well, never mind, it's all right. We knew full well that it'd get cold if we went north."

She didn't understand why Akela was laughing, but Mowgli laughed as well. Unlike those men she had seen on the train earlier, Akela's eyes often sparkled, and his complexion, even with his stubbly whiskers, was a healthy pink, and his lips were red, like a girl's. Was it fever that made his face look better than those sickly complexions? Whatever the reason, his face made her feel secure. The train pulled out smoothly, its wheels rumbling through the rice paddies in the darkening twilight.

6 December 1945
Homeless People Head to the Mines

"Let's do our very best" … Exchanging firm handshakes one after another, passengers and station workers alike cried "*Banzai*" at the top of their lungs. Smiling faces nodded from windows as the train pulled out. Sixty-one homeless people, who have been coldly and cruelly disparaged as "tramps who have lost their spirit," left on 5 December from both Tokyo and Ueno stations with a burning desire to work in the mines in Kyushu and Hokkaido and increase the production of coal. Ten headed for Hokkaido, while the other 51 departed for Kyushu….

15 December 1945
A Nighmare Tale—Treatment in the Mines

Aizawa Tadashi (age 22) and Endō Kunikatsu (16), applicants for the Japan Peace Construction Community, left in high spirits on the 5th of this month for the Tagawa coal mine in Kyushu, but returned suddenly and called on Under Secretary for Trade Toyota on the 14th to complain about conditions.

"On the day we arrived we were given only a small amount of boiled rice mixed with barley and three slices of pickled *daikon* for lunch. We received even less for dinner, and then the following morning our rations were cut even more. There was no *miso* soup, and we had to ask the farm families in the village for some salt, which we licked up. We had been told that we would get about four cups of rice per day, so we were surprised when we were given so little, and they lied about paying the round trip train fare to Kyushu and a 100-yen advance per person. Because of that we were increasingly worried about our salary. We asked them about it directly and were shocked to hear that our take-home pay would be about 30 yen a month, even though they had told as at the employment

office in Kanagawa before we went to Kyushu that we would make eight
to ten yen a day, or at least 300 yen a month. In just four days 20 people
out of a group of 52 deserted the mine, and all of those who had gone
there with us from Kanagawa Prefecture had left by the 10th, which was
the day we returned."

5 September 1946
Allied Council for Japan—Mr. Ryder Describes Terrible Working Conditions

...[T]he reasons for the decline in coal production: (1) before and during
the war the majority of coal miners were Koreans, but this has changed
now and Japanese laborers are not experienced at doing the work; (2)
food supplies are scarce, which means that miners must spend a lot of
time searching for food; (3) workers are anxious because equipment and
machinery are old and labor conditions are bad....

24 November 1946
More than Fifty Children Fall Prey to Scheme

Village of Sugatagawa, district of Kawachi, Tochigi Prefecture. Utsunomiya police are investigating the defendant Iinuma Shōjirō (34), who
told a 14-year-old boy he would give him a job at 80 yen per day plus
meals, but then sold the boy to the Hazama Corporation's Murata construction camp at Ōsawa village in Mitaka, Tokyo. In Utsunomiya City
the defendant similarly sold three young men aged 17 and 18 to the same
camp. He has also sold more than 50 orphans of the fire bombings and
other homeless children at Ueno and Kita Senju.

25 January 1947
Homeless People Head for Hokkaido Mines

On the 15th of this month a large number of homeless people were
rounded up by the police in Ueno and forcibly sent to homeless shelters.
At the time 20 people from the Meguro welfare dormitory, 3 from the
Yodobashi shelter, 13 from the Arakawa shelter, and 14 from the Ueno
worker's dormitory—a total of 50 out of all the homeless people rounded
up—applied for and received jobs at the Meiji Coal Mining Company,
Number 2 Mine, in Shoro just outside Kushiro in Hokkaido.

6. Children of Eve

The little child who had already died of his illness was screaming, *The Law! Forget not the Law!*

His little body was cold, and it was dusted with a white powder. The white powder fell on Akela as well. And on the other little ones who were still alive. The windows had been closed, and the children were breathing quietly. Only the one child who had died was running around, shrieking in a high-pitched voice. No one could control him. Almost as soon as they realized he had a fever, the little one had died, just like that. He was such a small child he didn't understand what it meant to have died. The dead child was looking for Akela—his "older brother" who had told him so many stories about Akela and Mowgli. Akela wanted to run away from the dead child.

The Law! Forget not the Law!

The little one came running toward Akela, his eyes glittering, his hands outstretched. White powder was scattering all around....

Akela awoke to the sound of his own groaning. He raised his right hand to brush off the DDT powder only to realize he was on an overnight train heading for Ueno. It was Mowgli who was asleep with her head resting on his chest, not that little child. The two of them were sitting in the vestibule. This train was just as crowded as the others had been. Because it was a long-distance night train, a lot of passengers had brought large pieces of luggage with them, and whatever they couldn't place on the luggage racks, they set in the middle of the aisle. At each stop the train got more crowded. As soon as they boarded, the two of them had given up on getting into a car, settling instead in one of the vestibules. At least the toilet was close by, and they would be able to get off the train easily.

Akela had definitely caught a cold, which embarrassed him. To make matters worse, the little frog Mowgli was showing strange devotion and kindness to him, and so he fell into the kind of depression typical of a sick person. He couldn't help feeling weak and wondering if the time had come when he should give up the great name Akela. Mowgli spread her newspapers over his body, which he had already covered with his own, and wrapped a towel around his neck. She placed her hand on his forehead and rubbed his arms and legs. She even sang to him—she may have been intending to sing a lullaby, but instead sang the words of an Ōtsu Yoshiko hit, "Happiness is here" ... *When a storm rages, and the rain also falls* ... These snatches of popular song were mixed together with songs she had learned during Mass at her Christian school: *Suffering in this vale of tears, children of Eve, wandering, yearning for the light of salvation* ...

Listening to her flowing voice, Akela soon drifted off to sleep. It seemed his fever had gone up. His body was weak, and when he opened his eyes, the outlines of things were blurred, as if his eyeballs had melted. They hadn't been able to make it to Aomori, let alone Siberia. If they hadn't gotten caught in the rain, they would never have ended up in this pathetic state. Akela offered that excuse to his four-year-old self, who had had no problem sleeping in a graveyard in winter. And to his father, who had silently snuggled up with him.

Mowgli had fallen asleep, her head nestled on Akela's stomach and her legs tucked around his head. She was probably exhausted from her bout with diarrhea. Still, they were lucky it wasn't dysentery. Had that little one died of dysentery? Dysentery or typhus—either way, he had died of a contagious disease. His hair was close-cropped, like a priest's, and the area around his eyes was always red and inflamed. He died of a contagious disease just as he was finally adjusting to life at the Children's Home. The voice in the dream crying *The Law! Forget not the Law!* continued to echo in Akela's ears.

Drowsy, Akela retraced his memories. Other children had died. Three of them … or was it five? Akela's mind had not been all that clear back then, and his earliest memories of the Children's Home were even more faded and distant than his memories of living in the graveyard. Perhaps it was because he was constantly sick. And it wasn't just him; all the kids were like that. The nurses would wrap green onions inside soiled gauze and hang them around the children's necks. They tied the same thing around their own necks, and always wore hospital masks. Once, when he saw the badly chapped hands—bright red and actually bleeding—of the nurse named Kazuko (Akela called her his big sister Kazu), he actually rejoiced. You're the same as me, he told her, and his big sister Kazu had nodded, her face glum. When one of the children died, he watched as the woman who had established the Children's Home with her husband—the woman Akela always called "Mom"—hugged and comforted the nurse called Toyoko (his big sister Toyo) as she sobbed. Akela wanted to imitate Toyo and cry, so that he would get a hug too. When he tried imitating her, he started to cry for real. As a result, Akela gained a reputation as a kind-hearted, sensitive child. His big sister Toyo had muttered to herself, "When people die, where do they go? If the child had to die anyway, it would have been better if he had died along with his mother and father. By dying alone, he'll get lost on his way to the far shore, won't he? Why did such a small child, who didn't even know his own name, have to die all alone?"

The train slowed down and stopped at a station. Akela heard the station announcement—*Yamagata ... Yamagata.*

Ten passengers got off. The passengers who were getting on struggled with large pieces of luggage as they tried to push ahead of one another. Barbaric monkeys came pouring into the car, baring their teeth, shoving each other with their arms, blocking each other with their legs, cursing at one another. The commotion woke

103

Mowgli, and she got up.

"I'm hungry. Is it morning already?" she asked.

"How could it be morning? It's still dark out."

Just as he was answering her question, a group of passengers came crowding into the vestibule. There wasn't much he could do about it, so Akela also got up and pulled Mowgli's shoulder over closer to him.

"It may be late, but they're making a terrible racket anyway. Everyone seems agitated."

He pulled out Mowgli's wristwatch and checked the time.

"9:30. No wonder we're getting hungry, it's about time to eat. It's good to have an appetite. But let's wait until after all this fuss dies down before we buy a *bentō*."

Groans arose among the passengers, and children were crying loudly. The train was overflowing with people, and there was very little free space left. Yet there was no end to the number of people boarding the train. Feeling oppressed by this crush, Mowgli replied in a low voice, "That's okay by me. I don't have to eat right away. Where are we?"

Akela laughed and said, "I get the strange feeling it's Yamagata."

"Yamagata? Where I ate *ramen* this morning? So that means this train is heading back to Tokyo?"

"I guess so. But we're going to get off on the way, so it doesn't matter to us. In any case, so long as it's raining like this, it's better for us to stay on the train."

The way they were sitting in the cramped vestibule—legs scrunched up, backs bent forward as far as they could go, faces pressed up against their knees so they were staring into each other's eyes—made it look as though they had been stuffed into a grotto in a rock. A cold wind mixed with rain came blowing in from the open door. The bodies of the people around them had been partially soaked, and the smell of rain wafted up.

"If things stay like this, we won't be able to move at all," Akela muttered absently.

"I'm used to it being this crowded on the morning trolley," Mowgli answered sleepily, "so this is nothing. As long as we can sit down like this, it's fairly comfortable."

The backs and arms and legs of passengers, all tangled up, pressed in on them from all sides. Akela pushed back with both hands. The backs of some men sitting on the floor right in front of them also invaded their space, and each time they pushed nearer, Akela and Mowgli would have to take turns driving them off with their legs.

The departure bell rang, and finally the train took off. Mowgli rested her face on her knees again and sighed. Whenever she rode a crowded trolley on her way to school, some large hand would stretch out from somewhere and grope beneath her skirt. That hand, which was no different from the hand of the men who wanted to kill girls, would squirm, and the man would push something warm against her panties. If she just stood still, she'd be murdered. So Mowgli would twist her trembling body with all her strength, stamp on the man's feet, and run away. Why should she have to be killed in such a weird way, just because she was a girl? Why did men like that have to be everywhere in this world? If some other world existed, she wanted to escape there. Still, she had trousers on now. She had become a boy and could get by without having to experience such terror. Mowgli was constantly discouraged by the fact that she was a girl, which is why she didn't feel the slightest regret at being transformed into a boy. Akela's plan had made her happy. Was Akela disappointed in girls? She wanted to know for sure, but there was no way she could ask him that question. Because however much Mowgli pretended to be a boy, however much Akela continued to treat her like a boy, they could never forget the fact that she was actually a girl.

Akela, his eyes half-closed, spoke in a low voice. "Mowgli, do you know what happens to people when they die? I sometimes wonder where they all go, and I can't help feeling weird thinking about it. For instance, what becomes of a dead baby that's been left in a graveyard?"

Mowgli peered into Akela's brown eyes. A white shadow that seemed to be her face flickered in his eyes.

"Adults say we go to Heaven, but …" Mowgli whispered. "When you go above the clouds, there's only black space all around. And under the ocean and the ground, it's all coal and water and magma. Dead people can't possibly be in places like that. When Ton-chan died, I was still just ten years old, but I thought people shouldn't talk about childish things like Heaven. It was all just a lie. I thought I could find out on my own, but I still don't understand. After Ton-chan died, I became afraid of death. Until then it hadn't bothered me. I often dreamed that I died, and I couldn't decide whether it was better to die or go on living."

"Really? Why is that?" Akela whispered.

"I don't know. Maybe it's because ever since I was a baby there's been nothing but memorial services or visits to a grave. Or maybe because I was told that my dad was in the grave. But when Ton-chan died, I'm not sure why … but it felt completely different. It didn't take very long for him to turn into a corpse and be cremated, and then he was just suddenly gone. Yet I felt that there must be something left of him somewhere. Do you know what I mean?"

Akela nodded, blinking. Mowgli continued talking, as if to herself.

"But I didn't know where that something was. It wasn't like he had become a ghost hovering around. Or like he had flown off to the North Star and was living there. There's a cross hanging in every classroom at the school I go to now. Christ is dying on those crosses. It's really scary. And there's the Mass too. They use words I don't understand, and the priest holds up a large gold cross, and then he eats and drinks something by himself. The students who are Christian wear veils, and they eat what the priest divides up and gives to them. It looks like a rice cracker, and they say that if you carelessly bite down on it the blood of Christ will flow. It won't stop bleeding, and you'll be smeared with blood and go to Hell. But if you eat it the right way, you'll go to Heaven and God will take good care of you. But I doubt if Ton-chan and my dad have any connection to a Heaven like that. I can't go, because it wouldn't be right for me to be the only one. You know, you can see Christ's heart from the outside, and there's a hole in his heart, and the blood is flowing out. They say Christ suffered and died because we're full of sin. And because he died, any child, no matter how bad, can go to Heaven, as long as they sincerely repent and receive that rice cracker. But … it's hard to put into words … I feel like your jungle is a Heaven that comes after death. Ton-chan and my father, and your father too have all become beautiful birds in that jungle. Or maybe they've become wolves, or snakes, or bears, or elephants, or black panthers or deer, or tigers, or—they could be rabbits, foxes, bugs, or even flowers or grasses in the jungle. They become whatever they want to be, and together in the jungle, they carefully guard the Law and live at peace…. I'd be really happy if there was a Heaven like that, but … all this is what you taught me, you know."

Akela kept his eyes closed for a while, as if lost in thought. Thinking he had fallen asleep, Mowgli was about to give up on getting any response when he opened his eyes and began to talk.

"*The Jungle is large, and the Cub, he is small.* There is also this saying: *Wood and Water, Wind and Tree, Wisdom, Strength, and Courtesy, Jungle-Favor go with thee!* This is "The Outsong" the animals sang as a parting song. Once the man-child Mowgli was grown up, he obeyed Akela's last words and left the jungle to return to the world of man. Baloo the bear, and the python Kaa, and the black panther Bagheera—these three animals had been Mowgli's guardians. But Baloo was doddering and going blind. On the other hand, Mowgli was a human, so it took him a long time to grow into an adult. No matter how long the animals waited, he didn't grow fur on his body; he didn't grow fangs. He had no tail, and his ears and nose didn't work all that well. Even when he reached my age, seventeen, he still wasn't fully grown. If an animal lives to be twenty, that's really old … with the exception of pythons and elephants of course … so Mowgli returned to the human world. However, he actually continued to live on as a companion of the jungle. He could always return to the jungle, and the jungle would always continue to look after him. In other words, the jungle is a place that exists before humans are born into this world, and it's where they go after they die. I understood that for the first time just now … those who die when they're little kids probably become butterflies in the jungle. And my father is what? Probably a skinny water buffalo. My mother died in an air raid. I wonder if she and my brother and sister are deer or hares? When I die, I want to be a wolf, I suppose. What about you?"

Conjuring an enchanting image of jungle scenery in her mind, Mowgli answered,

"Let's see ... I don't want to be an animal. A flower would be good. Maybe a cosmos or something."

"Damn, you're talking just like a girl. Become something that has more spirit," Akela urged her. He was smiling.

"All right, I'll become a lizard. Lizards are beautiful, and they're good at escaping."

"You're thinking small, as usual. At least be a big lizard. Like a dinosaur or something."

Mowgli gave a little laugh at Akela's words.

"I'm different from you," he continued. "I've hated death since I was a kid. I didn't understand anything during the time I was in the graveyard, but after my dad died, I kept thinking, I don't want to die, I don't want to die. I'd greedily devour anything I could eat. I'd tell lies just to please adults, and I'd avoid getting into stupid arguments. I couldn't stand the thought that I might die unexpectedly and be thrown away like garbage. If you die by the side of the road, they just cover you up with a mat, and that's it. I have no idea how they treated my old man. His bones and ashes are in a dusty urn on a shelf in a community temple. No matter how much time passes, we have no connection to things like graves. We spent all that time wandering around a graveyard, but it was stupid, because graves have nothing to do with us. I don't remember my dad or me ever once putting our hands together to pray at a grave when we were in the graveyard, and so we were punished, that's for sure."

"I often played with Ton-chan in a graveyard in the neighborhood. We never prayed there. But we haven't been punished for that yet."

Mowgli's voice sounded sleepy. Though their bodies were still crammed in among the other passengers, they actually felt comfortable. They maintained their position, enveloped by their own warmth. Of course, that would last only as long as they didn't move. If they went to the toilet, there was a chance that someone would take the space they occupied. Mowgli had wanted to go, but she gave up out of fear of losing their position, and instead cocked her ear toward Akela to listen to his story. If she could fall asleep again, then perhaps she could get by without having to go to the toilet. Eventually there would be fewer people in the vestibule, and she could bear up for now. It seemed that her diarrhea was under control, and since she had pooped herself out, her stomach ought to be empty. Now all she had to worry about was Akela's fever. Mowgli kept staring intently at Akela's slightly red face, his moist eyes with their thick lashes, his red lips surrounded by the stubble of his whiskers.

"There were Christian graves in the graveyard as well. They had to be Christian, since they were in the shape of a cross. I wonder if Jesus's Heaven is a separate place where everyone else goes? It shouldn't be. To my Pop and Mom at the Children's Home, God always meant the Shinto gods. But I never saw them pray in front of the *kamidana* shelf. When a little one died, they didn't have any money for a funeral.

We were told to just bow our heads and say our farewells, and that was it. Now that I think of it, they'd have a mandarin orange brought to the little one who died.... It seemed as if they could no longer believe in their gods. They lost three of their own children in the war, but they told us that because the dead returned to the energy of the universe, the flowers that bloomed in the neighborhood, and the kittens born to stray cats there, and the angleworms in the stream out back were all connected to the children who had died. Really, what they said is not all that different from saying that everyone goes back to the jungle. Next time I see them, I'll tell them about that. They may have already figured that out, but ... Pop was an elementary-school teacher in the old days, so he was really smart. He taught us all sorts of things. Stories about the Russian Revolution, the new country for Jews, about Gandhi of India ... Do you know about Gandhi? Just to look at him you might think he was a beggar priest, but he was a really great man. He used passive resistance to gain independence for India, and when he told people they shouldn't fight over religious or class differences, people hated him for it and killed him."

Just then Mowgli raised her head and whispered, "What should I do? I have to go to the toilet. Can I go?"

Akela raised his head as well and sighed. "You do? That's really inconvenient. When we get to the next big station, can't we just go on the platform and pee outside?"

"I can't do that," Mowgli answered, frowning.

"Do you have to do number one or number two?"

"I'm not sure. Both."

"Well, I guess it can't be helped. Anyway, go ahead and try. The toilet is right over there. It's so crowded, it's probably best to crawl over."

Hesitating for a moment, Mowgli put both hands on the floor and, crawling on all fours, spoke first to a large butt in front of her.

"Excuse me, could you let me pass? I want to go to the toilet."

The big butt moved a little, and she heard someone, she didn't know if it was a man or a woman, say, "You gotta take a crap?"

"It's diarrhea...."

"Oh, all right. Look, go through here."

The space widened, and Mowgli twisted her body through it. Next a large brown bag was blocking the way. Making a detour to the right, she told some men who were sitting there, folded up in a heap, that she had the runs and couldn't hold it any more. They shifted the upper part of their bodies to the side, their faces sullen. Making it over that valley pass, she moved between the legs of a person sitting on a piece of luggage and passed over the back of a woman holding a child. At last she reached the spot in front of the toilet. The door had been left open, and several passengers were sitting inside. They were all old, and two of them appeared to be women. Sitting on newspapers, they had towels wrapped around their necks, and were eating rice balls.

Mowgli stood up and, as she had before, made her request. "Excuse me, but *I* need to use the toilet.... Sorry, but it's diarrhea."

One of the old people nodded and answered, "Go on in, we don't mind."

The other old people nodded, but made no effort to move. When Mowgli just stood there, the old person spoke to her again.

"No one's gonna look. We don't mind. Hurry up and go on in."

Mowgli remained lost and confused. If she could just hold out, that's what she preferred to do. How could she poop in a place with people present? Yet if things continued like this, she'd probably poop her pants. It was one thing for her to soil her pants and trousers, but if she ended up pooping on the floor, everyone there would be furious ... *What the hell are you doing, smearing that filthy stinking crap all over the place! You got shit on my valuable luggage! Throw this brat from the train!*

Mowgli made up her mind and went in. She stepped up on the raised part of the floor and straddled the toilet bowl. The old people turned to the side, or turned their backs to her. They closed their mouths sullenly, as if they wanted to say they sure weren't in this sort of place because they liked it, and looked down. Mowgli closed her eyes, quickly pulled down her trousers and panties, and squatted over the toilet. She thought of nothing, she looked at nothing. And in that way she was able to become just like the father and the child she had heard about from Akela. The father and the child, who always had diarrhea, would fart loudly, and then there would be steam under their butts, and shit all around the graveyard.

By the time Mowgli, her face strained from the tension, returned to her spot next to Akela, the train had arrived at a station. They heard the station announcement ... *Yonezawa, Yonezawa.*

Hearing that, Akela got up and said, "This looks like a big station. I'll go buy some *bentō* for us."

He violently pushed his way through the crowd in the vestibule and went outside.

A lot of people got off at this station, but several times that number began pushing and jostling to get on. It finally occurred to Mowgli that this train was probably so crowded because it was the last one of the day headed to Tokyo. People could make it to Tokyo by tomorrow morning only if they took this train. It looked like most of the passengers were headed for Tokyo. Their luggage was stuffed with all kinds of things—rice, *kabocha* squash, potatoes, and the like. As she waited for Akela, Mowgli pulled some toilet paper out of her bag and stuffed it inside her panties. She hadn't taken any with her when she went a few minutes earlier, so the inside of her underwear felt a little damp. She figured that as a precaution from here on out she could use it as a diaper. The toilet paper they'd taken from the department store was a very valuable commodity, but she had already used up a lot of it.

109

The departure bell rang and the whistle blew. Akela wasn't back yet. The train swayed heavily and she heard the sound of the couplings crashing together between the cars. The door was open, and a chilly night rain blew in. If Akela missed the train, what would happen to her? Holding her breath, Mowgli stared at the door. The train gradually began to pick up speed. A swarthy face emerged from among the passengers, a hand stretched out, and then Akela's familiar body appeared.

"Whoa, that was close, that was close. Just a little more and I would have been thrown from the train. I was holding the *bentō* and tea, and so I couldn't use both hands. It was really hard getting on. I couldn't find a vendor anywhere, and all I could buy were these crummy-looking rice balls."

Roughly pushing his way through the passengers, he sat down in his original spot, and immediately opened a brown paper wrapper. They were pretty pathetic-looking rice balls, and though they were accompanied by pieces of *takuan* pickle, there was only the tiniest sliver of pickled plum inside. Instead of *nori* seaweed, they were wrapped in some kind of leaf they had never seen before. Three of them lined in a row. They were hardly sufficient, but their taste was unexpectedly satisfying. It was already close to midnight. The train rushed past smaller stations and, blowing its whistle occasionally, continued on through the darkness. The people around them, each assuming his or her own cramped pose, were closing their eyes. A few slept soundly, but most were barely dozing, surrendering themselves to a light sleep. Even though both the car and the vestibule were a crush of people, a stillness, like fear, bore down oppressively in the stagnant air. They could hear a baby's fretful voice in the distance. The clack of the train wheels echoed, and the two of them began to feel drowsy as they whispered to each other that tomorrow they would eat their fill of whatever they desired.

A woman screamed nearby, and they opened their eyes. All at once there was a big commotion around them, and people began looking over their bags and checking their breast pockets.

"My ticket's gone! And my purse has been stolen!"

Where was the woman who was shouting? He couldn't tell anything other than that she was close by. No matter how much she screamed, none of the passengers moved, and the conductor was nowhere in sight. Inside the car, things quickly returned to that earlier choking silence, and the rhythmic clatter of the wheels continued. Akela and Mowgli fell asleep again.

"Hey, what the fuck are you doing?"

"Asshole! I can punch too!"

"Owww! What the … you goddamn sewer rat!"

A fight broke out between a two men inside the car. At the same time the high-pitched, wailing voice of another man rang out.

"My luggage! It's gone! Has anyone seen it! It's a wooden box, about this big! I'm begging you, please look for it! If I can't find it, I'll have to kill myself!"

As the clamor grew louder, a woman's voice rose up.

"Isn't this your box here? It wasn't here before. Does anyone remember? If it's here, it must be yours. Somebody tried to steal it and carry it off, that's for sure."

Almost before they knew it, the quarreling voices had dissipated. Akela and Mowgli looked into one another's face, and then looked at the watch. It was past three o'clock. The people sleeping next to them woke up, and their whispering voices mingled.

"Looks like they found it. He's lucky."

"There are so many thieves around, you can't fall asleep."

"A lot of murders lately, too."

"Yeah, it's scary. *Really* scary."

"I guess ... but I'll tell you what really scares me. When the cops raid."

"How about this train?"

"Who knows ... nothing happened in Yamagata ... it's possible they'll be waiting for us later at Oyama, Ōmiya, or Ueno."

"I've heard the cops eat the rice they confiscate."

"It's disgraceful ... damn corrupt bastards."

Akela and Mowgli closed their eyes and tried to go back to sleep. However, it only grew noisier around them, and they were hungry, so they only dozed fitfully. Mowgli was having a dream. She was locked up in a chicken coop with more than a dozen birds and was trying to get away from their beaks. It had been Mowgli's chore when she was seven or eight years old to feed the four or five chickens they raised at home, and to hunt for eggs. There were times when the chickens wouldn't so much as look at her, but sometimes they would get excited and attack with their beaks, trying to drive her off. Their beaks hurt. The chickens were mean and violent, and they didn't know anything besides how to sleep or be angry.

Akela was walking along the banks of some river, he didn't know where. The river breeze was cold, and his cheeks were frozen. There was no else one around on either bank. When the wind blew, white ripples stood up on the surface of the river, and the withered grasses on the banks swayed and rustled. The sky was dark. The wind would probably bring on a blizzard. Akela was walking barefoot. White, frozen rice paddies spread out around the river. He couldn't see any houses or trees, and he couldn't very well rest in a place like this. Akela continued walking. Looking at the river, he saw a large white bird drifting along. Was it a swan? Just then the white bird bent its neck over to one side, and its whole body tipped over. Was it dead? Akela felt disappointed as he watched the current carry the body of the bird slowly along the surface.

"Everyone, off the train! Off the train!"

111

They heard a man shouting from the platform. The door had been opened from the outside, and the people nearest the door had picked up their luggage and were already getting off.

"Hey, it's the cops!"

"This early in the morning? Terrible...."

"Shit, those arrogant bastards...."

Mowgli and Akela were still groggy. They were inundated by the voices of the passengers around them. Some people had opened the door opposite the platform and were quickly tossing their luggage outside. Men dressed as police officers burst into the train like mountain bandits, brandishing billy clubs and shouting in shrill, sharp voices.

"Hurry up, get off! Take all your bags and get off! It's an inspection!"

Akela took Mowgli by the arm and, helping her get up, whispered. "I'm not sure, but it looks like they're going to inspect baggage. We should be okay. Still, keep your mouth shut."

Jostling with the other passengers, they stepped down onto the platform and saw police officers staking out the train, pistols drawn, four or five officers for every car.

The sky was still dark, and the air was cold. Mowgli's body began to shiver. Still half-asleep, she couldn't grasp what was going on. It felt less real to her than the dream she had been having just a few moments ago. Then the words "Gestapo" and "Auschwitz" came back to her. She had learned them from reading *The Diary of Anne Frank*. Thinking that under no circumstances should she let herself be separated from Akela, she clung to his arm with both hands. She began to shiver more violently. Her teeth chattered and her eyes teared up. She felt as if she might pee her pants. If they found out that she had skipped school without her mother's permission to go with Akela and that, to top it off, she had transformed herself into a boy, they'd probably send her to the gas chamber. If she could at least die together with Akela, she'd be able to die peacefully. Would Akela be treated as a child, or would he be sent off to a concentration camp for adults? Did they separate men and women at the camp?

"Hurry up! Line up in six rows!"

The officers' pistols flashed in the blinding glare of the light bulbs on the platform. Although the policemen screamed at everyone to form six rows, the passengers were surprisingly unafraid of the police. Some people were washing their faces at the drinking fountain, some men were pissing at the far end of the platform. Some of the policemen were lording it over the passengers, ordering them around as they began to search through their luggage. One after another they tossed large bags out of the train. A sign on a pillar on the platform read *Utsunomiya*.

"You got documents permitting you to transport this stuff? You know damn well that if you don't, we'll confiscate it. Next! What's this? What the—it's rice.

Rice! You've got barley in here too. A real pig, aren't you? This won't do. The limit's 3.6 liters! 3.6 liters!"

The cop pulled a heavy-looking cloth bag, a tin can, and a bundle wrapped in straw out of a piece of luggage, and dumped the contents into a hemp bag that a man wearing an armband was carrying. Rice, barley, potatoes. A short distance away, the cops were also confiscating the food of a woman who had children with her. She had broken down in tears. Some people were clenching their fists and heaping abuse on the cops.

Akela was shocked at what was going on, and muttered, "Damn, this is awful. Are they still conducting raids for black-market rice? It's exactly the same as when I was a little kid."

Mowgli was rubbing her teary eyes and runny nose on Akela's sleeve. He wanted to warn her not to be too frightened, so that she wouldn't attract the cops' suspicion. But by then some policemen had moved closer to them, and he had no choice but to keep silent.

A pair of cops finished examining the rucksack and cloth bundle of the passenger in front of them. He wasn't carrying more than regulations allowed, so he didn't have to complain about having anything confiscated. Next, it was Akela and Mowgli's turn.

"Just the two of you?"

Akela nodded silently.

"Where's your bags? Is that all?"

The younger of the cops opened their cloth bags and peeked inside.

"Have you two run away from home? Well, have you? You that know if you run off to Tokyo with no place to live, you'll end up homeless and some really bad creeps will snatch you away. Or are you pickpockets working the train? You have any other accomplices?"

"Let 'em go. They got nothing. Next!"

The older cop could have cared less about Akela and Mowgli, and he moved on toward the rear of the train.

The younger cop clicked his tongue, glared at Akela, and then moved on. From the looks of him, he wasn't all that much older than Akela. Dirty popped zits gleamed on his cheeks and forehead. Akela wanted to spit on that filthy monkey face, but he restrained himself for Mowgli's sake, and continued to look down. When all was said and done, a monkey's words were nothing more than meaningless, vulgar noises.

"We're okay now. You can go over there and get a drink of water. You want to wash your face too?"

Her eyes red, Mowgli looked up at Akela's face and shook her head side to side. She continued to cling to his sleeve with both hands.

"Dammit, I told you not to be so scared. Oh well, it can't be helped."

They heard angry voices and people crying behind them. When would they be allowed back on the train? Did these cop-monkeys have the right to delay a train this long? He glanced around the platform. They had made every single passenger get off, but he couldn't even begin to guess how many people there were.

Twenty minutes passed, and finally the cops told everybody waiting in their line that it was okay to get back on the train. Akela and Mowgli went over to the drinking fountain first. They washed their faces and gargled, and, after drinking some water, stood at the edge of the platform. The sky appeared to be getting lighter. Two sparrows were twittering softly and hopping around on the roof of the platform on the other side of the tracks.

"It looks like good weather today. If it *is* good, we'll be able to get our strength back."

Mowgli nodded. She finally loosened her grip on his sleeve.

"You know, it was natural for you to be scared. Even my heart was pounding at first. Those guys had pistols, after all. To top it off, they were treating us like pickpockets."

"They asked if we were runaways," Mowgli whispered.

He glanced at her face. She was still close to tears, but her mouth was a little more relaxed and she was starting to smile. Akela felt reassured.

"But it pisses me off," he continued, "they're so rude! We may look like runaways, but we were brought up in Tokyo!"

Mowgli giggled.

"I had no idea at all that the cops were still conducting raids. Nobody sells black-market rice anymore, so …"

"What's black-market rice?"

"You don't know about that? After the war, when they didn't have any rice in the shops, people sold what they could bring in from the countryside at really high prices. You could make a lot of money that way. Excuse me, but, could you turn that way for a minute? I'm going to take a piss here. Do you want to try taking a pee outside too? It's not hard to do, at all."

Mowgli was flustered and moved away from Akela a little, turning her head aside.

"Hmmph … she won't even give it a try," Akela muttered.

He loosened the buttons on the fly of his trousers and pissed a stream of water onto the tracks. Glancing over at the platform across the way, he spotted the word *Nikkō*. He could see a painted picture of a gaudy shrine that had been built in a forest. A poster with a picture of three monkeys had been plastered on the wooden planks of the wall of the waiting room. He could make out the words *Nikkō National Park … International Tourist Site … Tōshōgū Shrine … Lake Chūzenji*.

"Nikkō? Hey, look at that! Maybe we can get to Nikkō from here. The weather's good, so why don't we go have a look? Nikkō's a famous place. See, it says there it's an international tourist site. Since we're on a trip, I'd like to do a little sightseeing."

"Sure!"

He heard Mowgli's clear voice behind him.

1 August 1946
90% of Passengers Violate the Law
Angry Voices from Train Windows Rage at the Inequity of Government
Policies—An Account of a Ride on "The White Rice Express"

There are trains called "The Devil's Express" where a lot of crimes take place, and there are also trains that people call "The White Rice Express." They come up to Tokyo, running through the rice-producing region of the six prefectures of Tōhoku. They're like rice chests ... or livestock cars. Crammed with rice and passengers, these trains are targeted by the police, and somewhere along the way to Tokyo they will get caught up in the whirlwind of a raid. Armed police dressed in gaiters and wielding pistols will suddenly surround a train and order everyone off, driving people and possessions out onto the platform. Mountains of rice, barley, and potatoes will be piled up and confiscated with no compensation. Amid the frenzy and confusion of pushing and shoving and pressing, there have been reports of incidents when shots were fired.

One evening at 9:52, the 404 from Akita to Ueno slipped into Yamagata Station. The local police station regarded this train as an enemy, and on this particular night seventy-three policemen armed with pistols fortified their positions. Men wearing armbands claiming they were from the Food Rations Authority spread out large linen sacks and stood alongside the police interrogators. About 2,000 passengers had luggage filled with all they could carry. The amount of food taken without compensation this one night came to almost 480 liters, and the police swept away goods that were being illegally transported across prefectural borders. The train, which was considerably lighter after the raid, departed after a delay of forty minutes.

As they were about to depart, however, voices cursing the police and expressing outrage were hurled from the train. Rather than consider the consequences of their actions, people continue to go out to the countryside to buy rice, only to have it confiscated over and over in the same way. Having grown used to it, they seethe with rage and hurl insults, cursing a corrupt government. This time the railway police entered the train cars and seven thefts occurred during the confusion. In one case, a mother had her legal amount of rice, her breakfast, and her children's clothing taken from her.

They climbed up the platform stairs, followed the notice boards where the words "Nikkō Line" were written, and descended a similar set of stairs. They checked the timetable. It indicated that the first train out was the 5:20. They only had to wait for twenty minutes and they'd be set. On the platform they had just left, passengers were already returning to the train, and the policemen were standing by themselves under the bright electric lights. Mounds of goods confiscated from every car were left behind, like the carcasses of animals. Akela and Mowgli wanted by all means to avoid being stopped and called over by the cops again, so they went back up the stairs and headed for the ticket gate in the station. Akela paid the fare adjustments and bought tickets to Nikkō. In the meantime, Mowgli went to the toilet and finished her business. To her relief, her diarrhea seemed to be under control. Stepping outside the gate, they saw that the sky was just barely light. No shops were open yet. Two or three people, who apparently planned to board the same train as Akela and Mowgli, passed through the gate. In the deserted, dusky plaza in front of the station, they saw two trucks, guarded by cops, waiting to take away both the confiscated goods and the policemen who had carried out the raid.

A whistle blew, and the train headed for Ueno pulled out. Looking back at the platform, they could see cops cutting across the tracks and moving toward them. Other cops were in a line, passing along the bags containing the items they had confiscated. Akela suddenly grabbed Mowgli's hand and hid behind a pile of lumber in the plaza.

They silently crouched down with their backs against the wood. After a few minutes Mowgli whispered to Akela, "Are there really that many thieves working the trains?"

Akela whispered back, "There must be a lot, for sure."

"Will the policemen eat the rice that they took? If they do, they're pretty much thieves themselves."

"Any way you look at it, they're monkeys, and so they'll do anything. I'm really hungry now. I hope we can get some *bentō* around here."

"Has your fever gone down?" Mowgli, remembering that he was ill, peered into Akela's face.

"I feel hungry, so maybe it has."

"That's a good sign. I'm hungry too. And I'm sleepy. This is Utsunomiya, right? It's much farther south than Yamagata, but it's still cold. Will it warm up when the sun comes out?"

Akela nodded and stared at the tracks in front of him. White flowers were blooming all over. He was lost in thought, wondering if they were the flowers called cottonweed. Looking more closely, he saw small pink flowers blooming there as well. From where they were crouching, he couldn't tell what kind of flowers they were. Milkvetch? Clover? The smell of moist sawdust wafted up from the lumber at their backs, and he thought he was going to sneeze. The blue of the sky was shifting to a slightly different shade. He could hear sparrows chirping as well, but he had no idea where they were.

Since she didn't get a response from Akela, Mowgli gave several little yawns, glanced up at the sky, and then gazed at the white flowers. It occurred to her that even though they had not traveled to distant northern provinces, flowers were in full bloom here as well. But flowers bloomed everywhere, not just in Heaven. The jungle Akela had told her about, however, was not everywhere; it was a Heaven-jungle, which absolutely no one could get to while alive. A jungle that not even Akela had actually gone to yet. Even so, after she died, she wouldn't be very happy if she became a big lizard. She didn't like crocodiles, and wasn't sure if becoming a snake would be any better. Mowgli began to picture various kinds of snakes in her mind. Pythons, cobras, rattlesnakes, vipers, striped snakes, rat snakes …

Akela peeked out from behind the lumber toward the plaza and stood up.

"Okay, the cop-monkeys are all gone. If we don't hurry to our platform, we'll miss the train. It's about to leave."

The two of them made a spirited dash for the train, running through the ticket gate, going up and down the stairs. The train had already arrived at the platform. Their momentum from running carried them onto the car, which was practically empty. Flustered, they grabbed the seats nearest to them, and caught their breath. At the same time the departure bell rang and a short whistle blew.

"Aw, hell, the *bentō*! We forgot about them!" Akela muttered in chagrin.

"Never mind. *I* can hold out until we get to Nikkō," Mowgli responded. Judging by the tone of her voice, she was unconcerned.

She stared out the window. The sky was changing over to the colors of morning.

"By the way, Mowgli, have you ever been to Nikkō?"

Akela spoke in a low voice, all the while nonchalantly studying the faces of the two old women seated across from them on the other side of the car.

"I went there on a trip in elementary school. But I don't remember much about it. There wasn't much water at Kegon Falls, and I remember wondering if people could really commit suicide at such a place."

The old women both wore similar plain kimonos. They were clutching their cloth handbags, and their eyes were closed. They didn't really look like tourists. It seemed that most of the people on the train were locals. There was no question that this was more comfortable than the night train, which had been crammed full of people, but the fact that only locals rode this train meant that Akela and Mowgli couldn't let their guard down. Their Tokyo accents might invite unwanted curiosity. Then again, this place was near Tokyo, so a Tokyo accent probably wasn't all that rare.

"What do you mean, suicide?" Akela whispered back.

"Someone famous committed suicide there. It's weird that anyone would want to kill himself there."

"That's right. If you really mean to kill yourself, you can do it anywhere."

"I think if you're going to commit suicide, it's better to do it at your own house. Or if you could do it at a crematorium, that'd be even better, right?"

"A crematorium?"

"Sure, that way you avoid the hassle of having someone take you there after you're dead."

Mowgli was speaking seriously, with conviction. Akela was bewildered and stared at her nose and soft round cheeks.

"Well, maybe, but when it comes right down to it, I don't think many people would want to commit suicide at a crematorium."

"Well if it was me, I wouldn't mind, but ..."

"I think it'd be all right to do it in a graveyard. Dying in a graveyard would be pleasant, for sure."

"But if you die in a graveyard, they still have to take your body to a crematorium. It's different from the past, because nowadays everyone has to be cremated. Every corpse in Tokyo. Perhaps it would be best to dig a special grave and tell people who want to commit suicide to please go right ahead and use that hole. If they had such a hole, then my father and the others could have died at their ease. If they had died in a place like that, then your father wouldn't have had to go to the police box to report their deaths, and there wouldn't have been all the bother of having to take the bodies to the crematorium. There were three bodies, so it was a lot of trouble. Of course, if there was such a hole, then we could never have become Mowgli and Akela."

Akela nodded with a sour expression. Mowgli yawned loudly. The strength left her body, and she rested her head on his shoulder.

"You're still a little feverish. Don't you feel a chill? Come to think of it, we left our newspapers on that other train, didn't we? We'll have to get some more. I was wondering earlier if we wouldn't be killed by the Gestapo. That was terrible, wasn't it? It would be horrible to die in a gas chamber."

"Enough already. Try to get some sleep. I'm going to sleep too."

Doing as Akela told her, Mowgli finally shut her mouth and closed her eyes. The odor of her brother's corpse being cremated rose to the tip of her nose. A sickening sweet scent that clung persistently to the inside of her head. A stagnant scent that was a mix of lilies, of melon and face powder, and of fish. That scent was all that was left of her memories of the crematorium. Did all bodies smell the same, no matter who was being cremated? She had a hunch that perhaps it was the smell of the incense that they burned at the crematorium. Whenever it came back to her, Mowgli's body would melt away and turn to thick water.

Akela closed his eyes and searched his memory. He had once heard a similar story about a hole where people go to kill themselves. But who could have told him such a story? Had it been one of his "older brothers" at the Children's Home or a classmate from middle school? There was a boy who was so smart he seemed to have been head of his class from the time he was a toddler. He had burn scars on his cheeks, and though he was by far the smartest kid at the orphanage, he was gloomy and introverted. Perhaps that was why, unconsciously, Akela was drawn to the boy and spent a fair amount of time with him. Yet they weren't really friends. Was he continuing his studies at high school these days? In any case, Akela had the feeling it was that boy who had told him the story of the hole, but he couldn't be sure. Somewhere, in a far-off desert nation, there was a hole that waited for the dead. People who wanted to die because they were sick, or desperate, or grieving would travel to that hole and throw themselves into it. The hole was located in sandy soil. It was shaped like a mortar, similar to the circular pits made by an ant lion. Once you threw yourself in that hole, no matter how much you might regret having done so, it was impossible to crawl out. There were so many sick people in the hole who were on the verge of dying that, apart from starvation, or dehydration, or sunstroke, it was possible that you might die of a communicable disease like typhus, or cholera, or smallpox. With a perfectly serious expression, the boy told Akela that the people who had prepared that hole must have been very wise, and that such a hole is a necessity for human society. When a person's in despair and thinks that he might want to die, that hole should be the criterion for deciding whether or not he really wants to—a person should ask himself if he wants to die so badly that he'd be willing to enter that hole. If he finds the whole idea disgusting, he can change his mind, because that means he's not really sure about dying.

About an hour later the train reached its final stop, Nikkō Station. They were still fast asleep when the conductor woke them. Flustered, they hurried out onto the platform. The morning light was almost blinding. They looked up and saw a pale-blue sky overhead. It was a simple thing, but it made them feel happy as they headed for the exit. The other passengers were all headed toward the gate—people who had come to work in the town, or people bringing goods and foodstuffs. Children about Mowgli's age were mingled in among them. Apparently they weren't going to school. Were they going to work as dishwashers, or to do cleaning at a temple? A large information board for tourists stood at the exit of the whitewashed station building. The names of famous tourist spots like the Nikkō Shrine and Lake Chūzenji were listed there, and the board indicated, according to the number of the bus, how long it would take—ten minutes, or thirty minutes—to get to those various places. Akela and Mowgli, however, didn't feel like reading it, because it was too complicated. Bus stops were located in front of the station, and the plaza was filled with the morning light. Suddenly, they spotted four or five trucks parked there. Akela and Mowgli instinctively ran back into the station, and peeked outside once more.

Those trucks were used to transport police companies. They looked just like the ones at Utsunomiya. Except now there were even more of them. Were they pursuing Akela and Mowgli? The question flashed across their minds. They knew it was ridiculous, but at that moment they couldn't come up with another reason for the trucks to be there. Mowgli began to tremble. The ominous word "Gestapo" once more stormed through her body.

On closer inspection, they saw that the men in the trucks weren't just police. In fact, most of them were from the Civil Defense Corps. They were wearing navy blue work jackets lined with red stripes. Even so, each of them carried a long stick, which made them just as dangerous as the police. A company of men carrying tools like scoop shovels and pickaxes got on the bed of one of the trucks. There were six trucks in all, as well as a jeep and several hunting dogs. The word "manhunt" drifted up to Akela's mind. Had some violent criminal escaped into the mountains? Passersby were staring fearfully at the trucks from the edge of the plaza. Since the police were taking their time to conduct a roll call of the Civil Defense members and to prepare the equipment, it did not look as though the manhunt would begin any time soon.

Akela wanted to try to find out a little more about what was going on, but Mowgli was trembling and clinging to him and would not let go. She was on the verge of tears, and there was nothing he could do about it. So he put his arm around her shoulder and they sat down on a nearby bench. There were about a dozen people on the other benches, waiting for the next train, including several men who were intently staring out the window and talking together quietly. Akela tried to eavesdrop on them, but from where he was sitting he couldn't make out what they were saying. At first he thought it didn't matter if he could hear them or not, but then he felt that he wanted to find out what was going on. He suddenly stood Mowgli up, moved with her to a seat next to the men, and nonchalantly peered through the window, just as they were doing.

"Once you've murdered one, I suppose it doesn't matter how many more you kill."

"It becomes a habit."

"Since he committed the murders during wartime, I suppose he wasn't afraid the bodies would be discovered."

"I heard that the murderer was a soldier in the South Pacific."

"Yeah, they say he was discharged from the army before the war took a turn for the worse. Probably the only thing he learned was how to mistreat women."

"But still, why did he have to pick Nikkō to commit his crimes?"

"Yeah, what a nuisance this is. I wonder if they'll ever catch him?"

"They'll poke around in the woods until they find somebody else's bones."

"I heard they found the body of a woman in Lake Chūzenji. She was naked."

"Aren't they pinning the deaths of all the unidentified bodies they've found recently on the same guy?"

"Well, one thing's for certain. He's definitely murdered eight young women, so even if they blame him for a lot of other crimes, he can hardly complain, can he?"

"The more they search, the more bodies they'll find."

Just then a red-cheeked station attendant poked his face into the waiting room. He appeared to still be in his teens. His voice sounded angry.

"I'll start taking tickets for the train to Tokyo, so line up!"

The men stood up, mumbling and sighing, and left the waiting room. The others also filed out one after another.

"I'm getting on this train too. I hate this place. C'mon, let's go somewhere else. Pleeease." Mowgli suddenly stood up and tugged on Akela's hand.

He hesitated. "But we've gone to all this trouble to come here."

"Then I'll go by myself. Goodbye."

She let go of Akela's hand and ran out of the waiting room alone. He ran out after her, feeling angry. *The little brat, she can't even buy a ticket!* Mowgli was already lined up in front of the ticket gate.

"Hurry up! It's about to leave!"

The departure bell rang out over her voice.

The station attendant couldn't ignore the bell, so he told Akela, "You can get your tickets on the train. In any case, get on."

Mowgli went through the gate ahead of him and got on the train right in front of them.

"Hurry up! Hurry!" Mowgli yelled in a sharp voice.

Akela moved like an automaton, leaping in through the train door. The wheels of the train had already begun to slowly move. After standing in the vestibule and catching his breath, he muttered, "You're really pushy, aren't you. What the hell's up with that?"

As she tried to catch her breath, Mowgli gave a sidelong glance at Akela's face, and stuck out her pink tongue. As she did, tears ran down the side of her face.

"I don't like scary places. We can come again later, that's for sure. I don't know when, but ..."

Akela reluctantly nodded. He wanted to ask her if she meant that the two of them *together* could come here again? But he didn't have the guts to do it. Mowgli also felt awkward after saying what she did. She wondered if it was true that they'd never be separated. Would they go on forever like this until one of them died? After all, they had sworn an oath: *we be of one blood*!

"Never mind. Given what happened, we couldn't have done any sightseeing without feeling uneasy. I figure there must have been a murder, but those men were talking about something really scary. Damn, it puts everyone on edge ... like the sensation you get when stepping on a swan."

"Huh?" As she wiped the tears from her cheeks with her fingertips, Mowgli cocked her head in puzzlement.

"You know what I mean, don't you? The sensation of *stepping on a swan*? I've never actually stepped on one, but it must be pretty unnerving. Because no one would want to do that to a swan, would they?"

What was he going on about? Did he mean something like "stepping in a swamp"? Mowgli nodded. She felt weird, but even so, she thought she understood what he meant clearly enough.

The train picked up speed. They moved from the vestibule into the car. There were still a lot of empty seats. They picked seats near the vestibule and sat down facing one another. Two middle-school girls wearing sailor-style uniforms and slacks were sitting in the seats across the aisle. They were both focused intently on an old magazine.

30 August 1946
Suspicions about Young Girl Murdered in Tochigi

Utsunomiya. New details of the Kodaira Incident have come to light. On 2 December of last year Numao Shizue (age 17), a fourth-year student at the Nikkō High School for Girls in Nishi-machi, Nikkō, said she was going to visit a friend, but never returned home. Early on the morning of 3 January of this year her body was found beside the arboretum in the same town, her throat slashed by what may have been a short sword. According to the autopsy carried out by the Nikkō Police Department, it did not appear that the young woman was raped. On the evening of 30 December of last year Baba Hiroko (age 19) of Nishimachi, Shintsukudajima in Tokyo's Kyōbashi Ward was strangled with her own muffler in the vicinity of Honjō, village of Nishikata, district of Kamitsuga in Tochigi Prefecture. The money she had been carrying was stolen. Hiroko was on her way to Nikkō to visit her older sister.

2 October 1946
Kodaira Interrogation Notebooks
12 Victims Listed
Tokyo Metropolitan Police Eager to Corroborate Evidence

In a little over a month following the arrest of the serial killer Kodaira Yoshio (age 42) on 20 August by Atago Investigation Headquarters, police have determined that Kodaira is responsible for the murder of five young women, and that based on his modus operandi he is certainly the perpetrator of a large number of previously unsolved murders of women whose skeletons have been discovered. Because police are satisfied that these murders can be attributed to Kodaira, they have at a stroke settled a number of unsolved cases. The Atago police now have their hands full trying to corroborate testimony and to finish disposing of the cases that have been resolved.

1. Midorikawa Ryūko (age 17) murdered (body naked, 6 August near Zōjōji Temple in Shiba).
2. Abe Yoshiko (age 13), murdered (13 June, parking lot in Takahama-chō, Shiba).
3 & 4. Kondo Kazuko (age 21), skeletal remains, and Matsushita Yoshie (age 21), body naked, both murdered (15 July and 28 September of last year, Kiyose-mura, a western suburb of Tokyo).
5. Miyazaki Mitsuko (age 20) murdered, (26 May of last year, air-raid shelter in Ōi).

Police have been able to find compelling evidence in the five cases above and have determined they were crimes committed by Kodaira. It appears certain that Kodaira committed the remaining murders as well, and it has been reported that he has already admitted certain details about the crimes. What we know is the following:

1. Skeletal remains found on Mount Shiba (discovered at the same time as the body of Midorikawa).
2. A strangled corpse found in a thicket in the village of Nishikata, Kamitsuga district, Tochigi Prefecture (30 December of last year: Baba Hiroko, age 18).
3. Skeletal remains found in a mountain forest near the village of Manago, Kamitsuga district (discovered in November of last year)—a Western-style umbrella found in the vicinity of the crime scene appears to have belonged to Nakamura Mitsuko (age 22), oldest daughter of Nakamura Yoshizō of Higashi-chō, Rokkaku-bashi, Kanagawa Ward, Yokohama, a woman intellectual who, as previously reported, had gone to Shibuya Station to buy a ticket a year earlier. Inspection of the crime scene has not proven this conclusively.
4. Skeletal remains found in a mountain forest near the village of Kiyosu, district of Kamitsuga, Tochigi Prefecture (discovered in February of this year)—it seems that the suspect has come close to confessing to the crime, but the body has not been positively identified yet.
5. Skeletal remains found in an underground room in Shibuya Station (discovered on 17 January of this year: Shinokawa Tatsue, age 17, murdered)—the case remains unresolved, due to a lack of physical evidence.
6. A drowned corpse was found in Lake Chūzenji (discovered on 13 June of last year). An aunt of the suspect testified that around that time Kodaira had taken the woman to Nikkō for sightseeing. Suspicions arose because the body was naked and the autopsy showed that the woman was about age thirty (the same age as Ishikawa Yori) and that she had no water in her lungs.
7. Numao Shizue (age 17), a fourth-year student at the Nikkō High School for Girls in Nikkō City, murdered (2 December of last year).

The conductor told them when he came around to collect tickets that the final stop for this train was not Utsunomiya, but Ueno. They looked at each other in surprise. Of course, that wasn't a bad thing, but Akela decided it was best to buy tickets for Ōmiya. If possible, he wanted to avoid going anywhere near central Tokyo.

When they arrived back at Utsunomiya, they again encountered a lot of passengers with luggage struggling to get on ahead of the others. Up to that point their car had been fairly empty, but now the aisles filled with people, the air became stuffy, and it was hard to breathe. Akela and Mowgli had been told that it would take less than two hours to get to Ōmiya, so they resisted the urge to move out to the vestibule and remained in their seats. A woman wearing a wide flared skirt and a flower-patterned scarf on her head and a man wearing sunglasses and a white neckerchief sat down in the seats across from them.

This train was coupled at Utsunomiya with a train coming in from the north, so it stopped for more than twenty minutes. While they waited, Akela was able at last to go out onto the platform and buy *bentō*. Feeling very hungry, he bought three of them. He justified the expense to himself, thinking that they might have problems if they didn't get enough nutrition.

He still felt feverish. He divided up the *bentō* with Mowgli and they ate. When his stomach was full, Akela began to smoke—the first cigarette he'd had in a while. He was feeling a sense of rivalry with the couple opposite him, who were smoking up a storm. But because he felt ill every time he took a deep drag, he decided to hold the cigarette lightly in his lips and puff away. Mowgli's face had a healthy glow as she quietly drank her tea. Her cheeks were round and the soft fuzz on her face was glowing. Akela tried rubbing his own cheeks. The stubble of his whiskers was getting longer, and he felt his cheeks were a little hollow. It was hard to believe it had been just noon yesterday when they had been soaked by the rain in Yamagata. It looked as though Mowgli was over her diarrhea. Perhaps this little one's body was much stronger than his. The realization that he might be the weaker one made Akela feel forlorn.

The rays of the sun beat down intensely outside the window, and the green of the paddies and the leaves of the trees glistened a dark color. Akela stretched out both hands and opened the window a crack. He closed his eyes and savored the wind that came in through the window. Though he was puzzled that it had suddenly changed from winter to early summer, he felt ravished by the softness of the mild breeze.

Other windows were opened here and there, and a pleasant breeze came wafting through the car. It was terribly crowded, but the faces of the passengers standing in the aisle did not wear the same bloodthirsty expressions as those of the passengers on the overnight train—perhaps because the train was at most just two hours away from the final stop, Ueno. Enjoying the breeze, Akela tried muttering the phrase *The sensation of stepping on a swan.* Images of a swan had been flashing off and on in his mind for the last few minutes. The swan wanted to say something to him, but he couldn't understand its language. *Stepping on a swan?* Of course it was forbidden to do such a thing. It was too cruel. Didn't swans sing just before they died? He had seen a swan once, in a park somewhere. A large bird, pure white, with a long neck. It was so big that, had he been a child, he could have climbed onto its back and flown up to the sky. But the wings of the swans in the park were clipped, so those birds couldn't fly anywhere. Could swans with clipped wings continue to think of themselves as swans? At some point he had seen swans floating not on a pond in a park, but on a great river. Akela had been walking along the bank in winter. Snow was flickering, and the surface of the river was white with ripples. There was no one else there, just him. No wait, there had been a dog nudging up close to him. Akela was

124

freezing in the cold wind. And on the bleak surface of the river, a swan. The Swan was passing by. *The Swan—*

Akela opened his eyes, and nodded excitedly. *That's it! I've got it! If you can find just one clue, then everything will fall into place.* He immediately clutched Mowgli's shoulder and whispered into her ear, "Listen, let's give up the names Akela and Mowgli. From now on you'll be Capi, and I'll be Remi."

In order to stop Mowgli from turning her face toward him in surprise, Akela continued to whisper, "Weren't you singing a song from *Nobody's Boy* yesterday? You know the words: *helpless children of Eve suffering in this vale of tears.* There was something about it that kept bugging me, something not right about it, but I couldn't put my finger on what was wrong. At some point Mowgli has to leave the jungle and go back to the world of humans. Because he was originally human. Akela grows old and dies in the fight with the Red Dogs. You understood all that, right? But now I think that Akela was actually my dad, because he expended all his strength in the jungle and died. Isn't that right? And I was kicked out of the jungle, because my old man was dead. I was kicked out because the jungle is the world after you die and before you're born. We were both fated to have to come back to the Man Pack. And now that we have, we can't use the names Akela and Mowgli anymore. Do you see?"

Mowgli nodded mechanically.

"So now that we've come back to the world of humans, I've thought of better names for us. We're Remi and Capi. Those names are perfect. You see, I often read the book *Nobody's Boy* as well. Remi and Capi are constantly chasing after a barge called *The Swan* that's moving along a river. Remi's real mother and his real little brother are living on that barge. But none of them are aware of that. It's that kind of story."

"But isn't Capi a dog? I don't want to be a dog." Mowgli's face looked dead serious as she whispered back to him.

"Well, Capi is a dog, but he's much smarter than Remi … and he's always guarding Remi. Capi is the more experienced traveling performer, and when he and Remi are learning how to read and write from their master, Capi always remembers more quickly. In any case, that's what it says in the book. You shouldn't mock him just because he's a dog. You could be Remi, but in that case, what would I do? I can't become the master, and anyway, I'm older and bigger, so it would be weird if I were Capi, wouldn't it? Capi means "Captain" in Italian. From now on the two of us have to live in the Man Pack without forgetting the law of the jungle … *Jungle-Favor go with thee!* You understand, don't you?"

Mowgli nodded deeply to show that she did understand. She was in fact surprised at herself for being able to comprehend Akela's thoughts, and for being convinced by them. She knew the story of *Nobody's Boy* better than she knew *The Jungle Book.* Though she still objected a little to being a dog.

Akela, who was now Remi, looked satisfied. He smiled at Mowgli, who was now Capi.

7. The Swan

The world was before me. I could go where I liked, north, south, east, or west. I was my own master.

For the Remi of *Nobody's Boy*, this thought was a cause of sorrow, not of joy; and because the seventeen-year-old Remi was still an adolescent, he understood that feeling. Because what really matters for a child is not fears about money or health, not the hardships of cold or heat. What matters is the feeling of security that comes when someone is looking out for you. What every little child wants more than anything else when they're on their own is someone who'll protect them. If they can't find someone like that, then even a dog is better than nothing. A lot of little ones are careless and get mixed up with bad types. Yet no matter how bad those people might be, the child will be happy so long as he feels he's being looked after. Back when the four-year-old Remi was living in the graveyard, he felt no anxiety, probably because he was not alone. Even at the Children's Home he basically felt all right. When he thought back about his time there, he remembered a dog at the orphanage. It was just a stray white mutt who hung around the place, but seeing him always made Remi and the other little kids happy. They'd feed him scraps of their own bread; they'd hug him and rub their faces up against his nose so that the dog might lick them. Everyone called him by a different name—Jirō, Shiro, Tom. No one thought of calling him Capi.

Remi, who had just left the Children's Home in March, was now grateful that the Capi accompanying him wasn't a dog, but a real live human. He still had his freedom to travel where he wanted, and, to top it off, he had a companion called Capi. She loyally followed him, and she even looked after him with the solicitude of an adult. When Remi told a joke, Capi would laugh; when she grew sleepy, she'd snuggle up to him so they could keep each other warm. Because she was smart, she was never intentionally thoughtless or indiscreet. She knew a lot about maps of Japan. Remi could keep going as Remi only so long as he and Capi were mutually supportive. It was completely different from being on one's own. Remi's master, Vitalis, had said as much: *Fate doesn't always torment humans who have the courage to fight. Be thoughtful and humble.*

About half the passengers got off the train at Ōmiya. Remi and Capi also stepped out onto the platform with the same expression of relief as the other passengers. But there was no reason for them to get off at this station, and no need to hurry toward the exit gate. They washed their faces and rinsed their mouths again at the water faucet. It was not yet ten in the morning. Because they woke up before dawn at Utsunomiya, the day felt surprisingly long. They went to a toilet next to the exit gate, and Remi used the scissors to trim the whiskers around his mouth. Unlike a razor, however, the scissors left stubble about two millimeters long. He remembered that Capi had wanted a toothbrush, and so he bought her one and realized he should probably get a razor as well. He studied his own face in the mirror carefully. As he suspected, he was looking a little drawn. His body somehow felt weak. It couldn't possibly be a serious illness, but if he didn't make a quick recovery it would be really difficult for Capi. Should he pick up some cold medicine at a drugstore? Capi's stomach seemed completely better now. But her body was sluggish from fatigue and lack of sleep, and her mind was becoming dull. Remi had asked her if they should try walking around town, but she had been reluctant and hadn't answered right away. So Remi had suggested that instead, since it was still early, they could try riding the Kawagoe Line. That seemed easier than walking around the town, so Capi smiled and nodded.

They boarded a train that was already standing at the Kawagoe Line platform. The engine was diesel rather than steam, and that difference alone gave them both a sense of familiarity, a sense that they were getting back closer to Tokyo, since only electric trains ran inside the city.

To their surprise, their diesel train took just twenty minutes to reach Kawagoe station. Since it was the end of the line, all the passengers got off. Remi and Capi had no choice but to get off as well. They decided to sit down on a bench on the platform for the time being and wait for the next train. If they got on the private railway line that ran from this station, they could have headed for Ikebukuro in Tokyo. Remi knew that, but said nothing. He was convinced they must never go back to Tokyo, and he was not about to change his mind. Remi worried that Capi would forget all about him and make a dash for home as soon as she realized Ikebukuro was within walking distance of her house. Of course, he couldn't be sure she wouldn't run home no matter where they were, but he didn't want to end his journey with her just yet. The time they would spend together had only just started.

While they were waiting for the next train, Remi began to tell her all he could remember about *Nobody's Boy*, just as he had told her about *The Jungle Book*. Capi knew the story, but there were many parts she had forgotten: for example, how Remi came to be abandoned and raised in a poverty-stricken farm family; why he had to be sold to his master, the traveling performer Vitalis; how he learned his art from his master and was able to perform plays with Capi, two other dogs, and a monkey. At the beginning Capi's role was to keep an eye on Remi so he wouldn't run away. Capi was a white poodle who sported a policeman's cap. He was the leader of the animals in the troupe, and could read clocks and human emotions. Whenever he sensed that Remi felt lonely, Capi would come over to lick his hand. "You're not alone," Capi seemed to whisper softly. The master gave the role of the Fool to Remi. It was a role intended to highlight the cleverness of Capi and the monkey named Pretty-Heart.

128

The play they all performed, *Mr. Pretty-Heart's Servant, or The Fool Is Not Always the One You Think*, was a pantomime. Since it starred a monkey and a dog, there were of course no speaking parts. Pretty-Heart is a retired English General who earned fortune and status during the wars in India. His clever servant Capi, who has been with him all that time, is getting old, so he decides to hire a new servant and entrusts Capi with the job of finding one. But instead of finding another dog, Capi brings back the human child Remi to be the new servant. Pretty-Heart is extremely wealthy, so he thinks he should be granted the pleasure of bossing around a human being. However, Remi plays an uneducated boy from a poor farm family who has no idea about how to use the napkins placed on the table or how to set out plates or use a fork. All he can do is stare blankly at those items with an idiotic expression. He ends up blowing his nose with the napkin, which he then ties around his neck. Pretty-Heart laughs heartily at that, while Capi is shocked and rolls over on his back, his four paws pointing to the sky. The people of the town who gather on the side of the road to watch the performance are greatly amused. They toss money to Capi, who is now walking around on his hind legs carrying a bowl in his mouth, and admire the fact that truly both the dog and the monkey look clever compared with the idiot human child.

After they'd sat on the bench for about thirty minutes, the next train arrived. Apparently it was headed for Higashi Hannō Station. They got up, stretched, and boarded the train. Once more the houses around them gradually disappeared, and rice paddies spread out around the tracks. They could see the bluish shapes of mountains ahead of them. They opened the windows wide and felt the pleasant sensation of the air flowing over their bodies. There weren't all that many passengers on the train, perhaps because it was right around lunchtime, and no one was standing in the aisle. Presently, they arrived at the next-to-last station on the line. Everything had proceeded smoothly up to this point, but once the train stopped, it didn't move again. There was no announcement, so it was apparently all right to stay on board. Even so, they had no idea why the train was sitting in this station. The other passengers looked as though they understood the situation and sat silently, as if resigned to it. The silence in the car was oppressive.

"Are they having engine trouble?" Capi whispered to Remi.

"What are they waiting for?" Remi muttered.

A woman dressed in work trousers was in the seat in front of them. She looked angry as she explained the situation.

"Accident ... a derailment. Didn't you know? It's been all over the news."

A young man next to her—probably a college student—smiled tolerantly at them and said, "You couldn't have known that the accident site was close by, could you? After all, this isn't the Hachikō Line."

Remi simply nodded in response, shrugging his shoulders and scratching his head as though he were apologizing. He didn't want to cause them problems by talking any more, so he turned his face toward Capi, sighed with a mournful expression, then folded his arms and pretended to be deep in thought. Fortunately, neither the woman nor the student was the talkative type, and they remained quiet too. Their expressions suggested that they didn't want to bring up the topic of such a horrible accident again.

Fifteen minutes passed before the train finally came back to life and began to move. The eyes of the people on the train all turned in unison to the right. Following everyone else's lead, Remi and Capi stared out the window too. The train was now running slowly beside a river. A cliff loomed high overhead, and the river sparkled. Yellow and white flowers were blooming along the bank, and all around was an expansive pastoral landscape. A single cylinder from the engine stood alone on the riverbank. It resembled a memorial pillar, and they caught a glimpse of what may have been bouquets of flowers and incense that had been laid around its base. Remi and Capi were still gazing at the scene, their mouths agape, when the train arrived at the final stop, Higashi Hannō. Even after they had stepped out onto the platform, the story of the derailment stayed in their minds. It must have been a major accident. When had it happened? They could easily have found out by asking a station attendant, but neither of them wanted to do that. People might wonder how they could know so little about the derailment, and become suspicious.

They paid their fare adjustments, went through the exit, and looked up at the train schedule. They had to decide where to go next. Although it was a small station, both the Kawagoe Line and the tracks for the Hachikō Line ran through it. If they took the Hachikō Line, they could go to either Takasaki or Hachiōji. In addition, there was a station for the Seibu Ikebukuro Line next door, and if they took a train from there, they could they go as far as Agano, or they could go to Ikebukuro. Ikebukuro was out of the question, and because they had had a bad experience at Nikkō, they didn't want to go near the mountains of Agano, if at all possible. Having ruled out Takasaki and Agano, Hachiōji was the only option left. They would continue to cut around Tokyo, heading south.

"The next train to Hachiōji leaves in about forty minutes. It's just noon and I'd like to get something to eat, but there don't seem to be any shops around here," Remi said.

Capi glanced around to make sure no one could hear and replied, "I think I've been here before, on a school trip. The name of the station sounds familiar."

"Whatever. In any case, it's the middle of nowhere."

Remi sounded out of sorts. Just like the Kawagoe Line, the Seibu Ikebukuro Line next door could easily take them back to Tokyo, and he was worried that she might realize that. He moved away from her and went outside. In the midday light, the plaza in front of the station looked blindingly white. A clear blue sky spread overhead, and the temperature had gone up considerably. He could see the bluish shapes of a line of mountains in front of him.

"Is it okay if I go over by the tracks? The flowers are blooming." Capi came up from behind him, then ran off to the side of the station. Remi hurriedly ran after her. It was hot, so he pulled off his sweater. Eyeing Capi from behind, he thought she looked like a poor little vagabond. Her clothes were too big for her, making her look all the more like some malnourished little kid. Remi sighed, thinking with satisfaction she was just like a puppy that has no concept of physical danger.

White flowers and long-stemmed yellow flowers were blooming alongside the tracks and between the ties. There were also small red flowers. Capi walked beside the tracks, humming some random song. She could never even get close to any railway tracks in the middle of Tokyo, and flowers like this certainly didn't bloom by the tracks in the city. Trolley lines were laid on square stones, and the tracks of the Yamanote Line were laid on a bed of small brown stones. Flowers did bloom on embankments, but because the embankments were blocked off by wire fencing, you couldn't get close to the flowers. She had often heard stories about bad kids who had crossed the fence, fallen from the embankments, and been run over by a train and killed. Even though the tracks here were the same as the tracks in Tokyo, the flowers seemed to be blooming in a carefree way, just as they pleased. Two yellow butterflies were flitting along, entwined. A brown dog was walking about ten meters ahead of them, sniffing at the flowers. Capi could hear the buzzing of insect wings. The rails shone white in the sunlight. She opened her mouth and began to sing

"We praise thee, O God, We acknowledge you to be the Lord, All the earth doth worship Thee, Everlasting Father ..."

"Hey! Capi? How far you going?"

She heard Remi, but pretended she hadn't and kept on walking. She walked beside the rails, bathed in sunlight. It was a simple pleasure, but it made her feel exhilarated. Swinging her cloth bag around, she sang even louder.

"The angels, and all the Cherubim and Seraphim unceasingly proclaim ..."

The brown dog turned toward Capi and came running up to her, wagging its tail. Then it began walking at her side.

"Haven't you gone far enough? I'm hungry. And tired."

Laughing, Capi looked back at him.

"No way! Even the doggy is having a great time!"

"It's only because he thinks you'll feed him something. If we don't get back soon ..."

"And just when I was feeling good."

In the bright sunlight, Remi almost looked to her like a much older man, someone who was ill, and for an instant she felt afraid. But almost immediately, the Remi she knew came back. Perhaps his partially shaven whiskers had made him look like a somber adult. Or perhaps he was feverish again. Capi was a little worried, but then she reconsidered, figuring that being out in the sun ought to cure Remi's illness. Phrases like "basking in the sun" and "disinfected by the sunshine" popped into her mind.

The brown dog walking beside her, wagging its tail, suddenly barked and ran off to the left of the railroad. Something big and black was lying near the edge of a paddy. The dog ran toward it, barking furiously. Capi descended the embankment and went over to take a peek. A huge mass was squatting in the grass—it looked enormous. Square holes that resembled windows were arrayed along its torso. Not a single pane of glass was left in them. The right side had been crushed, and the back end of it tapered out like a conch shell. It was the wreckage of a passenger train car. The roof on the right side was twisted, and the window frames had been crushed and torn and were bent downward. The dog continued to bark with white froth bubbling around its mouth, and its howling sounded like a scream. It ran to the left, to the right, it moved away a little, then came back again. Yet it absolutely would not come within a meter of the wreckage.

"Is this a car from the accident? Dogs know the smell of dead people," Remi muttered as he came up beside Capi. She nodded, and began to back away little by little. Through the sound of the dog's howling she could imagine corpses crushed in the passenger car, blue hands and feet sticking out of the windows, the bleeding figures of people who had been thrown from the train. Their groans and cries crashed like waves and echoed in her ears. Surrounded by the green of the grass, the black train car and the injured people and the corpses writhed like a single living organism.

"A lot of people died here, that's for sure. Instead of a memorial marker, they've set this car here. There're probably flowers and incense on the other side," Remi remarked as they walked back to the tracks.

Facing the wrecked car, he put his hands together and slightly bowed his head in prayer. The dog, having barked itself hoarse, looked exhausted by the time it returned to them. Glancing over at Remi, Capi hurriedly put her own hands together and apologized to the people in the accident for herself and for the dog. *Please forgive us for disturbing you. We just came here out of carelessness. We didn't know anything about the accident. So please don't hold it against us. Even though you died, I sympathize with you, knowing how you must regret leaving so many things behind. So please don't do anything bad to us. Please don't mind us, and sleep in peace. Well, goodbye.*

26 February 1947
Hachikō Line Train Overturns
1,000 Shoppers Killed or Injured

Urawa—At about 7:50 on the morning of 25 February, just as a six-car train filled with shoppers reached a curve on a steep hill about 500 meters south of Komagawa Station on the Hachikō Line, the coupler between the second and third coaches came loose, and the last four cars toppled and fell from a cliff about five meters high. The workers on the train did not notice the accident, and discovered what had happened only after the engine and remaining two cars entered Komagawa Station. Railroad service was suspended. Approximately 1,000 passengers were killed or injured. A rescue team of linemen from the Hachiōji, Kawagoe, and Ōmiya rail districts was dispatched, and people from neighboring villages, including doctors and nurses, reported to help. They took the injured who had been caught underneath the train by trucks and buses to hospitals in Hannō, Moro, Kawagoe, and Ōmiya. However, because the hospitals couldn't accommodate all the victims, the houses of local residents overflowed with the injured. As of one o'clock that afternoon, the Saitama police released their report, announcing that the number of dead had reached 178, the number of seriously injured about 300, and the number of people suffering minor injuries about 500.

27 February 1947
Death Toll Reaches 190

Urawa—According to a report released by the Saitama Police at noon on 26 February, 178 people were pronounced dead at the scene of the major accident on the Hachikō Line. The number of seriously injured taken to area hospitals was 265; 77 to Kawagoe, 74 to Hannō, 23 to Ōmiya, 80 to Moroyama, and 11 to Ogose. Of those 265, 12 have since died. The total number of dead has risen to 190, and a number of victims are in critical condition.

It would take about forty minutes to reach Hachiōji from Higashi Hannō.

The brown dog had followed them all the way to the station platform. It sat down beside them and, whenever they looked its way, wagged its tail. Capi was concerned, wondering what they should do if it followed them onto the train, or kept running after them, chasing the train. If that happened, wouldn't they just have to reconcile themselves to getting off the train and continuing their journey with the dog? When she mentioned that to Remi, he told her not to worry, that the dog would give up while they were waiting, but Capi continued to fret as she and the dog looked at each other.

The train pulled into the station. They got on board, and when they looked back at the platform, the dog was still sitting there, quietly watching the two of them. Remi assured her that the dog killed time every day by wandering around the station like that. Capi, a little disappointed, waved to the dog. The train started up, but the dog made no effort to get up. Had the dog actually joined their party, then their journey really would have been like the one in *Nobody's Boy*, and they could have had fun teaching the dog tricks.

The diesel train of the Hachikō Line proceeded with ease through the verdant scenery.

The dog Capi's family had once owned had been taken by the dogcatcher and put to sleep. Another dog of theirs had eaten rat poison and died. They never had any dogs after that. Then her brother died. The dog that had been taken by the dogcatcher was a white mutt that had once lived at some other house in the neighborhood. It couldn't do any tricks. It just dug holes in the garden. Capi would straddle the dog's back, or pick up its hind legs and make it walk on its front legs. She even attached its leash to a mandarin orange crate once, hoping to make a kind of dog sled. She tried to get it to jump through hoops or walk a tightrope, like the dogs in a circus. Not once did it even try to live up to Capi's expectations. Their other dog—the one that died in place of the rats—was a little Spitz. It wasn't much fun since it just barked nervously all the time. Not the kind of dog that made Capi want to teach it tricks. She and her brother were always together with the white mutt, constantly playing with it—or, more precisely, always tormenting it. That dog was quiet and patient, even when they knocked it over, or forced its mouth open, or stuck blades of grass up its nose. It never got angry and bit them. One time, her brother decided he would try riding it, but the dog was crushed by his weight and actually had the poop squeezed out of it. After that, the dog always ran away whenever it saw her brother.

Remi was sitting alongside Capi on the Hachikō Line, absorbed in contemplating the differences between wolves and dogs. It seemed certain that dogs had the power to sense the presence of spirits. In old folktales, for example, a fox could change into a woman and trick men, but a dog could immediately detect the fox's true form. And what about wolves? He couldn't remember any such stories about them, but that didn't prove that wolves didn't possess such powers. Because dogs live together with humans, they're often being observed, and their behavior recorded. But since wolves can survive even when there are no humans around, there are a lot of things about them that humans don't understand. Even though ghosts wander around the jungle, wolves, unlike dogs, are probably never afraid of them. They don't distinguish between the world after death and the world they live in. The difference means nothing to them. Dogs aren't like that. They have become part of the human world. And like humans, dogs know the difference between life and death. They fear death and cling to life. When he thought about it, there were probably no other animals as fragile and pitiful as thoroughly domesticated dogs. When a dog is separated from humans, it has no choice but to become a cruel wild dog that knows nothing of the Law. It was the same even for Capi. If Remi continued to protect her, she would grow human-like. No matter how much Capi tried to do things beyond her abilities, she couldn't go on living by herself. Remi was a necessity for Capi, and Capi was a necessity for Remi as well. If Capi weren't around, Remi would quickly be overwhelmed by the loneliness of his isolation. This was exactly a case of *The Fool Is Not Always the One You Think*.

They arrived without a hitch at the end of the line, Hachiōji Station.

The two of them walked into the town and went to a *soba* shop first. Capi ordered *ramen* again. Remi ordered chicken and egg over rice. The shop was crowded.

Mothers with their children. Workers from the neighborhood. Even old folks eating a late lunch or an early snack, slowly slurping *soba* or *udon* noodles. Yamagata, Hachiōji … the interior of *soba* shops everywhere looked pretty much the same. Remi and Capi ate and ate without once lifting their heads. They bought some soft ice cream, which Capi had been dying to try, and went outside. While they licked their ice cream, they walked side by side down a street of shops decorated with artificial wisteria blooms. They spent fifteen minutes in front of a toy store looking in the show window, then they stared at the dried viper, Korean carrots, exotic mushrooms, and other curiosities lined up in the window of a Chinese herbal medicine shop. After enjoying a demonstration by a sewing machine salesman, they found a small drugstore, and Remi went in by himself. He got cold medicine, a toothbrush, toothpaste, a razor, and, just in case, some medicine for diarrhea. He looked around the store, wondering if there wasn't something else he needed. He spotted a tin of fruit drops, and he bought that for Capi as well.

Hachiōji was, for the two of them, an unexpectedly splendid city. There were lots of people mingling in the shopping district, and because it was located within the greater Tokyo region, the dialect was not all that different from their own, which made them feel at ease. As Remi had expected, Capi, who had been waiting outside, was thrilled to receive the candy. At once she popped one of the lemon-flavored drops into her mouth, and had Remi pick out a flavor he liked. When Remi shook the tin, a white mint-flavored drop rolled out. He casually tossed it into his mouth. There were very few white mint drops, only two or three to a tin, so Capi quickly stuffed the candy away in her own cloth bag.

Going around behind the shopping district, they found a temple and went in to take a look. There was a small graveyard within the temple grounds. Picking a spot with good sunlight, they decided to rest awhile. They hadn't had enough sleep, and their bodies felt heavy.

"It's not right for outsiders to spend the night in a tiny graveyard like this."

Remi spoke with evident pride. He seemed to be implying that his own graveyard had been a *real* graveyard. In contrast, this cemetery was only about ten meters in width from end to end. The gravestones were new and decorated with fresh flowers.

"It's quiet here. It feels good. I feel like taking a nap."

Leaning her head up against the gravestone next to her, Capi closed her eyes. The strong rays of the sun shone down directly on her face. Remi spread out his bag and sweater on the ground and sprawled out, leaning up on one elbow. Tearing off the slender leaves of some weeds there, he scattered them on the ground and began to talk, as though he were speaking to himself.

"But still, when I'm dead and my body is scattered, can I return to the jungle then? Humans die in so many ways, so …"

Her eyes still closed, Capi answered him. The images of corpses from the train wreck and the howling of the dog came back to her beneath the orange-tinted insides of her eyelids.

"Sure, you can go to the jungle."

"But suppose your head was completely crushed and washed away in a river, and your right hand decomposed and dissolved in an ocean far away, and your torso was devoured by a man-eating tiger in a completely different place, and … If that sort of thing happened after you died, you wouldn't be able to make much sense of things, would you? People believe that if their bones are buried in a grave like this, it's easier to go on to the world after death, right? That is, they can go to the jungle."

Attracted by the presence of living humans, two large black flies began to buzz around. They kept landing on Capi's nose or on Remi's earlobes and lips, and whenever they were shooed away, they would buzz around with even greater energy, as if they were enjoying themselves.

"But graves don't have much to do with the dead, do they?" Capi continued, "Once you're dead, you don't really care about anything in this world. So it must be the same for the way you die. If that's not the case, then people who have been murdered and dumped in a lake or left in the mountains wouldn't know what to do or where to go if their bodies were never discovered, even though it's not their fault."

"And so they can't become Buddhas, and they'll come back and haunt this world."

A dog was barking in the neighborhood, then a car horn sounded. They could smell the scent of grass and dirt warmed by the sun.

"Maybe, but when you die, your brain dies too, so everything completely disappears, doesn't it? The fact that you were human, or that you were a woman … those sorts of things must disappear as well—become something like the wind—and when they do it's a good feeling, and then gradually you move to another place and arrive at the jungle, and you dissolve into the jungle. I've never seen Ton-chan's ghost, not even once."

Remi was brushing away the two flies. He exhaled in a way that wasn't quite a yawn and wasn't quite a sigh either.

"I don't get it. What's the point of a graveyard, then? I guess you're not supposed to leave a corpse just anywhere. Is that why people feel they have to prepare a special place to bury bodies? During the war they didn't have any choice, but if you bury bodies in common graves just anywhere, it'd get so that you couldn't stroll down the streets without having to watch where you walk. Pretty soon the whole town would become a cemetery. When I was little, I never saw any ghosts in the graveyard. I never even had the sense that they would come out. But then again, the dead wouldn't be hanging around places like a graveyard, would they?"

"Well, they might come and hang around once in a while," Capi answered, her voice drowsy. "Like the wind. Maybe once in a great while they feel like going to visit a place they liked. That's what we call a ghost, for sure. And so I can't see Ton-chan's ghost, but I've felt his presence…. A ghost won't go near the person who killed her, though maybe she'd call on her companions and they'd punish the criminal."

"If the criminal is crazy, it wouldn't bother him at all, no matter how many ghosts appear."

"Does it really make a man feel good, to kill a woman? I don't get it—why do they want to kill just women?"

Remi was stumped and couldn't answer right away. He sighed and continued to tear off blades of grass, tossing them at the two flies still buzzing annoyingly around his face. Remi had absolutely no idea why such men kill only women. In the jungle, at least, no creature would kill members of their own species who were weaker than they. The difference between male and female was clear. Stupid males who targeted only females didn't exist in the jungle. There may be females who killed males they didn't like, but females, who give birth to children, had to be protected for the sake of survival, no matter what. That was the law of the jungle. However, because human men and women don't live in the jungle, they don't know that Law. Male animals and men are different. He had the feeling that the difference between male animals and men was greater than the difference between female animals and women. There was something odd about human males. He didn't understand the meaning of a man. Remi had a man's body, but that didn't mean that he could understand what being a human male meant. In appearance, he spoke like a man, he gestured like a man, he occasionally soiled his pants with wet dreams, and he took pride in the fact that even when he felt like he wanted to masturbate, he wasn't like some monkey obsessed with it, and did his best to control himself. Still, he couldn't bring himself to think that such things had anything to do with what it meant to be a human male, and he had a hard time understanding the Man Pack. After he graduated from middle school, he would hardly ever hang out with kids his own age, so he didn't have a very clear idea what it meant to be seventeen. Did guys who were raised by their real mothers try to become more macho in the Man Pack? There had always been women around Remi—the nurses at the orphanage, and "Mom" as well. But how were those women different from a real mother? Remi speculated that guys who were fussed over by their real mothers were the kind who contrive to kill women. But he couldn't just carelessly blurt out what he really thought. After all, people naturally would assume his views were jaundiced and his suspicions baseless because he hadn't been raised by his real mother. Society tended to assume that it was a boy like Remi, who had never known his *real mother*, who would become a man of dubious character.

"Men who kill women are the same kind of guys who don't give a second thought to killing a puppy. It's useless wasting time thinking about crazy men since there's nothing you can do about them. Still, you have to be careful. You don't want to get murdered."

Capi didn't respond. She seemed to be fast asleep. Remi sighed once more and closed his eyes. His heart had begun to beat intensely. He suddenly felt weirdly disturbed, wondering what Capi could be thinking. She did not yet identify herself as Capi, and she didn't believe in Remi as Remi. Even though Remi and Capi had to trust and believe in one another purely, without the slightest shadow of a doubt.

As Remi began to doze off, something painful began striking the top of his face. He yelped and instinctively grabbed that painful black thing with his right hand and stood up. He saw that he had grabbed a bamboo broom filthy with dust.

"You damn mutts! Get out! Get out!"

An old man, his head shaved like a priest's, his face bright red, was screaming in a high-pitched voice and tugging with both hands on the broom he used to sweep the graveyard, trying to get it back out of Remi's hand. His screaming woke Capi, and she stood up behind Remi in confusion. It made no sense to fight in a place like this. Their adversary was a weak old man. Even so, Remi was angry, and so he screwed up his mouth as much as he could, like some villain in a play, and spat at the old man. Then he let go of the broom and stood up. Turning back toward Capi, he gave her a wink and said, "Let's get out of here."

They returned at once to Hachiōji Station, and Remi carefully checked the train schedule. Taking the Chūō Line toward Tokyo was out of the question, and since he had learned that Kōfu was the hometown of Capi's mother, he wanted to avoid going in that direction as well. He felt they had no choice but to get on the Yokohama Line and keep heading south. If they went south, eventually the ocean would spread out before them. No matter what, it wouldn't be so bad if they could enjoy themselves at the seashore. The weather for tomorrow looked good, and even if there was no way they could go swimming, they could do other things, like chasing crabs or gathering starfish. When Remi mentioned his idea, Capi happily agreed.

The Yokohama Line is a commuter railway just like the Yamanote Line in Tokyo. So when they got on a train a little after four o'clock, it wasn't all that crowded. A group of middle-school students, apparently heading home from school, noisily boarded the train. Remi and Capi stood beside the door, wordlessly staring outside. The rural landscape, which had nothing special to recommend it, passed by. The middle-school girls in this region were dressed in trousers—not work trousers, of course, but school trousers identical to those worn by the boys. The boys all had buzz cuts. They gathered in small groups of several students each, laughing excitedly and absorbed in gossip. Just listening to their voices made both Remi and Capi feel exhausted and depressed.

After about an hour they reached the final station, Higashi Kanagawa. They changed right away to the Keihin Line, and it was about six when they arrived at Yokohama.

The sky was still light, but they weren't all that hungry, and the station was overflowing with commuters. Rather than hang around such a busy, confusing place, they decided to keep going, so they got on the Yokosuka Line. This train too was crammed full of passengers, each headed home. Even so, Remi and Capi were definitely moving closer to the sea. Station by station. To the sea. To the sea.

The passengers finally began to thin out after they passed Kamakura, and the train was even emptier at Zushi, but they still had not reached the sea. They continued to stand near the door and wait. The sky grew dark, and the yellow lights of the houses began to flicker. Just when they caught a glimpse of what they thought looked an expanse of sea, the train pulled into Yokosuka Station.

Most of the remaining passengers got off at this stop. Remi and Capi had the feeling that their eyes had caught a flash of something that looked like the sea here as well. The car was almost deserted, which actually made it more difficult for them to speak or move around as they would have liked. Two or three men, perhaps company employees, were reading newspapers. A young couple in raincoats was smoking cigarettes, while two middle-aged men with overnight bags were whispering something back and forth.

The train finally arrived at its last stop, Kurihama Station. When they stepped out onto the platform, they realized that night had fallen. The figures of the other passengers disappeared with hurried steps, and the station grew cold and quiet.

"This is as far as it goes. What should we do?" Capi asked in a small voice.

"Maybe we should have gotten off at Yokosuka. In any case, let's go outside and get something to eat. There has to be some place around here. Since we've come all this way, let's head for the seashore after we eat. It's still early." Remi answered, stretching.

An evening breeze was beginning to blow. They caught the scent of the sea—a sweet, damp smell. Breathing it in gave them an appetite.

"I came here once from school to go swimming in the sea. This is the place the American, Perry, came in his Black Ships. I remember seeing that stone monument and anchor," Capi whispered, moving toward the ticket gate.

"Your school sure takes a lot of trips. My elementary school only went to nearby places. Lake Sayama or Nagatoro."

"Yeah, but my school's no good at all. It's full of arrogant boys who boss the girls around. If you don't listen to what they say, you get pushed down the stairs. I had Ton-chan, so I didn't have time to play with my classmates. Now that I mention it, there was a man here who was like Ton-chan. His name was Maabō. He'd wander around the town, and everyone teased him to amuse themselves, yelling things like *Hey Maabō, where you going*, or *You stink, you stink, wash yourself*, or *Try eating this rock*. My classmates would chase after him too, yelling *Maabō, Maabō*."

"Monkeys everywhere. I'm sick of 'em already. At least from now on they won't trouble you anymore."

As they neared the ticket gate they both clammed up. Capi didn't have a chance to ask him why monkeys would no longer trouble her. But even so, she had a vague sense that's how things would turn out. And if Remi said it was so, then perhaps it would come true.

A small, dark plaza opened out in front of the station. The lights of the shops across the way were shining forlornly in the darkness. A person on a bike was cutting across the plaza, while a woman cleaned up in front of a restaurant where a glass door had been propped open. People who were going to take the train headed for Tokyo appeared a few at a time out of the darkness and began to gather in the station.

Remi and Capi entered the nearest restaurant. They were surprised to find the place full of customers—day laborers, some wearing split-toed cloth work boots, others in rubber boots. All of them were drunk, their faces red.

Remi and Capi sat in a corner, and the shop was filled with cigarette smoke. Strips of flypaper hung above each of the tables, swaying slightly, with dead flies stuck all over them. Remi ordered a fixed price meal, while Capi ordered chicken and egg over rice. If they both just sat there in gloomy silence, they would be more likely to call attention to themselves and, rather than being ignored, run the risk of being spoken to. For that reason, Remi decided to tell Capi about the journey that Remi and Capi had undertaken in the story.

"One time, when a policeman tried to chase the troupe—that is, the monkey, the dogs, and the child—from the street, a quarrel ensued, and the master, Vitalis, was thrown in prison. Remi didn't have much money, and he had to continue his journey with the dogs and the monkey until the day his master was released. Remi would cry from loneliness, and Capi, who was cleverer than any human, comforted him. And then Remi and the animals encountered the mother and child on *The Swan*.... Do you remember *The Swan*, Capi? It was a large flat-bottom boat, like a barge. Two horses walking along the bank pulled it slowly along the canals and rivers. To tell you the truth, even now, I'm still not sure I understand what kind of boat it was. Remi was given a small room on the barge, and there was a bedroom for the child, who was ill, and his mother. *The Swan* was built in order to cure the boy's illness, and so there was a female cook and a pilot, who needed places to sleep as well. Of course they couldn't do without a kitchen either. They must have stocked up on a fair amount of food, but I wonder what they did for a bath and toilet? They'd need fuel for the bath, and a big pile of charcoal for the stove. They even needed feed for the horses. And where'd they dry their clothes? *The Swan* drifted along the river at its own pace for several months, and when you think about it, it must have been an amazingly large ship, but I'm not sure just how big, or what it looked like. But even though I talk about it now like it's just a fairy tale, I was fascinated by the story when I was little. I thought, man, I'd really like to ride on *The Swan*. Little kids are such idiots."

At that moment their food was brought to them, so they began to focus on eating. The other customers were noisily drinking, talking about a construction project somewhere. About a woman somewhere. As Capi busily tucked into her chicken and eggs over rice, she thought about *The Swan*, which Remi had told her he longed for—a boat silently moving along rivers and canals. Capi could only imagine it as a boat shaped like a barge with a room that seemed to be a greenhouse on top of it. A beautiful matron and a sick boy lived in that room. That matron was of course wealthy, and, as it turned out, she was Remi's real mother. The boy was Remi's little brother. As a result, in the end, Remi became wealthy, his brother got better, and everyone lived happily ever after. Did that ever make Remi feel envious toward the fictional Remi, who ended up with a wealthy, beautiful, kind mother? For her part, Capi preferred that *The Swan* be fated to have to sadly wander on forever. Indeed, at some point, before she was even aware of it, she had come to imagine it *was* just such a ship. Capi too had yearned after *The Swan* when she was in elementary school. The boy's illness would gradually worsen, the money would run out, the matron would grow old, and all that would remain on *The Swan* was despair. If she encountered *The Swan* under such circumstances, how frightening and beautiful it would look.

Remi, who finished his meal quicker than Capi, took some cold medicine and began to smoke a cigarette.

"Anyway, boats are good. The only ones I know about are the boats on the Sumida River. A boat like *The Swan* would never sail on the Sumida. Only filthy garbage barges or houseboats with families living on them. Babies crying among kettles and pots that look like trash, fluttering laundry that hasn't really been cleaned—those boats are nothing at all like *The Swan*. And yet, I still get the sense that living on boats like that is probably not all bad. Tiny dorm rooms on land are suffocating."

Capi finished eating and began sipping her tea. It was so hot she could only drink a little at a time.

"I tell you what, let's stow away on a boat. It doesn't matter where it's headed," Remi whispered.

Capi gave a laugh at his suggestion. She thought he was making a childish joke.

Before they left the shop, they took turns going to the toilet. As they were walking out side-by-side, one of the male customers called to them. "Hey, boys! You new around here? Did you come to play?"

Remi pushed Capi from behind and bowed his head slightly.

"It was too early to go swimming in the sea."

"So you're going home already? Have a drink first. If you smoke, then you can drink, can't you?"

"Let your little brother have a drink too."

"We've all been drinking since we were kids."

The men, their faces red, began to tease them, so Remi and Capi hurried outside

141

and ran back to the station.

"Dammit, what a bunch of loud-mouth creeps. Still, did you hear them, Capi? They called you my little brother."

"Yeah," Capi answered, "that's what they said."

"We're finally starting to look like brothers. If we stay together for a while, we'll even begin to look like each other."

"You really think so?"

Remi gave a confident nod. "I do. All right, then, let's go to the shore. Wait here a sec. I'll go ask a station attendant which way to go to get to the sea."

Capi did as she was told and stood in front of the station. She could see the light of the restaurant where they had just eaten. A bus was idling in front of her, its door open. The driver was outside, puffing on a cigarette and staring at Capi. Did she and Remi look like brothers to his eyes as well? Even though they didn't resemble each other that much? Remi had no real brother. He didn't have a real mother. Capi had both. Her brother was dead, but her brother was different from Remi. If Remi were to become another older brother for her, what would become of her mother? The thought set her head spinning. A real mother wasn't anything so great. In fact she wasn't all that sure that having a mother was much better than not having one.

Remi came back. If they walked straight along the river flowing on the opposite side of the station, they'd reach the sea. *That's right,* Capi thought, recalling the landscape from her earlier visit here. The river wasn't clean at all. Her school group had followed it from their lodgings. The muddy river had washed out the sandy beach where it flowed into the sea. Fishermen had been dragging their nets out, dogs had been running around them, Maabō had been chortling. They had had to do warm-up exercises on the beach. Capi's chest back then was completely flat. Now her breasts were beginning to fill out a little. Still, they weren't so big that the swimsuit she wore in elementary school wouldn't fit. Her new middle school had no pool, and as far as she could tell there was no summer school at all. Because she wasn't good at swimming, it didn't really matter much to her. Nonetheless, she couldn't remember ever having swum in the sea here. Would she really have come all the way here and not gone into the ocean?

They located the river right away, found the path that ran beside it, and took off walking at a leisurely pace in the dark. Here and there lights on the electric poles illuminated the sandy path, but the lamps from the rows of houses along the way did not.

It took longer than they had expected to reach the sea. It may have just seemed far because they had assumed it would be close by. The rows of houses ended, the electric poles disappeared from view, and the narrow path ended. The ground around their feet suddenly opened out onto a sandy beach. They couldn't tell by the light of the moon how far out the sand extended, or where the ocean began. But they could hear the sound of waves. A rhythmic sound, as though the waves were whispering to them. A moist sea breeze blew against their bodies.

"Look, the sea's right over there!"

"You're right! I can see white waves."

"I wish it was a little brighter."

"Still, I can make out something just offshore. Is it a fishing boat?"

"If it is, it's really huge. I can see others too. There's lots of boats floating around out there."

They moved closer to the edge of the shore, where the waves were breaking. They quickly removed their socks and shoes, and dipped their feet into the sea. It still felt a little cold on their skin. They ran along the water's edge in their bare feet, then came back the other way. They would move out into the sea, then rush back in a panic before the waves overtook them. As they were playing, their attention was constantly drawn to lights in the offing. It looked like a passenger ship. But why would a passenger ship be anchored in a place like that? Surely it wasn't the ghost of one of Perry's Black Ships, was it?

They proceeded a little way along the beach to their left and sat down, stretching their legs out. A white dog came up to them, then moved away. They saw the figure of someone walking a large black dog on a leash.

"It gets really cold at night, doesn't it. If we sleep here, my cold will get worse," Remi grumbled.

Hearing that, Capi spoke hesitantly. "Listen, can't *we* stay at an inn? It's not that I want to stay at an inn, it's just …"

"I've got the money, but if the two of us go to an inn, they're not going to let us stay without an explanation. I'm not a legal adult, and you're just a kid. If they say they need to check with our parents, we wouldn't be able to tell them a thing. So why do you ask? What's up? Do you feel like you want to take a bath?"

Capi cocked her head at Remi's question. "I was just asking, that's all."

"Because we can always go to a public bath, if that's what you want. We won't have to worry about being questioned there."

"Well, actually, I haven't been to a public bath since I was in kindergarten. The bath was really deep, and I almost drowned. It was scary," Capi said, scooping up some sand with her toes and letting it sift out little by little. The sand was warm and dry, and fell through her toes quickly.

"Really? The baths only come up to your knee at the deepest. I have to use a public bath now. The Children's Home had a bath, so I didn't know anything about public baths. On the other hand, we only took a bath once a week—once every ten days during the winter. I always took it with the big kids."

Remi put his hands between his legs and scraped together the sand around him.

"But, you actually knew your real father, Remi. That was enough, wasn't it?" Capi furrowed her eyebrows and muttered, as if talking to herself.

"What's that all about, all of a sudden?" Remi was surprised and peered into Capi's face.

143

She looked down and continued to talk. "I mean, after all, you were alone with your father all the time until you were four, and there wasn't anyone to interfere with you. In my case, I never knew my father at all, and my mother—well, I never feel like she's my mother. Sometimes I even think that maybe the person I call my mother is an imposter. A mother isn't as big or broad as children think. Maybe it's the same for all mothers who've been abandoned by their husbands, but in any case, I feel that with *my* mother, she used up the motherly part of herself on Ton-chan. I think she found it hard to think of me as precious to her in the same way she thought of Ton-chan. I was a lot healthier than Ton-chan—I was big and I could talk back to her, or keep secrets. I was just a boring, ordinary kid. And of course, I wasn't a boy. She told me to study hard, so I'd be able to get out and live on my own as soon as I could. She planned to go on living forever with Ton-chan. And I felt so sorry for her when Ton-chan died, because all the joy of living was gone for her. I could never be a substitute for him. If my father had lived, my mother would have been happier, and maybe she would have paid more attention to Ton-chan's little sister too. Even though she's a schoolteacher, the truth is, she's no fun at all. Yet she *is* my mother, of course, no matter how boring. I've moved beyond daydreaming that maybe we aren't actually mother and daughter, and so I've come to think a *real mother* isn't so great after all. That is, I think that you're much better off than me, Remi." Capi finally cut herself off, raised her head and stared at Remi.

"Dammit, you've got the luxury of talking like that. It's a terrible feeling not knowing anything at all about your own mom. I'm not like Momotarō from the folktale—some baby that pops out of a peach. I was born of a real, flesh-and-blood mother, so I'm always fretting about her, wondering what kind of a mother she was. If you don't know anything about your mom, then you feel inferior to all your mates who were brought up by their mothers, and you worry that maybe you're different from them somehow."

"But I feel exactly the same way. I don't know anything about my father, so immediately I tend to think there must be something strange about me. My mother is always looking at me as if I'm weird. She'd tell me to think of my homeroom teacher as my father and discuss everything with him."

Her voice sounded angry as she spoke, and so when Remi responded at last, his voice was sharp.

"But you know what kind of man your father was, right? He even has a proper grave. That's a big difference between you and me."

"At least you know the scent of your father. You know his body was warm, that even his poop was warm. I don't know anything like that. It's not that I feel lonely or bitter—in fact I hate such sentimentality. And yet whenever I hear you talk about your father, Remi, I can't help envying you because it reminds me that I don't know anything about mine. Your father never abandoned you and fled. That's right, isn't it?"

Capi's bluish-white face seemed to be floating in the moonlight. "Well, I think you may be right, but, I don't know what the truth is. All I know is I was brought up in an orphanage, and you were brought up in your own home, with your own family, Capi. It irritates me that you can't see the difference, because it's about the only thing I have to brag about. To tell the truth, it's because I'm envious of you ... but enough of this, already! It's gotten too complicated. In the stories about Mowgli and Remi, they find their real mothers and are completely happy in the end. I thought it was a bad idea to read those endings to the little kids, so I always omitted the parts about their real mothers. Stories like that would have been too hard for them to take. Even I would brood over the stories. I'd think, is having a real mother such a wonderful thing? And if it is, aren't people like us who don't know their mothers, terribly unfortunate? Yet somehow I don't feel that we are. Is it all a lie? And if it's a lie, why does it reappear in so many different stories? I can't help wondering what it all means."

Remi sighed, then Capi sighed, and they stared out at the lights in the offing.

"That's why stories like that are lies, because the authors are parents, not kids. If you teach children that a real mother is such a wonderful thing, then the children won't be able to run away. No matter how much they're bullied or mistreated, it's always the children who are at fault.... Still, I think if it's a parent like your father, Remi, then it's a completely different matter. I've kept the facts about my own father a secret at my elementary school and at my new school. It would be awful if people found out about how he died. But when I'm beside you, Remi, I feel as if your father is with me as well, and somehow that puts me at ease."

Remi was flustered to hear something so unexpected. He scratched his head. Sand was stuck to his hand.

"Anyway, we're Remi and Capi now, and so we'll always be together. Even if we argue about which of us had it better or worse, in the end there's not much difference."

"Oh, that's disgusting. You're saying we're exactly the same." Capi's eyes darted mischievously, and a smile rose to her lips. Feeling a sense of relief, Remi chuckled.

"Dammit, Capi, it's not good for you to act so girlish. You've got to be more like a boy, because it's a lot less awkward for me. By the way, those lights out there, they might surprise us and be *The Swan*."

He motioned with his jaw toward the lights in the offing. When he spoke, Capi focused, stared out at the sea, and said, "It looks like a passenger boat. But there are four ... no, five boats out there."

"Yeah, and for some reason I can't get them off my mind. There's something going on out there, that's for sure. If there wasn't, there'd be no reason to anchor in a place like that."

Remi stood up and gazed along the shore to his right, then to his left. Capi looked around in the exact same manner. At some point, before they were aware of it, a large number of dogs had gathered around them. Black dogs, white dogs, large and small dogs running around all over the beach, digging up the sand, scattering garbage.

"Wow, take a look at that!" Remi said. He sounded excited. "There's a boat over there. We don't have anything else to do, so let's go check it out a little. If things work out right, maybe we can stow away. If we could make it all the way to America, how great would that be!"

"But if it's a pirate ship, they'll kill us. And if it's a ghost ship, that's even scarier."

Remi hurriedly slipped his sneakers over his bare feet. Not knowing what else to do, Capi pulled on her socks and leather shoes. Her white cotton socks were now filthy. But if she didn't wear the socks, her shoes would definitely rub her feet sore. When they set off, four or five dogs noticed and followed after them. The dogs probably weren't strays, but it seemed creepy to be followed all the same. They avoided looking back as much as they could, so as not to excite the dogs, and continued walking forward, hurrying at a steady pace. Why were there so many dogs here? Were they always here, or did they come here just tonight? They had no idea what was going on, and gradually began to feel threatened, and were afraid to even exchange words with one another. If the dogs heard them talking, they might suddenly get angry and attack.

After walking for about a hundred meters, they came to a boat that had been left on the beach. Capi, doing as Remi told her, immediately hopped inside. Remi ignored the dogs and, with all his strength, pushed the boat into the sea. As the boat drifted out onto the waves, the dogs left behind on the beach started to bark at them. Remi pushed the boat forward against the waves, soaking his trousers in the process. His face grew red and his forehead sweaty. The water was now up to his knees, and was about to soak the thighs of his trousers. Remi finally clambered into the boat. The dogs were still on the shore, barking. Rowing with the oar, he stuck his tongue out at the dogs.

"How do you like us now? Goddam mutts! You know, maybe I'm imagining it, but ever since you became Capi, doesn't it seem like dogs have been tagging after you?"

"That's just a coincidence, but if they keep watching for us, we won't be able to go back there."

"There's no reason why we have to go back. This looks like the inner part of the bay, so we'll land at the promontory on the way back. I do feel a little bad for the owner of this boat, though."

Capi nodded and pulled out the tin of candy drops. Popping one into her mouth, she handed the tin to Remi. He stopped rowing, put a strawberry drop in his mouth, then tossed the tin back. If he could, he'd like to take off his wet trousers. But he couldn't do that in front of Capi, since then he would be wearing only his underpants. When they got out onto the water, the wind blew stronger and stronger and cooled him off. But if he continued rowing with all his might, he would definitely get hot. Remi's face took on an intense expression as he rowed with all his might.

The sea wasn't all that rough. Even so, Remi wasn't accustomed to rowing, and the waves were much stronger than he anticipated. Soon his hands and arms began to ache, and though he aimed to row straight ahead, the boat moved in a curve to the right. It didn't seem that it would be all that easy to get close to the boats in the offing. Remi had had enough after about twenty minutes and began to regret that he had taken the boat. Still, it was out of the question to go back now. It had been his idea in the first place, and if he gave up, Capi would make fun of him. In any case, Remi told himself, it would all be over eventually, and so he kept rowing ahead.

"Forward! Forward!" Remi muttered, imitating master Vitalis's way of speaking. It was vital to go one step, one step—no, one stroke at a time. After all, Remi kept walking through France even though he had no money. *Forward! Forward!*

An hour went by. Remi was drenched in sweat, and when he looked at his hands, the skin was torn and red with blood. His eyes were bleary, and he couldn't clearly make out Capi's outline, even though she was riding in the same boat. The surface of the sea was gently heaving, and it cast a sharp reflection of the white light of the moon. When they finally passed the promontory, they could make out the shapes of boats anchored in a spot they hadn't been able to see until now. One, two—five boats. The number kept increasing. Together with the boats that had already been in view, they could count more than ten of them. Perhaps it was the fault of the moonlight, but, just as Capi had remarked earlier, the boats all looked worn-out, like a fleet of ghost ships. Because each one was quite large, taken together they gave the impression that a single, manmade island had arisen from the depths of the ocean.

Remi stopped rowing and, with his eyes and mouth open, stared for a while at the fleet.

"What in the world is this? They can't be going off to war. For one thing, they don't look like warships."

Capi answered Remi, her voice quavering.

"Do you think this is okay? Let's quit and go back to land."

"No one's going to shoot and kill us. There's another boat closing in from the far side."

Aiming for the boat right in front of them, Remi used all his remaining strength to pull the oars. Ten minutes. Twenty minutes. Finally he reached the spot he had been focusing on, near the boat in front of them. The light streaming from the windows was blindingly bright. Having relied strictly on the moonlight till then, he'd grown accustomed to the dark. Rust was developing on the steel-plated hull, which towered over the surface of the sea, and it was encrusted here and there with something that looked like seaweed.

"This really is a ghost ship. Come on, let's go back. It's best to give it up."

Remi heard Capi speaking to him again, but he didn't answer. Instead, he continued to row toward the stern of the ship where a narrow rope ladder was hanging from the deck. He couldn't possibly make it back to shore in his present condition. He had exhausted his strength just to get this far. If he weren't allowed to rest on the deck for a while, he wouldn't be able to row the boat back to shore. When the crew saw the shape he was in—they could be Russian or American for all he knew—they'd probably think he was just some reckless kid and, after some good-hearted laughter, agree to take them back. How grateful he would be if they did that. That was how exhausted Remi felt.

He came right up to the bottom of the rope ladder. Remi put the oars in the boat, stood up and grabbed the bottom end of the ladder with both hands.

"Capi, you go up first and climb to the deck. I'll support the ladder from below, so don't be afraid."

"I can't do that." Capi's voice sounded fearful.

"Well, then, are you going to stay behind on the boat by yourself? I can't row any more, so I don't care what happens—I'm getting on the boat. If possible, I'm going to see if they'll let me sleep on the deck until morning. I guess that means you have no choice, Capi, but to board it as well. So come on, be brave and try to climb up. It'll be all right."

"But I'm afraid. There's definitely something weird about this boat. Why is it so quiet? It's not the middle of the night. I can row, so if we take turns, we can get back somehow."

"Enough already, just get on. We've gone through all this trouble to get here, and if everyone's gone ashore, what's the harm? Hurry up."

He sounded irritable, so Capi finally stood up. "What do I do about the bag?"

"Just slip the cord through the belt on your trousers and tie it up. No, that's okay—actually, I'll carry it for you. It's dangerous and you're nervous, so it's best to be as agile as you can."

Capi looked up and sighed. Then, handing her bag to Remi, she grasped the rope ladder with both hands and carefully placed her right foot on first, then her left foot.

"If you climb up like that, one rung at a time, you'll be fine. Just don't look down or do anything unnecessary."

Capi silently began climbing up—so slowly that it irritated Remi to watch her. Looking at the ladder up close, the spaces between the rungs were very large, and the footboards and rope were rough and thick. The ladder would sway a lot without someone at the bottom holding it steady. Capi had never climbed a rope ladder, but then again, Remi had never climbed one either. And his athletic abilities were nothing to brag about. He was worried about the moment when he'd have to climb up after Capi, since there'd be no one to hold the rope ladder for him. But he had no choice but to climb up.

How many meters was it to the deck? It was dark, so the outline of the boat probably looked larger than it actually was. Four or five meters … was it about that high? Capi reached the deck more quickly than he'd anticipated and disappeared from sight. Her appearance on deck hadn't seemed to cause any disturbance. Remi tied the cloth bags to the belt loops of his trousers, and finally began climbing. Like Capi, he went up slowly and steadily, progressing one rung at a time. It didn't sway as much as he had feared. But if he were careless and his hand slipped, he could easily fall into the sea. He groaned as a result of the pain caused by the raw, blistered skin on his hands, and his eyes teared up. He passed the round windows of the ship. Just a little further. His hands were slippery with blood. He would probably not be able to use his hands for a while because of this. He caught the scent of the rusty steel of the ship. Where was it from? If it was a foreign ship and the crew didn't understand Japanese, he would try showing them his hands first. They were fellow humans, after all, and would surely feel sympathetic and bandage them up for him. At last the deck was in sight. Just five rungs left. Four rungs. After coming this far, falling into the sea would be unbearable. He had to be careful.

Remi grabbed hold of the deck railing. He had to endure the pain in his hands one last time as he put all his strength into pulling himself up from the ladder and onto the deck. The instant he landed on the deck, he felt dizzy, and crouched down there.

"Hey, Remi. Remi!"

Turning his face toward Capi's voice, he saw her kneeling beside him, staring.

"Listen … this ship? It's just like I thought. It's a ghost ship. And now we can't escape. All we can do here is wait to die. That's what that man said. That man said he's going to die soon." There were tears in Capi's eyes.

"Don't give me that nonsense, all this talk of a ghost ship."

As Remi spoke, he glanced around the deck for the first time. It was faintly illuminated, tinted a yellowish hue by the light from a lamp on the mast. A group of people—so many he couldn't count them all—was lying quietly on the deck.

Through her tears Capi reported to Remi everything she had heard. "There's been an outbreak of cholera. They threw the bodies of the people who died during the voyage into the ocean. But then people just kept getting sick with cholera one after another, and those people went to the hospital in Kurihama, but because the people left here have been exposed to the bacteria, they aren't allowed to land. And since we've come on board, now we have no choice but to stay here too."

"Cholera? Why would they …" Completely dumbfounded, Remi glanced around the deck again. If this was true, were the people here just waiting to fall ill? There were so many of them. Five hundred, or maybe a thousand. Most were

149

wearing dirty underwear and lying wrapped in blankets. Even though a thousand people or more were crammed together there, it was strangely quiet. Remi began to tremble. Then he noticed that a man near them was waving the two of them over. Apparently it was the same man who'd spoken to Capi. Remi's body was stiff with fear, but he wanted to learn more about the situation, and so gradually he and Capi moved closer to the man.

"You two are real idiots, you know."

The man was sprawled out, supporting his head on one arm and jeering at them. His eyes, caked with yellowish mucus, looked sunken and hollow. His face was swarthy and unshaven, his teeth were yellow, his neck and hands had a yellowish tinge. His shirt had cords in place of buttons in front. A dirty soldier's cap rested on his head.

"Now you'll suffer the same fate as the rest of us. The same as everyone else, 'cause all these ships have been quarantined. We somehow made it this far, but now we can't take the final step and land, and we haven't got a thing to eat. You're way better off getting cholera and going to the hospital. If you stay here, you'll starve to death. We've been here like this for more than ten days. We finally make it back to Japan, and now look. It's fucking unbelievable. Speaking of that, how in the hell did you get here without being spotted? Oh well, they probably figured no one would want to come near a ship like this."

"Where did you come from?" Remi asked, finally finding the courage to speak up. He still didn't fully understand what was going on.

"All these ships are from Guangzhou. You two don't have any idea where that is, do you? Man, you people back in the homeland have it fucking easy. You look like you're well fed. Man, I'd really like to tear into your flesh."

Capi made a weird sound and moved to a spot about two meters away. The man opened his mouth and laughed. His breath was incredibly foul smelling, and, instinctively, Remi also backed away a little.

"Shit, and here I thought I was lucky not to have died in battle. I never figured I'd die in a place like this. This quarantine is probably an order from the Americans. When the war was over they never wanted to see any more of us soldiers, that's for sure. But I can tell you I sure as hell didn't become a soldier for the fun of it."

"Knock it off! You're getting on my nerves!"

"Stop whimpering to those kids!"

"Yeah, just shut the fuck up!"

Voices from all around roared over them like a wave. But no one lifted their heads or moved a muscle. It looked as though they were all either asleep or sunk deep in their own thoughts. However, the group, as one body, intently studied Remi and Capi. If they tried to make a run for it, they sensed that the group, like a pack of wild dogs, might suddenly attack them, tearing and eating their flesh. Remi was overwhelmed by that weird, uncanny sensation.

There was a disturbance a little ways off, and the crowd stirred. They formed a circle, and one man was left in the middle. The man was screaming and vomiting what looked like gastric juices. Men wearing white gowns and masks appeared from somewhere, placed the vomiting man on a stretcher, and then disappeared again. Perhaps there was a device they couldn't see from here that would transfer the stretcher from the deck to a boat.

"What the—that can't be cholera. We were all vaccinated. Anyone who gets cholera would have to have been infected already. I wonder if he has typhus, or smallpox?"

The man they had been talking to earlier was muttering to himself. Looking back and forth between Remi and Capi, he laughed in a low voice. Remi saw there was no need to keep on talking to a man like this. So he made up his mind and, urging Capi on, tiptoed quietly further back toward the stern of the ship. He didn't know what people might say to them if they made even the slightest noise.

Remi was wondering if there were only men on board when they came across a group of women who had gathered in the shadow of a lifeboat. The women looked at them but didn't utter a word and made no effort to get up. There was one woman who was groaning and tossing and turning. Even if they weren't sick with cholera, all of the people there looked ill. Remi, who was exhausted, thought to himself, *Whatever's happening, enough's enough already. I'm going to sleep here. I'll think things over after I wake up.* After signaling to Capi with his eyes, he set his bag down on the floor and, using it as a pillow, lay down. Capi did the same thing, lying down face-to-face with Remi.

"There's not much we can do now, so let's wait until morning," Remi whispered, staring at his own hands, which continued to sting painfully.

"Cholera's contagious. You get infected before you know it, then you die. And listen, we're probably already infected. After all, we haven't had a vaccination."

Capi's small round face was pale and drawn.

"If that's true, there's nothing we can do about it, since we can't escape. I never expected something like this would happen, but it'll work out somehow, so don't worry."

They were quiet for a while, then Capi began whispering again.

"Even if we die of cholera, it's not as scary as dying in a train wreck, or being murdered in the mountains. I didn't want to die just yet, but it's okay, I guess. If we die like this, I wonder if they'll throw our bodies into the sea?"

"That's only if you're in the middle of the ocean. They wouldn't throw bodies away this close to shore. That would just spread the cholera germs."

Suddenly, close by, a woman began to groan, as though she were wailing. In response to that voice another woman began to cry.

"Oh, it hurts so much, it hurts!"

"I can't stand it! I can't stand this pain!"

The people in white robes did not appear for these women, and soon they fell silent. Apparently they weren't suffering from cholera. Remi and Capi closed their eyes, and tried to escape into sleep.

But thy hands are loosed and weak, and the blood has left thy cheek
But thy throat is shut and dried, and thy heart against thy side
Hammers: Fear, O Little Hunter--this is Fear!

Remi could hear the deeply familiar song of the wolves again. As in the song, fear was undulating through his body along with the pain in his hands. *I thought I was going to board The Swan, but got on a cholera ship instead. I guess my luck has run out. At least my old man died in a hospital. I'm going to die on a cholera ship. No, I'm not going to die. Will I die, or won't I die?* He remembered the words from Remi's story—"Unlucky people don't die all that easily or simply"—but they didn't really ring true. Those who were unlucky would be unlucky no matter what, and they would die all too soon. Remi's master had frozen to death by the roadside on a winter evening. Remi should have frozen to death as well. However, because he'd held Capi close to his chest, he didn't die in the end. For some reason, dogs are resistant to the cold. Remi had the feeling there were other stories in which people had been rescued by dogs from the midst of snow. He felt that he had his own Capi, even though she wasn't a dog. The moment Remi dies, Capi will die as well. Then the two of them would return to the world of the jungle. And if Remi doesn't die, Capi won't either. The two situations were similar. All the time he was wondering what kind of disease cholera is.

For her part, Capi also scrunched her body up as small as possible and tried to resign herself to her own death. *God, please help me. I'm praying to you. Please let me die without suffering too much. And you too, Ton-chan, please help me. I'm really scared. I never thought I'd die of cholera, but I won't say I'm dissatisfied. Since everyone is going to die eventually, I suppose cholera is as good a way to go as any. But I don't want to die a painful death. At the moment of your death, does your consciousness fade? I don't even know that.*—*Comfort us in sorrow and in woe, grant us your strength in pain and suffering, save us at the hour of our death.*

Tears came flooding to her eyes and nose from deep inside Capi's body. Because Remi was there, she was not alone. There were a lot of other people there as well, besides Remi. Still, she felt terribly alone. An image of her family's grave and the urns containing the remains of her father and of Ton-chan drifted up in her mind. At the time they interred Ton-chan's ashes and bones, she had confirmed that there really was some kind of hole hidden in front of the grave, and that they would be able to set the new burial urn of her brother beside the old burial urn of her father. Soon another pure white urn would be set in place next to those two. Even though it would be pure white at first, soon it would turn a dull color, like the urn of her father.

When they close the stone top, the hole will become pitch dark. Mother will be the sole survivor and continue to decorate our grave with flowers. She'll probably clear away all my things soon after, just like she did after my brother died. Will mother cry at my death as well? When she gives me a funeral, will I be able to see it or not? Death is when your body no longer belongs to you, and maybe that's why it feels so lonely.

Tears kept streaming from Capi's eyes. The ship was filled with people weeping. When she listened carefully, it seemed those weeping voices were echoing to the night sky, like the voices of a choir. Overlapping those voices were other voices familiar to Capi, singing to God.—*Agnus Dei, qui tollis peccata mundi, miserere nobis. Tantum ergo Sacramentum. Forgive us our sins, and deliver us from evil. When Mother hears that I died of cholera, she'll be surprised, because she didn't know I became Capi and was with Remi, and she'll never understand at all why I was on board a ship like this. Ahh, my stomach really hurts. It's diarrhea from cholera, for sure this time. My head hurts too. My chest aches. If I go to sleep like this, will I ever wake up again? Grant us your strength in pain and suffering, save us at the hour of our death.*

Capi fell asleep to the rocking of the ship.

At some point in the middle of the night, Capi woke up needing to relieve herself. She was beginning to suffer from diarrhea. Remi was asleep right next to her, his breathing healthy and regular. Apparently he didn't have diarrhea yet. Raising the upper part of her body, she looked around the deck. She didn't have the courage to go looking for a toilet on her own, and waking Remi would have been no help to her at all. Capi lay down again, and tried to resist the urge to go. A cold sweat broke out on her forehead. A nasty chill ran through her body. She couldn't hold out any longer. Finally a warm liquid squirted out. She was going to die soon anyway; and since she was going to die of cholera, she couldn't help it if she soiled herself. Still, when all was said and done, there was something sad about dying smeared with your own waste. As she pooped her pants, she couldn't hold back her sobs. Her poop didn't give off an odor. It ran down her legs from her panties, and soaked the area around the hips of her trousers. The warm, sticky sensation made her feel like retching. Apparently there was nothing more inside her stomach, for only fluid came out her mouth. Her vomit smelt more unpleasant than her poop, perhaps because it was close to her nose. She couldn't control her nausea. When she rolled her body over to vomit, diarrhea squirted from her bottom. Her whole body was covered in sticky filth. Remi was paying no attention. Everyone around her seemed to be deliberately ignoring her. Because each of them was suffering from illness, they were not inclined to notice how much Capi was suffering. She could hear groans. And sobbing. She heard voices that sounded like animals she couldn't identify. While she was crying, she continued to vomit and shit herself. Gradually her consciousness began to drift away. The ship was swaying. She could hear singing voices on the ship.—*Qui tollis peccata mundi, miserere nobis.*—Her mother's weeping echoed in her ears. The sound of the waves swelled and flooded over her.

Capi let out a single deep breath. Her body gradually grew cold. The whole of the night sky began to sparkle brightly, illuminating the ship where Capi was lying.

10 April 1946
Cholera on Repatriation Ships
250 Quarantined

(Yokosuka) The number of cholera patients on the V-75 Liberty-type transport ship carrying 4,038 veterans, which arrived at the port of Uraga from Guangzhou on the 5th of this month, grew to 15 on the 7th and to 16 on the 8th. As of the 9th, the number of patients quarantined at the Kurihama National Hospital, including those suspected of having the disease, has risen to a total of 179. Of those, 16 cases have been confirmed. There has also been an outbreak of what is suspected to be cholera among 77 patients on the V-69 transport that arrived at Uraga from Guangzhou on the 9th.

For this reason, all the passengers on board the transports have been prohibited from landing, and traffic in the vicinity of the Kurihama isolation ward and Kurihama Hospital has been cordoned off. The authorities are carrying out vaccinations for the 30,000 people living in the area of the seacoast. For the time being, fishing is prohibited in the vicinity of Kurihama and Uraga.

10 April 1946
Unemployed Have Highest Rates of Illness
Breakdown by Occupation of Typhus and Smallpox Patients

According to a survey carried out by the Tokyo Metropolitan Social Welfare Bureau, the number of typhus patients had reached 1,704 as of the 5th of this month. Breaking this number down by occupation, the unemployed are the largest group at 446 people. Next come office workers at 115, students at 58, and factory workers at 52.

Travel by train is seen as especially high-risk for infection. The breakdown by age group is as follows: the highest rate of outbreaks have occurred among individuals between the ages of 21 and 25, who are normally at the peak of health. There are many patients, both male and female, between the ages of 16 and 45.

There were 1,269 cases of smallpox as of the 5th, and, as with typhus, the highest number of cases, 392, have occurred among the unemployed, while office workers account for 156 cases. In contrast to typhus, vagrants account for 86 cases, workmen for 78, day laborers for 50, and factory workers for 48.

The contrast with typhus is conspicuous in that there are many cases of smallpox among children between the ages of one and five.

26 April 1946
A Metropolis of Cholera on the High Seas
Repatriates Short of Food

As of the 25th, 16 ships carrying up to 80,000 repatriates have been anchored off the coast of Uraga as a result of a quarantine that followed an outbreak of cholera on 5 April. In order to prevent the cholera bacteria from entering the country, a strict ban on traffic has been put into place. The situation regarding food supplies on the ships has not been clear up to now, though the Japanese Shipping Control Association and the Repatriation Welfare Bureau have declared there to be sufficient food on board. However, according to officials who, since proceeding with the quarantine, have from time to time assessed conditions over the past twenty days, the reality is that almost all the officers and men on the ships have used up the foodstuffs they brought with them and are just barely able to make gruel out of their portable rations. The most desperate ships have been out of food for two days already.

There are an additional nine ships with repatriates from the region of Guangzhou who are suspected of carrying cholera. These have yet to arrive in port, and within a few days the population of the floating metropolis here will eventually swell to 120,000 or 130,000. In response, Kanagawa Prefecture has been working hard to provide food relief, but at a time when the city of Yokohama has also been pleading for additional rations of rice, the situation is close to desperate, and the Ministry of Agriculture and Forestry has been asked to step in to provide aid as soon as possible.

26 April 1946
New Outbreak of Typhus

The number of cases of typhus, which had begun easing up a little during the last ten days of March, has been on the increase again recently. 129 cases were reported on the 20th, 128 on the 21st, and 188 on the 22nd. There was a record number of cases, 203, on the 23rd, and 192 on the 24th. As of two o'clock on the afternoon of the 25th, the total number of cases had surpassed 5,400.

8. One Blood

Her body swayed and her head bumped into something. She opened her eyes and saw Remi's shoulder. His big earlobe. Capi blinked and sat up. Remi opened his eyes just a crack in response to her movement. They found themselves in the same old surroundings, a crowd of people crammed together. But now, apparently, they were sleeping, huddled together in the vestibule of a train, not on a ship. They could hear a station announcement coming from outside—*Numazu, Numazu.* And over that announcement came the loud reverberations of other voices ... *Bentō! Tea and bentō!* As soon as she heard those words, Capi remembered the pain in her stomach, and glanced down at her clothes to make sure she hadn't soiled herself.

"You were sleeping really well," Remi said as he stretched and got up.

Her voice still drowsy, Capi muttered, "They said it's Numazu. That's so weird. When did we get on this train?"

"Obviously we got on this morning," Remi replied offhandedly, his eyes bloodshot. "Why does every train have to be this crowded? It's really annoying. You want to eat our *bentō?*"

"Sure, but it feels like I got diarrhea again. It may be cholera. I thought I was dying of cholera. Must have been a dream."

Two *bentō* boxes and tea were already sitting on Remi's lap, and when he handed one of them to Capi he said in a low voice, "I bought these a little while ago at Odawara. Listen, don't say things like 'cholera' out loud. Everyone's jumpy about it, and we'll get kicked off the train."

Capi nodded, untied the cord around the box, then whispered, "I have to go to the toilet before I eat."

When she stood up she noticed that the palms of Remi's hands were glistening an odd color. They were splotched red and brown, and blood was seeping from them here and there. Apparently their ride in the rowboat last night really *had* happened. But she couldn't tell if what happened afterward was real or a dream.

Capi cut through the people sitting or standing in the aisle, and headed for the toilet. Though it wasn't as chaotic as an overnight train, passengers filled the car to overflowing and the vestibule was packed with people and luggage. People were standing in front of the toilet as well, blocking the way. When she brushed them aside with her hand and opened the toilet door, the departure bell rang. The train gave a jolt and began moving.

With nothing else to do, Remi went ahead and began eating his *bentō* without waiting for Capi to get back. It was so meager he felt disappointed when he glanced at it—it contained some small *inari* sushi, some slices of *konnyaku* gelatin, taro,

156

burdock root, and a few dried sardines.

He was unable to find any other kind of *bentō*, so he had to take what he could get. He didn't consider himself all that picky about food, but the portion was very small, and it seemed he couldn't help feeling hungry all the time. Each time he used his chopsticks his palms hurt. He pulled a roll of toilet paper out of his bag and stuck some onto the bloody spots. He had rubbed his skin raw, but there weren't any major cuts or anything. Remi recalled that the previous evening he had eaten dinner in Kurihama—a meal of cold croquettes. They went down to the shore after that and got into a rowboat. What had happened next?

The subsequent course of events was veiled in darkness for Remi as well. He remembered they boarded a cholera ship that had arrived from China and been quarantined. After they went to sleep, someone, some authority, must have noticed them, realized that they had simply wandered astray, and ordered them back to shore at once. Obviously they hadn't been forced into the sea, for if they had been, then surely they would have woken up. Had they been moved into a boat while they were still asleep and carried back somewhere near the vicinity of Yokosuka? And was it there that the two of them, in a state between dream and reality, had changed trains for the Tōkaidō Line? Remi was bothered less by the question of how they got on this train and more by the fact that cholera is contagious. If someone had given them a vaccination while they were asleep, there'd be no problem. But if they had just been released from the ship, then the cholera bacteria would already be running riot inside their bodies, wouldn't it? Capi's diarrhea was a concern, and he was worried about the sluggishness of his own body. If they fell ill with cholera or typhus, they would have to go to a hospital, no matter how they might want to avoid it. Because cholera and typhus were different from other diseases, they'd die if they didn't get treatment. On the other hand, if they went to a hospital, they'd be investigated for sure. Capi would be sent back to her mother right away, and the police would take Remi in for interrogation. He had willfully taken a child along with him without telling her guardian; and even though Capi had happily followed him of her own free will, society would view his behavior as criminal. A child belongs to the parent. But Remi was different. He didn't belong to anyone. Social judgments didn't apply to him. And yet a contagious disease was something else altogether. Just then it occurred to him that stories about contagious diseases never came up in the worlds of *The Jungle Book* or *Nobody's Boy*, even though there should have been some fear of communicable diseases around Remi and Akela. India's Gandhi would surely have taught them to prepare for this sort of situation. Terrible contagious diseases, as well as groups of people who seemed on the verge of starvation, swirled all around that beggar priest. Yet Gandhi would walk barefooted, calmly and genially, among throngs of people with all sorts of illnesses. Probably even infectious diseases would have been surprised by his attitude and become his followers. How could the man have attained a state like that? Remi should have read the book about Gandhi more carefully.

Capi came back from the toilet.

"How are you?"

"Not so bad," Capi said, opening her *bentō* and beginning to eat.

"I've got some medicine for diarrhea, so take some after you finish eating. I'll take some cold medicine. The worst thing that could happen to us is to get sick."

Capi chewed her food with such energy that one could only assume that she was really hungry. She finished very quickly and, with a contented sigh, began to drink her tea. Looking up at the ceiling, she gazed at the light streaming in through the window in the door, then said to Remi, "Shouldn't Mount Fuji be visible from around here? Do you think we can see it?"

The instant she spoke, a young woman sitting in front of them answered in a curt voice, "We already passed it."

Startled, they looked at the woman's face and nodded ambiguously in reply. The woman wore red lipstick and had a large mole in the middle of her cheek. Next to her was a swarthy man, and beside him were two old women in work trousers sitting with their backs to them. Men wearing dirty army clothes were also standing around. Capi was disappointed, and closed her mouth. She had to be as quiet as possible when they were among other people. She recalled her promise to Remi, and she also remembered that she had been told she should pretend to be a mentally slow child.

They fell silent and took their medicine. Clutching their knees, they dozed off, giving their bodies over to the swaying motion of the train. No matter how much they slept, they always seemed to be able to sleep more. Stopping at frequent intervals, the local train made its way along, its wheels rumbling loudly. Because it was a day train, passengers got off and on, a few at a time, except when they reached a larger station, where the waves of people getting off and on clashed violently, creating a disturbance each time.

Capi continued to feel a dull pain in her stomach. However, perhaps thanks to the medicine, she didn't have that feeling of pressure, of having to take a poop. As she dozed, she dreamed she was back in her own house. She was sleeping in the six-mat room, curled up on the futon she always used. Remi was sleeping in the futon next to her, and her mother was wiping his forehead with a towel and whispering something to him, and Remi was responding in a sleepy voice. Thinking that he was being pampered like a small child, Capi wanted to laugh. Light was streaming in from the garden; small rustling leaves were dancing in. As she became more awake, she realized that her mother was holding Remi's body and wailing. Had Remi died? Capi wanted to cry too. Remi's head had slipped from her mother's arms and was rocking back and forth. A shadow flitted across the hallway fronting the garden. The pitch-black boy and Remi's father were just then quietly disappearing, moving off somewhere. The six-mat room grew dark, and the bedding was flooded with water. Although the water continued to rise, her mother took no notice of it and held

Remi's corpse tight. If they stayed like this, they would all be washed away. The futon would grow heavier and sink into the depths of the water.

In his dream, Remi was chasing furiously after Capi, who was fleeing toward Mount Fuji. Because Capi was a dog, she could run fast and squeeze through any opening. In Remi's mind, towering Mount Fuji was a long, thin, cone-shaped mountain that had a cheap sheen to it, as if it was made of celluloid. Remi's feet slipped on the celluloid, and he could make no headway up the slope. Looking up, he could see cracks here and there, and a mold-like undergrowth. Small animals seemed to be lurking there. Capi was wagging her tail, happily peering into cracks and sniffing at the undergrowth. Remi was so irritated he couldn't stand it. Next time, when he caught her, he'd put a leash on her. That way Capi would learn a lesson. The job at the electric appliance store that he had just begun in April had been hard on Remi. He had to carry heavy packages, and the wires and the glass of the vacuum tubes that pricked his fingers seemed to be pursuing him. And he didn't want to go back to the company dorm. Capi was running around, pretending she knew nothing about those things. She was still just a little child. She was a child now, but at some point she would be an adult. In the meantime, he had to teach her all sorts of things. *After the law of the jungle came the principles of traveling artists.* Rules such as: *In this world one cannot live by kindness alone.... You can tell a master by his dog....* Or: *Rely on your feet, and you will only proceed straight ahead ...* like the mendicant priest, Gandhi. Gandhi continued on and on, straight ahead, in his bare feet. Until the moment when his final step was pierced by a bullet.

At Hamamatsu they each had another *bentō*.

Capi's diarrhea was cured for the most part, but now Remi began to have the runs. And he seemed to have a fever as well. In order not to be overcome by his illness, he tried sleeping and eating a lot. That was, for the time being, the treatment that came to Remi's mind first. If a person keeps up his strength, then most diseases will subside. On the other hand, if a person is malnourished, then any disease could be fatal. Soon after Remi had moved to the Children's Home he contracted pneumonia and was hospitalized. His health had just improved when he again fell ill, this time with pleurisy, and was confined to bed for quite a long time. There was no doubt that he'd contracted those diseases because he had been malnourished. He suffered from trachoma, pinworm, tympanitis, rashes, bronchitis, hernia, and frostbite. Those maladies weren't considered illnesses, and the doctor who would come around from time to time would simply disinfect him, or give him medicine. During that time in his life he was always shabby and dirty, he had pains and itches here and there, and there were many excruciating nights. More recently he got so that he rarely caught a cold. He was sure this was because his diet had improved.

Thinking about these things in his past, he ate every last bite of his *bentō*, even though he had hardly any appetite. He then went to the toilet. His shit spurted out, and he vomited the boxed lunch that he had just eaten. He was dejected, figuring that his meal had gone completely to waste, and he was filled with anxiety, wondering if this might be the beginning of a serious illness after all. He returned to Capi's side and popped a double dose of both the diarrhea and cold medicines into his mouth. His palms continued to smart where the skin was blistered and peeled.

"What's wrong?" Capi whispered.

"I think I caught the runs from you. You seem pretty healthy, though."

Remi spoke sarcastically, but he couldn't help himself. Capi's cheeks were glowing cherry pink. Her lips and eyes were a clear, beautiful color. Remi's lips, on the other hand, were dry and white, like the shriveled peel of a mandarin orange.

"Diarrhea?" Capi immediately stretched out her right hand and felt Remi's forehead. "You really do have a fever, don't you? Your cold has come back, that's for sure."

As she spoke, Capi's face betrayed her grave fear—*This can't be cholera, can it?* A similar fear rose up in Remi's face, and he stared back at Capi.

"If I take plenty of medicine and sleep well, I'll be as good as new, just like you."

"I'm sure you will. Okay, well, you'd better lay your head on *my* lap and go to sleep."

He really didn't want to be cared for by a little kid like this, but under the circumstances he had no choice. Necessity knows no law, so Remi put his head on Capi's lap and tucked in his arms and legs. Capi placed one hand on his head and supported his chest with her other hand. Remi had chills, and his breathing was labored. He closed his eyes and tried to sleep. If he could just go to sleep, he would definitely be a little more comfortable. Capi's bony thighs pressed on his earlobes, and gradually they began to hurt him. Thin, undeveloped thighs, they were terribly uncomfortable. Even so, their warmth spread into him. Passing through the scent of her used clothes, Capi's smell tickled his nose. Even though her body should have been quite filthy, it had a clean smell that reminded him of strawberries. From time to time her stomach touched the back of his head and conveyed its softness. A stomach that brought to mind a tiny frog. Remi felt a peculiar admiration that it was still very much the body of a child. Many times he had let small children sleep on his lap, but he himself had never before slept on a little one's lap. It might make Capi angry at him, but he wanted to think that perhaps a *real mother* might feel like this. Or perhaps Gandhi's lap might feel like this. These were of course foolish associations in his mind, but ...

Over and over, every twenty minutes or so, just when he thought he would finally fall asleep, Remi would have to get up and run to the toilet. Eventually he was able to sleep for a while, because his stomach was emptied out and his diarrhea under control. While he slept, they passed through Gifu. Capi also continued to doze. In her dream she had become a real dog, barking inside a cage in a pound.

Once they passed through Gifu, there were fewer passengers on the train. They continued to doze, not understanding why the train was so empty. After about an hour, they reached a station called Maibara. Capi learned for the first time that this was the end of the line, so she woke Remi and they went out onto the platform. Because they had assumed that the Tōkaidō Line would go all the way to Osaka, they couldn't think clearly, and their legs wouldn't move. They were forced to get off at Maibara, having absolutely no idea what kind of station it was. From what they could see, it was dark and dreary. There were, however, a lot of platforms.

"Look over there, at that train. It's bound for Osaka," Capi said in a relieved voice. She pointed at a train that had stopped at a platform a short distance away.

"You're right. Shall we get on? It's a pain being put off at a half-assed station like this."

"Yeah, but it looks like we'd better hurry. They just announced that it's about to leave."

Capi started to run, but then hesitated, remembering that Remi had a fever. Remi, however, took off with all the speed he could muster, just the same as when he was feeling good, and dashed up the stairs. Capi hurried after him.

The two of them jumped onto the train just as the door was closing. Panting heavily, they stood with their backs to the door. Remi crouched down. Startled, Capi squatted down beside him as well.

"What's wrong?" she whispered. "Does your stomach hurt?"

Remi took a deep breath, and in a hoarse voice answered, "It hurts, but … I'm feeling dizzy. Shit! But we had to make a run for it or we wouldn't have made it."

"I guess I shouldn't have told you there was a train headed for Osaka."

"Damn, are you kidding? Heading for Osaka is better than staying in that half-assed station. There's food in Osaka, and hospitals."

Capi nodded and looked around. The car was crowded, but she stepped inside anyway, just in case she might find some empty seats. It was already past 8 p.m., and people returning home from work were nowhere to be seen. Capi's stomach was constantly growling from hunger.

Leaving Remi, she walked through the car by herself, looking for seats. She finally found one seat that an old man was occupying with a large bundle wrapped in a *furoshiki*. Working up her courage, she spoke to him.

"Excuse me, mister, but I'm traveling with someone who's sick, so could you let him sit here?"

The old man, who was wearing a black deerstalker hat, glared at Capi, but he didn't refuse her. She ran back to Remi and got him up. Even though he was much larger than she was, she supported him on her shoulder in a way that anyone who saw him would understand he was sick and led him to the seat she had found.

The two of them stared at the old man, who clicked his tongue and stood up. He

161

set his bundle in the aisle and stood next to it.

"I'm getting off soon anyway, so go ahead and sit down."

"Oh, but you don't have to …"

As Capi stammered out her words, Remi immediately flung his body into the window seat and closed his eyes.

"It's all right, never mind. It looks like he's really sick."

"Thank you so much."

Capi bowed her head and sat down next to Remi. Young men, college students perhaps, were sitting in the seats across from them. They began to speak to her.

"What's wrong with him?"

"Yeah, he looks like he's in real pain. Is he anemic? Did he hurt his hands?"

Capi made a distraught, helpless face and replied as childishly as she could. "Well, you see, he really overdid himself, even though he has a cold and all …"

She couldn't very well tell them that it might be cholera. At the same time, she wanted to see what would happen if she did tell them. Would everyone run away, she wondered, leaving just the two of them in the car?

"How far are you going?"

"Osaka."

"In that case, you'd better let him sleep. It'll take about two hours to get there."

Capi nodded quietly and turned her face toward Remi. Was he pretending to be asleep? He was grimacing, his eyes shut tight. A thought came to her, and she took off her jacket and put it over his body. Remi didn't move a muscle. Sighing, Capi snuggled up to him and closed her eyes. If both of them slept, the college boys would give up and go back to their own world. After a few moments, she could hear the students and the old man chatting.

"I heard that some smallpox patients escaped again. Why in the world would they do that?"

"Because they're worried about their families and their jobs. It's a real hardship for them to be suddenly locked away in a hospital."

"I've also heard rumors that there's been an outbreak of the plague."

"Good god, they do everything they can to control it with vaccinations and DDT, but I wonder how much they *can* do to suppress it.…"

"Armed robberies, bandits, murders, whole families committing suicide—all are the result of losing the war."

"There was a robbery in my neighborhood. The victim was hit on the head with an iron bar."

"The way society's going, it's possible that someone will suddenly shoot you with a pistol and kill you."

"That's right. Kids like them have no compunctions about committing really atrocious crimes. When there's no order in society, kids are the first to go bad."

"But it's always kids and young people who are being sacrificed. There was a family suicide that happened in Kyūshū … six kids were killed, starting with the oldest son, who was seventeen, right down to a four-year-old child. They say the cause of it was trouble between the adults. It's a horrible story, no?"

"Yeah, but take that big train robbery. That was pulled off by kids.…"

"Sure, you're right, but for the kids it was fun, a thrill.…"

"It's scary to think they may have done it out of revenge.…"

"And in Tokyo, vagrants …"

"They say they were starving.…"

"The atomic bombing in Hiroshima …"

"And because of that, first your hair falls out.…"

When they arrived in Osaka, it was after ten.

Thanks to the medicine, Remi's diarrhea was under control, but his fever had gone up and his strength had drained away. Perhaps because of the fever, his hands were dried out and the pain had lessened. The toilet tissue was still plastered to his sores, and if he forcibly pulled it off, his hands would start bleeding again. If he just left the tissue alone, it would probably peel and drop off at some point. He said that he had better eat something nutritious, in order to recover his strength. Capi, whose stomach was already growling, had no objection.

Although it was late, a lot of people were passing through the station. Just like at Ueno, many had spread newspapers on the floor and were either sitting there, nibbling at some food and dropping crumbs all around, or sprawled out asleep, disheveled. Apparently they were waiting for tickets to go on sale at the ticket window.

After finishing their business at the toilet, they went outside. The plaza in front of the station was sunk in darkness, but orange lights flashed here and there across the way, flickering unsteadily like the lights of fishing boats on the sea. Remi and Capi proceeded forward, heading for those lights. Unlike the interior of the station, the plaza was quiet, without much activity, and there were no cars to be seen. Paper trash had been blown into one corner of the plaza, and there were several dogs curled up there. The orange lights were coming from the acetylene lamps of stalls. The odor, identical to what they had smelled at Ueno, assaulted their noses.

"It looks like it's too late, doesn't it? Only a few shops are open." Remi's voice betrayed his disappointment.

"But there's grilled chicken and potatoes. Look, over there. There's *udon* too." Capi spoke excitedly. Everything looked delicious. Her mouth was watering.

"Yeah, I guess. I was hoping to eat something a little better than this. Oh, well. Shall we try the *udon*?"

Two young men, military caps on their heads, sat at the *udon* stall. They were drinking saké, and bowls of noodles had been placed in front of them. An old woman with a baby strapped to her back was preparing the noodles. Probably the grandmother. The mother was nowhere to be seen. The old woman and the two men were sullenly quiet. Was there something about Remi and Capi that they didn't like?

"Two *kitsune udon*."

Remi ordered diffidently. Feeling sick in a strange land, he felt extremely vulnerable. When Remi and Capi approached the front of the stall, a dog came up to their feet and started sniffing around. A dirty gray dog with mange. The two of them took turns trying to shoo it away, but the dog paid no attention to them.

The old lady prepared the *udon* quickly. Even though her back was bent from the weight of the baby, her hands were quick and agile, and when she poured the soup into the bowls, she didn't spill a single drop from the large ladle.

Each bowl of the *kitsune udon* contained a square piece of fried tofu. Remi and Capi piled a mound of green onions, which had been chopped and set out in a dish on the counter, onto the noodles and sprinkled some chili pepper over the top. They then took their bowls and, blowing on the hot noodles, began slurping them up. Capi ate with great gusto and joy, but Remi was bothered by the bizarre sweetness of the soup. The *udon* noodles also tasted heavy to him, and as he ate he began to feel like throwing the bowl away. But if he didn't eat here, his illness would just get worse. He was afraid he wouldn't get well, so he forced himself to eat. The dog continued to sniff around their feet and wouldn't move away. It stared up at them intently, following the movement of their hands, then walked about, staggering, trying to rub its mangy body up against their feet.

"… So where'd she go?" One of the men muttered in a melancholy tone.

"She's just like a dog. She'll come back at some point," the other man said, glancing indifferently at Remi and Capi.

"You best not run off without paying. Two bowls, twenty yen. Come on now, hurry up and pay." The old woman sounded angry. Remi was flustered and fished two ten-yen coins from the pocket of his trousers. He set them on the counter.

"What the hell is this? You think you can fool me with counterfeit money?"

At the old woman's words, the men leaned over to look at the coins.

"Wow, you're taking this joke too far. It has *Japan* and *1952* written on it."

"They're ten-yen coins for sure. Really well made. Interesting, but these won't do you any good. What happened, sonny? Did you pick 'em up somewhere? I doubt you could have made this kind of fancy coin yourself."

Feeling dizzy, Remi stared at the coins the two men were examining. Was something going on? He couldn't muster the strength to think. It felt like he had become trapped, unawares, in a bizarre dream because of his cholera fever. Even in his dream he felt bad and wanted to lie down and go to sleep right away.

"This is no good, sonny. Don't you have any money at all?"

Remi shook his head absently.

"Damn guttersnipe trash. I had a feeling this would happen. Look at his hands, all diseased and blistered."

"Got anything in your bag, sonny? Something you could use in place of money? If you don't want to get the cops called on you, you'd better find something, fast."

Remi looked back at Capi, who was standing behind him. Her mouth was open, like some witless child, and tears were welling up in her sleepy eyes. Remi felt like crying too. He quickly peeked into his bag, then pulled out the empty lunch box he had brought with him from Tokyo, and the new scissors and razor he had bought.

"For street orphans they're sure carrying a lot of things."

"That's too much for two bowls of noodles. This lunch box is enough. What d'ya say, granny, that'll do, won't it? Look there, it's a real nice box. All shiny like that."

"You better put away your scissors and razor, sonny. You could trade just the scissors for almost four kilos of meat, so put it away and take good care of it."

Without a word, Remi put the scissors and razor back in his bag, then gazed into the old lady's face.

"Aww, never mind, what's done is done. But you listen up, young man, you be careful from here on. You pull any foolish tricks, and you're gonna run into serious trouble."

Bowing his head slightly, Remi moved away from the stall on wobbly legs. Capi followed after him, her head hanging down. The mangy dog was clinging to their legs, and if they weren't careful, their legs would get tangled up and they might trip. The edge of the plaza was terraced, and they sat down for a moment on one of the steps there. Capi nestled up against Remi and whispered to him.

"It looks like we can't use our money here."

"So it seems." His reply was mingled with a sigh.

"What'll we do? We don't have any local money, so we're flat broke. It looks like we can barter, though...."

"Yeah, I suppose." Remi nodded. Had his fever gone up a lot? Everything was swaying before his eyes. The *udon* he had eaten just now was coming back up his throat.

"Those people over there—they were kind to us, weren't they. I mean, letting us off with just your lunch box. Still, I want to eat something else. Those potatoes they're selling over there? Do you think they might trade one for my soap?"

"Damn, you still haven't eaten enough? If you really want to eat, go try to get one by yourself. I don't need any potato."

"Well, I'll try asking, just to see what happens. I want to find out a little more about the situation here." Capi stood up briskly and went back over to the stalls lined up on the plaza. The dog chased after her.

Remi supported his head in his hands and closed his eyes. Potatoes ... being flat broke ... everything paled compared to his anxiety over cholera. He felt like throwing up. His head was spinning. He wanted to cry out, pleading for an ambulance because he had contracted cholera. How did Remi die? Nothing was written about dying in *Nobody's Boy*, so he didn't know. Perhaps he became a rich old man and died paralyzed by a stroke. But that would be a disagreeable end. It would be better if the plot were rewritten so that Remi died of cholera before he could be reunited with his mother. Continuing to chase after his mother on *The Swan*, he thinks that he has finally found it, but when he gets on board it's a cholera ship, and Remi tragically catches the disease, collapsing and dying somewhere along the riverbank. Capi would protect his body and sing a song of mourning. *The Swan*, the real one this time, would slowly pass by that riverbank, unaware of what had happened.

"It went really well. *Good hunting all that keep the Law*! Right? Though I don't have any idea just exactly what the law of the jungle is."

Capi, who had returned with the dog in tow, sat down roughly and thrust a packet wrapped in dirty newspaper under Remi's nose. He felt the urge to retch again. He turned his face away and muttered, "I don't want any. Just hurry up and eat it."

"Okay, I love potatoes. I got three of them for one bar of soap. This bartering is fun. It makes you feel like you really got a deal. More than if you'd bought it with money."

Capi began to stuff her mouth with potato. The dog sat at her feet, waiting for her to drop a piece of the potato.

"You're an awful big eater." Remi was fed up. He glared at Capi. She couldn't say anything, her mouth full of potato, so she nodded several times instead.

"I'm going back to the station to use the toilet."

Remi stood up, his eyes glazed, and began to walk unsteadily toward the station. Capi walked behind him, still eating her potato. And once more the mangy dog tagged after them. The station lights looked blurry, opening out into a rainbow arc. Reddish lights, moving left to right, right to left, illuminated the sky here and there. Those were probably the lights of trains entering the station. Station announcements and steam whistles echoed in their ears like distant howls of wolves … echoes that seemed to call to Remi.

Hurry, climb up on our backs and ride! We'll take you to a beautiful, faraway place.

As they neared the station building, he groaned because of the glare of the lights. Bumping into the dark figures of passengers going in and out of the station, Remi seemed in danger of falling. Capi supported him and peered into his face.

"Do you feel worse?" she asked, placing her hand on Remi's forehead. "You're burning up."

Remi was gasping as he whispered, "In any case, I'm going to the toilet. I want to shit everything out. Don't worry. I'm not ready to collapse here yet."

Knitting her eyebrows, Capi nodded. Still, she didn't want to be separated from Remi. And he had no choice but to lean on her. When Capi helped support him, it was definitely easier to move around. They went into the station, Remi squinting at the bright lights.

"What happened to the dog?" He asked as a way to indicate that his mind was clear.

"It's not here anymore," Capi answered. "It knew people would get angry if it tried to come into the station."

"Did you eat all of the potatoes?"

"I can't eat that much. I wrapped the leftovers in paper and put them in my bag."

They finally reached the toilet. Remi started to go into the men's toilet, but Capi wouldn't let go of him. He stopped and said to her, "Aren't you going to the women's toilet?"

"It's okay. I'm a boy, after all."

And with that reply, Capi nonchalantly proceeded into the toilet. Remi said nothing more and, continuing to lean on Capi's small shoulder, went in as well. Several men were standing at the urinals and three or four men were at the sinks, shaving or brushing their teeth. Without a word, Remi let go of Capi and went into one of the stalls. Of course she could not go into the stall with him. As soon as he saw the toilet bowl, he felt a powerful urge to vomit. Squatting down on the floor, he barfed up all the *udon* noodles he had eaten earlier. Tears overflowed from his eyes. But that made him feel a little steadier. He stood up, pulled his trousers down, and straddled the toilet. Thanks to the medicine, his shit wasn't completely watery, but had firmed up a little, more like the consistency of gruel. He tried to see if there was blood mixed in with the diarrhea, or if he could see anything else ominous-looking, but, since it had fallen into the depths of the hole, he couldn't make it out very clearly.

Capi had finished first and was already waiting outside his stall, an anxious look on her stiff face. This was probably the first time in her life that Capi had ever gone into a men's toilet.

"You okay?" She whispered.

"Yeah, if I take some medicine after this, I think I should be okay," Remi smiled.

He rinsed his mouth at the sink, drank a lot of water, then swallowed three times the normal dose of the medicine. When he wet his hands, the pain came back. He dried the palms of his hands gingerly with the towel Capi gave him, then put tissue paper on his blisters.

"I just remembered, if you want to brush your teeth, go ahead. I bought a brush for you, but you haven't even used it yet."

"You haven't brushed your teeth either, Remi," Capi replied, "and you haven't shaved. Look at yourself in the mirror. You're starting to look like the monkeys you detest."

Flustered, Remi glanced at the mirror. It was terrible. Just as Capi said, his whiskers had grown out unevenly like weeds in a deserted lot, and his cheeks were hollow. The face reflected back at him was the very image of a monkey. He closed his eyes, then took a second look. This time a somewhat more decent face stared back at him. Nonetheless, even Remi thought his own face scruffy-looking and filthy. Could his beard really have grown this much in so short a time? Standing beside Capi, who was brushing her teeth, Remi let out a great sigh and averted his eyes from the mirror. He really wanted to brush his teeth like Capi, and shave as well. But he didn't have the strength to do that just now. Tomorrow morning, for sure, he would try to go back to cleaner ways. Remi told himself that once he was feeling better, the two of them would go to a public bath—to separate men and women's baths, of course. At the same time, his anxiety made him feel somber and desperate. If he didn't get better, if all that was left was dying of cholera …

Capi, who had finished brushing her teeth, smiled at Remi, her face lustrous with a healthy glow after she had washed it with the dried-up piece of soap that had been left there.

"You ready to go?" she said.

He hesitated. *When I was little was my face like this, like one of those figurines made out of taffy, even though I was malnourished?* Remi squinted and nodded.

He returned to the plaza in front of the station without help from Capi. The light from the few remaining acetylene lamps that had been visible a few moments earlier had been completely extinguished. Only the dim light of the bare bulbs of the street lamps remained, and the realm of shadows had spread. People's shadows could be seen drifting inside that realm. Or maybe that was just an illusion. They didn't feel like leaving the station and walking around the city, so Remi headed toward a railway underpass off to the right. Capi was worried and walked beside Remi, leaning up against him. The dog that had been trailing after them earlier was walking behind them again. They had given up trying to shoo it away. While they were in the toilet, the dog had obviously waited in front of the station, its ears straining, exactly like a loyal dog waiting for its master. Even so, it was a sure bet that this dog would soon abandon them. A masterless dog always acts like that.

A pitch-black hole was visible under the railway overpass. Apparently there was a tunnel-like passageway there. It was the perfect place to sleep until morning. Remi immediately moved closer to it. The passageway was completely sunk in darkness, and they could see nothing. They hesitated to step inside, but Remi told himself it wasn't as if they were deep in the mountains or any place where man-eating tigers or deadly poisonous cobras were lurking. Using the fingertips of his left hand to follow along a wall of damp bricks, he went about ten paces inside. The tips of his sneakers touched something. He bent over at the waist and stretched both hands in front of him. He fingertips touched something soft and warm wrapped in a cloth. He got his courage up and tried grasping it. When he did, someone groaned back at him.

"What the hell are you doing? Leave me alone!"

Remi backed away toward the entrance and, after making sure there was no one around him, sat down. "This place is full of people who got here before us," he murmured to Capi, who'd been clinging to his back the whole time. "Keep your voice down. Let's sleep here."

After touching Capi with his fingertips to make sure she was sitting next to him, he searched around in his pocket and pulled out a match. He struck one, and, after it made a small crack of light, the dark at once melted away. An image of people sleeping piled on top of one another like a pile of rags in the interior of the passageway floated before them. Their clothes, which had once been of various colors—were now filthy and worn and had all faded to the same color. Men and women. Children and babies. A woman was sitting up and feeding an infant at her withered breast. Some people had thin straw mats wrapped around their bodies instead of rags. Remi and Capi could make out crumbling wooden boxes and bamboo baskets scattered about, and in the interior they could see the figure of a child munching on a bread roll.

When the match burned out, the darkness suddenly became a mass descending over them. Remi lay down facing the wall, and used his bag as a pillow. Capi did likewise, resting her head on his legs. Remi stretched out both hands and, grabbing hold of her arm, pulled Capi up to a position where he could shield her with his own body. It was probably not a dangerous place, but Remi had a responsibility to protect her.

"What happened to the dog?" Remi asked.

Capi whispered back, "It's still there."

"Really? It must be a regular here."

"What'll we do if it doesn't leave us tomorrow? Should we keep it?"

"You must be joking. That filthy mutt? If we're not careful, we'll catch something from it. If it tries to stick with us, give it a swift kick in the ass."

"I don't want to catch anything, but I don't want you to kick it either," Capi said, her voice wavering.

"Damn! All right, then, suit yourself."

Remi yawned and closed his eyes in the darkness. Since he hadn't been able to see anything to begin with, closing his eyes didn't make any difference. He felt like he was dreaming already and hoping to have dreams within a dream. He put his right arm under his head and placed his left hand on Capi's back as she slept in the space between him and the wall. In this position, he should finally be able to get some sleep. With that thought, he exhaled and quickly fell asleep, as though he had taken a whiff of anesthesia.

Capi curled her body up in a little ball and held her breath, thinking she wouldn't be able to sleep because of her concern for the dog. She was worried that Remi might have cholera, and she didn't know if she would be able to avoid catching the disease. Remi had once used the phrase "stepping on a swan," and the ghastly feeling of trampling on something pure white and beautiful, like a swan, haunted her. She could see *The Swan*, which was made of glass, drifting along in the darkness. Remi, who was going to die of cholera, had laid his pale body down on that boat. His mother, unable to cry and frozen with despair, remained standing beside him. His mother was Capi, now all grown up. *The Swan*, reflecting a cold, sorrowful light, proceeded along the dark surface of the river. Four o'clocks were in full bloom on the riverbanks. Four o'clocks had grown thick in the garden of Capi's house, and her mother had no idea what to do about them. Red, white, and pink flowers floated up in the night darkness. Remi's father was standing there, his face ashen as he watched *The Swan* go by. A small naked boy was running around like a dog among the flowers.

Her butt was itchy. Immediately the itch began to spread out and around. Her stomach was itchy. Her thighs were itchy, and, still asleep, she began to squirm. She opened her eyes. The very instant she opened her eyes, the itchiness also awoke and mercilessly assaulted her entire body. Capi sat up and began scratching all over with both hands. At first she thought she might have caught the mange from that dog, but then she realized it was fleas.

"Capi, have you been bitten as well?"

She heard Remi's voice, followed by the sound of a match being struck and a blinding light bursting open and spreading out. Remi was also sitting up. His face was contorted, and he was scratching his back and his waist with his free hand.

"This is terrible. My fever seems to have gone up, my head's throbbing, my stomach hurts … I'm a wreck."

As Remi spoke, the match went out and his figure disappeared into the darkness.

"Didn't the medicine work?" Capi spoke in a whisper, all the while scratching her butt.

"This is a hell of a mess. If it's not a cold, I'm done for. Do you feel anything abnormal, other than the fleas?"

"No, I'm okay, except that I'm about to die from itching."

"You won't die from fleas, but—"

Remi started to say something, then fell silent. Presently he took a deep breath, exhaled, and, leaning close to Capi's ear, said quietly, "Listen to me. I'm still all right for now, but if I get to the point where I can't move, you leave me and go to the police. Don't say anything about me, just tell them that you've come from Tokyo and lost your way. If you do, they'll send you back home. It looks like you can get away without getting sick, so don't say a word about cholera."

"But what about you, Remi?"

Capi's voice sounded forlorn.

"Me? If I collapse like this, I'll be taken to the hospital at some point. Just like my old man was. It's best if you don't stay close to me. Because you'll survive."

"Don't talk that way."

In the darkness, Capi clung to Remi's left arm and began sobbing.

"I could never do such a thing. I could never leave you to die alone, Remi. I'll never abandon you."

Remi put his right arm around Capi's shoulder. He felt as though he was going to start crying himself. He didn't know if the source of his tears was his sadness at being sick or his happiness at hearing Capi's words.

"It's not certain that I'm going to die, but ..." he whispered, "and I don't want to be separated from you either, Capi, but still ..."

"Then we'll stay together. Even when we go home, we'll go together. My mother will be surprised, but I just know she'll understand. After all, Ton-chan's not around anymore, and the house is empty."

Remi could feel his chest grow hotter and hotter with emotion, and tears welled up in his eyes. It was lucky she couldn't see his face in the darkness.

"I'm so happy you said that for me, Capi, but society would never allow me to live with you and your mother. No matter how much we think we want to be together, society will never recognize us as true brother and sister. Your mother has to live in that society, and so she'd never let me even set foot inside your house. The Man Pack is terribly rigid. There may be exceptions, like the peasant wife—Mother Barberin, who raised Remi, but even she was so poor she couldn't stop her husband from selling Remi to the traveling performer Vitalis. I think about how differently the story might have turned out had Remi been her real child. Of course, poverty was a problem in her case, but what about Remi's real mother, who was rich? It never occurred to her that because she was rich she could have cared for children who had no one else to care for them. Instead she continued to search desperately for only Remi—for her own child. The Man Pack accepts only real children, or at best the children of relatives. If people didn't act that way, I suppose society would fall apart."

As he scratched himself all over, Remi spoke to Capi as calmly as he could. Remi, who had come from a graveyard, at least knew the truth that even though there are many touching stories in the world, things never really progress all that much. Now, when perhaps he was on the brink of death, he wanted to show his dignity to Capi, the cute puppy dog who knew nothing of the world.

"All right, all we have to do is get married. I'm really a girl, after all, so if we want to get married, we can."

Capi was squirming as she spoke, scratching all over.

"We can't get married. What nonsense. You're just twelve years old...."

Remi was truly in a panic, and his face flushed crimson. In the darkness, however, Capi couldn't see his panic.

"But what if we told my mother that we're married and can't be separated?"

171

"Do you have any idea what marriage is?"

In spite of himself, he sounded as though he was scolding Capi.

"It's living together. Eating meals together, going to the baths, and eventually having kids," Capi answered hesitantly.

Remi was perplexed, and chose his next words with great care. "To get married, Capi, you have to be an adult first. It's awkward enough that your body is still a child's, but your way of thinking is childish as well. They say the sign you've reached the first stage of adulthood is what they call your *period*, and you haven't even reached that stage yet, have you, Capi?"

"They taught us about that in fifth grade. No, but my breasts are already getting a little bigger."

Remi was becoming even more flustered, and he swallowed hard.

"Damn, this is stupid. No one considers such a thing a sign of adulthood. If you just wait a little, the first stage will come to you, Capi. But even that's not enough. At the very least, you have to be about my age. If not, no one will take the marriage seriously. Otherwise, I'll be treated like a pervert and reported to the cops."

"Why?" Capi whispered, sighing deeply.

"Because for now you're still a kid who needs your mother's protection. Because you belong to your parents, you don't have any qualifications to decide anything on your own. That's why I said that the Man Pack is so rigid and constraining."

"You don't think you want to try doing something dirty to me, Remi?"

This time, Remi's face blanched in the dark. For a second he felt hatred toward Capi and clenched his teeth. But he reconsidered, because now was a time when the two of them might have to go their separate ways. With some reluctance, he spoke to her.

"I come from a graveyard and was raised in an orphanage, but I'm not a monkey. So don't ever mention such a low and vulgar thing to me again. I'm really hurt that you don't understand even that much. So, listen up, okay? Maybe one of these days, sometime in the future, we may get married. But until then, it's enough just to think about what's happening now. That's all we can do. And what are we now? Remi and Capi. I'm happy being that. Understand?"

Remi sensed that Capi was nodding.

"If I can die as Remi," he continued, "that's my true wish. But if I don't die, even if we're separated for a while … then, that's right, in five years or so we can think about getting married, and I'll be able to come and live at your house, Capi. Still, I don't know how it'll turn out. Because in five years, you'll no longer be Capi. You'll be a woman by then."

Remi cut himself off, and Capi was lost in her thoughts for a while.

"I'm sorry," she said at last. "There are so many perverts out there, and I was worried, thinking that since you're a man, Remi, you might be one of them. That their *wieners* might get big and they'd force themselves on me. It's disgusting, and scary.... Doesn't your *wiener* get big, Remi?"

Remi's heart contracted and he held his breath. Just talking about it was enough to give him a hard-on. He took a deep breath and put all his efforts into speaking calmly.

"You ask that without really knowing anything about it, don't you? Naturally sometimes it gets big. It's necessary for the survival of the species. But still, how should I put this? Listen, Capi, you fart, right? Well, sometimes a man's penis will fart, even when it doesn't have anything to do with the survival of the species. But you don't need to know that kind of thing, Capi, and I don't want you to know."

"But Ton-chan was always playing with his wiener, and there are perverts out there, and there are men who want to murder little girls. I don't think you can just tell me that I don't need to know anything. I toyed a little with the idea that if you wanted to try touching my breasts, Remi, it'd be okay. And if you did, I'd want you to tell me whether or not you got an erection. But you don't have to go out of your way to do that sort of thing. My boobs aren't really filled out yet; they're more like the size of the swelling you get after being bitten by black fly. Even that may disappear soon. Given the way they are, it might be best if I could really turn into a boy. If I did, would you want to be with me all the time, Remi?"

Capi squirmed and scratched her stomach and her sides.

"You're still a kid, Capi, not a woman and not a man, and since this is the only time in your life when you can be a kid, you'd better enjoy this time. We'd both better. I need to go outside. I'm getting the runs again, and I feel like I'm going to throw up. It's all right, don't worry, I'm not going anywhere."

Remi stood up, staggering.

"I'm going with you."

"No, you wait here, Capi."

Despite what he said, Capi followed after him. After all, she felt forlorn and lonely. She was worried about cholera, and she felt she couldn't let him out of her sight. Her consideration warmed his heart, but it embarrassed and annoyed him, especially at a time like this, when he was going to take a crap.

The sky over the plaza was already turning white. The bare bulbs of the street lamps were still on, and the air had cooled enough that it felt chill on their skin. A large truck was passing along the road that ran along the far side of the plaza. Bicycles were also whizzing along. Some women carrying large bundles wrapped in *furoshiki* on their backs were walking along the edge of the plaza, and a large black cat was cutting leisurely across the middle of the plaza, moving toward the station. Remi walked beside a brick wall to his right, then went around behind some concrete drainpipes that were stacked up there.

"Wait over there on the other side," he said.

After making sure that Capi was out of sight, Remi dropped his trousers and squatted down. His stomach hurt, as if needles had been stuck into it. His eyes swam and his head hurt. His body itched all over. The raw skin on his palms began to sting again. After exposing his bare ass to the morning air and waiting a few moments, a hot liquid streamed out. Remi groaned. His ass had been rubbed raw because of his fever and his diarrhea. Because he hadn't brought his bag, he didn't have any toilet paper. He fished around in his pocket, but couldn't find anything to use; so he gave up and pulled his pants back on just as he was. Next he carefully inspected the liquid. Only a small amount remained. A urine color dyed the whitish gravel, but he couldn't see any blood.

He realized the dog had come near him. It was the same mangy dog that had been hanging around them since last night. It paid no attention to Remi, but stuck its nose in the puddle left on the gravelly surface and began sniffing. Even though it wasn't a smell that should have aroused its appetite, the dog wagged its tail and tried licking it with its tongue. Remi suddenly kicked the dog hard in the side. He kicked the dog two or three more times until it gave out a yelp and ran away.

"Stop it! What are you doing?" Capi ran up beside him, yelling. The dog went running off.

"Why pick on the dog? It may be a dirty old mutt, but it hasn't done anything wrong."

Remi exhaled, his shoulders heaving, and glared at Capi.

"It's disgusting, so stop talking like a girl. That dog ... it tried to lick the stuff that came out of my butt, as if it was the most natural thing in the world. If I have cholera, that damn dog will get it too, right? That's why I stopped it."

Opening her mouth just slightly, Capi glanced at the puddle on the ground. "Do dogs get cholera?"

"I don't know, but anyway it'd be taking a risk, wouldn't it?"

"Yeah, maybe. I thought that because I said some weird things you suddenly took it out on the dog. And when you're focused, you can be kind of intense, Remi."

Capi's face showed her disappointment. No one, not even an animal, can help being afraid when an opponent is stronger than they are. Remi sympathized with her and allowed his voice to show how tired he felt.

"It's just the kind of brute strength you get in an emergency. Dammit, I feel light-headed. These drain pipes are perfect, so can we sleep inside them for a little while? The other place has so many fleas, I can't stand it."

"Sure, the pipes are better. I'll bring the bags over, so just wait."

Capi dashed off to the tunnel under the rail overpass. The concrete drainpipes were piled up in the shape of a triangular mountain—three on the bottom, two in the middle, and one on top. They were about a meter in diameter, so they were plenty wide enough for the two of them to lie down together and sleep. Due to the weight of the pipes themselves, there was no worry about the mountain collapsing. Remi pulled himself up the mountain, and slipped inside the drainpipe at the top. Cobwebs stretched across it, and fine gravel was scattered inside. He stuck his face out of the pipe and called out to Capi, who had come back from the overpass.

"Capi, up here! The view's great!"

Capi laughed, and, carrying the two bags in her right hand, she cautiously pulled herself up. In situations like this, Capi's high-quality leather shoes limited her movement. Remi was just now struck with admiration that she had been able to climb that rope ladder on the cholera ship so well in shoes like that. Now they looked only like worn-out shoes, completely stained through with sand and mud.

Capi, who had reached the top drainpipe, imitated Remi and stuck her head out, looking across the plaza in front of the station.

"Wow, what a great feeling! I can see forever. We should have slept here from the beginning."

"It was completely dark last night, so of course we couldn't see a thing."

"What are we going to do about these fleas. I wonder if we shouldn't take off our clothes and crush them. It seems like there's still a ton of them."

Remi smiled sarcastically, then muttered, "If we don't do anything, the fleas will all jump over to you, since your body looks a lot more delicious than mine."

"Dogs are gathering over there," Capi said.

About ten dogs were loitering around the left edge of the deserted plaza, which was growing more visible in the light. They couldn't tell from the drainpipe if the mangy dog that had been with them earlier was among them. There was a large black dog, and a small brown one, a skinny spotted dog—dogs of various sizes and breeds, their heads hanging down, searching for something that had fallen on the ground. Remi furrowed his brows, remembering the dogs at Kurihama. Why was it that wherever they went, there were so many damn dogs separated from their masters? Was it because Capi had taken a dog's name?

Four middle-school boys carrying worn-looking rucksacks on their backs came walking toward the station from the right side opposite the spot where the dogs were gathering. They had probably come to the station early intending to catch the first train out. A woman with a child in tow came walking along the side of a building, directly across from Remi and Capi, that had been half-destroyed in the war. The woman was wearing work trousers and dangling a heavy-looking handbag. Her child was about five and shuffled along in dirty, baggy trousers that resembled Capi's. A whistle rang out from the direction of the station, followed by the sound of a dog howling. When one dog howled, the other dogs began howling. The middle-school students stopped in their tracks. The woman accompanying the child also stood still. The large black dog headed toward the students. When the other dogs noticed what it was doing, they began to follow. The head of the black dog was hanging low; its gait was unsteady. Nonetheless, as it headed toward the students its pace gradually quickened. The black dog in the lead growled, then tried to spring upon one of the students. The students immediately screamed and fled. The woman also picked up her child and fled. The dogs, however, paid no attention to her and pursued only the students. In an instant the dogs, frothing at their mouths as they ran, were close to catching up to the students.

"Help! Mad dogs! Help!" The woman began shrieking.

"It's horrible. We've got to do something!"

Capi hurriedly climbed down from the drainpipe and began looking for stones to throw at the dogs. Remi got down after her and took off running toward the dogs. At this moment he had no choice but to forget he was suffering from cholera. The black dog had seized the trousers of one of the students in its teeth, and the student screamed and fell to the ground. The other three students were surrounded by dogs and could no longer move even a step. Capi stuffed her pockets with some small stones that were just the right size to throw at the dogs and came running after Remi. The woman continued shrieking in a constant wail, but no one came rushing out in answer to her cries. The pack of dogs leapt at the students from all directions and began to bite them. The three boys were crying and wildly waving their arms and legs.

Remi first moved close to the black dog and kicked it in the stomach. When he kicked it a second time the dog let go of the student's leg and turned, growling, to face Remi. Saliva was gushing out of its mouth, and its eyes were a muddy red. It was a genuine mad dog. Remi quickly pulled off his sweater, waved it around to distract the dog as he backed away. Capi, who had come running up panting and out of breath, threw stones at the pack of dogs assaulting the three students. One small stone hit the spotted dog in the head. Perhaps it would have been better if the stone had not found its mark. The spotted dog turned toward Capi and, white foam dripping from its mouth, started growling. Drawn by its voice, the other dogs all shifted their attention away from the students and began stalking Capi. Even the black dog started to draw a bead on her.

Remi yelled, "It's no use! Hurry, make a run for the drainpipes!"

He grabbed her by the arm, and they dashed off. The pipes were about fifty meters away. It would take about nine seconds. They'd be all right, they'd escape somehow. Getting rabies on top of cholera was no joke. To top it off, there were so many dogs opposing them, they might be bitten and mauled to death. Even Akela in *The Jungle Book*, following the battle with the pack of *dhole*, had exhausted his strength and died. Remi stumbled on something, his knees buckled, and his hand touched the ground. At that instant, several dogs jumped on him, seizing the legs of his trousers and the sleeves of his shirt in their teeth. Capi let out a loud sob that sounded like air escaping. Waving his sweater around, Remi scolded her.

"What the hell are you doing? Hurry up and get out of here! Right now! I'll get away somehow."

As he was yelling at her the dogs bit into Remi's wrist and the thigh of his trousers. His body flushed hot and trembled, more out of anger than pain. *Shit, I am not going to let dogs eat my flesh. Will that mangy dog that was hanging around* us last night try to help me? Or is it angry at me for kicking it, and glad to see its fellow dogs attacking like this? A sharp pain gripped his calf. As if in triumph, two of the dogs had mounted Remi's body and were tearing at his clothes. Remi rolled over and tried to push them off with his hands and feet. The dogs bit his hands, and tried to pull and tear at his feet. Groans and tears and blood all came pouring out at the pain that coursed through his entire body. The smell of blood and the smell of dogs. *These beasts are decaying even while they're alive. The smell of my blood isn't decayed. I thought I was going to die of cholera, but instead I'm going to die like this, in the most miserable way. My blood's gushing out everywhere. An awful lot of blood. It's hot and steam is rising off it. The stinking mouths and bodies of these dogs are wet and red with my precious blood. These beasts intend to eat me up. I have to hurry and escape. I'm not Akela now, I've completely transformed into a human, and the dogs will eat my flesh. It would have been much better to have died of cholera.* The flesh on Remi's cheek was bitten away. The flesh on his stomach was torn as well. The wind passed through his body, and his temperature dropped. He recalled the scent of the blood he had sniffed in the graveyard. The same smell as now. There had been so much blood then, he had been surprised. The blood of three people formed a pool. And in that pool was the blood of Capi's father. *My life began with the smell of blood that was partly the blood of Capi's father. Will it end with the smell of my blood alone? Isn't this all a bit too much? That I've lived to this moment in order to be eaten by dogs? Isn't my life even more pathetic than my father's? What a terrible end!*

The howl of a dog—one dog separate from the pack of rotting dogs—came flooding into Remi's ear like a shaft of light. It resembled the *Death Song* of the wolves—a clear voice with a hint of sadness that echoed through the morning sky. Remi followed that howling voice, turning his eyes toward its source. There, reflected in his bleary eyes, he saw Capi standing atop the drainpipes. She had transformed into the figure of a pure white dog, her face turned up toward the sky, howling out a song of sorrow. *Wow, she's singing really well, isn't she? Capi's now seeing off my life, which began with the smell of blood that contained her father's blood. There's an extreme symmetry to my life and death. But at least I didn't end up dying alone. Capi is here for me.* Remi smiled. The pain in his body was absorbed into her singing voice.

We be of one blood! We be of one blood!

Her howling voice reverberated in Remi's ear, sounding as though she was singing those words. The dogs, their teeth bright red with blood, ripped away his earlobes and his nose. They ripped open his throat, and tugged at his legs, and the life drained from Remi's body. Atop the drainpipes, Capi shed tears and poured forth her beautiful song of sorrow, all the while using every bit of strength to continue her howling so that her song might fill the sky all over the world.

We be of one blood! We be of one blood!

177

20 February 1947
Young Woman, 22, May Have Been Mauled to Death by Stray Dogs

A little after 9 a.m. on the 19th, Yoshikawa Ryūtarō of Nakamachi, Kara-suyama in Setagaya Ward, Tokyo, reported to the Seijō police station the discovery of the corpse of a small-framed woman, about 20, in a field behind his house. The woman had apparently been mauled and killed by wild dogs.

According to Yoshikawa, at around 10:30 on the evening before the discovery, right after the earthquake on the 18th, he heard the howling of wild dogs and the screams of a woman several times and saw three large dogs squatting out behind a barn that belonged to the family. A number of wild dogs always gather in the vicinity, and it appears that the woman was attacked by this pack.

Poor Results for Stray Dog Hunts

The office of the Public Health Inspector for the Tokyo Metropolitan Po-lice hired four groups to carry out a wild dog hunt on successive days in various areas. In December of last year they killed 55 dogs; this January they killed 78; and by February 19 they had killed 30 more. Because each group of two men must go around one jurisdiction per day, four groups are not nearly sufficient to do the job.

3 July 1947
Child Killed, Others Injured by Stray Dogs in Yokosuka

Yokosuka: At around five o'clock on the afternoon of the 1st, Gotō Hiro-shi (8), oldest son of Gotō Shirō of 503 Hemi-chō in Yokosuka City, was attacked, along with five friends, by a pack of seven stray dogs on a hill behind his house. He died as a result of bites sustained all over his body. The other five children barely escaped the danger, but the dogs chased them to the bottom of the hill and bit the stomach of Kudō Hideko (7), third daughter of Kudō Isamu of 519 Hemi-chō, causing a minor injury.

Also on the 1st, at around five o'clock in the morning, Hosaka Yōko (23), the oldest daughter of Hosaka Aiko of 1062 Hemi-chō, was bitten on her left leg and suffered for a week. On the morning of the 2nd, Ōno Satoko, age 3, oldest daughter of Ōno Shigetarō of 235 Iriyama, was seriously injured when she was bitten several times on her right shoulder and back. Because there have been other victims of attacks, the Yokosuka police have begun a series of full-dress hunts in cooperation with youth groups.

9. Not Always the One You Think

The dull sound of the announcement inside the station struck her ears, and Capi opened her eyes. *Takarazuka. Takarazuka.* "Really? Mother, they said it's Takarazuka …" she began to speak to her mother, but then, seeing Remi sitting next to her, it gradually dawned on her that she was still continuing her travels with him. His whiskers were long; his face resembled a raccoon's. He was fast asleep, his mouth hanging open. She remembered that he was sick and put her hand to his forehead. His fever had gone down, which meant that he probably did not have cholera. She carefully inspected his face and ears, his arms and trousers. There were no marks showing where dogs had bitten him, and no trace of blood. Capi tried rubbing her own face. There were no wounds. Her clothes weren't torn. The itchiness from the fleas had gone away. Relieved, she stretched out. When she did so, her stomach rumbled. *That reminds me*, she thought, and searching around inside her bag, she pulled out last night's potato, which was still wrapped in newspaper. Breaking it in half, she began munching on it. The cold potato was hard and bland, and because it smelled of the newspaper it wasn't very tasty. She wanted to eat freshly boiled potatoes with butter on them. Capi couldn't help sighing. After that she wanted to eat eggs over rice. And corn. Capi turned her eyes toward the interior of the train car. It was crowded, just like all the others, with people crammed into the aisle. She couldn't help feeling that at any moment now her mother and older brother would appear there. And when she realized that such a thing was impossible, it struck her instead as strangely curious that they wouldn't appear to her. Capi had no idea where this train was headed. She had heard of the theater, the Takarazuka, with its all-female cast. They had performed the song "When the Violets Bloom" in their 1930 revue. But why, she wondered, would a station in such a faraway province as this be named for that theater? She couldn't remember exactly when, but once she had a notebook decorated with violet flowers. The notebook had been included in a supplement of a magazine for little girls, and when her mother saw the flowers she began to sing "When the Violets Bloom." That was when Capi first learned about the song. Staring out the window, she began to hum it in her head. She didn't know the lyrics, so she had to make do. The scenery outside the window suddenly changed, and she was looking at mountains. The green of the trees had a wet sheen in the fine rain, and yellow and blue flowers were blooming amid clumps of grasses. They had not gone north, yet flowers were blooming everywhere. The train's whistle rang out. The passengers all began to shut their windows. As Capi wondered what was going on, the train entered a tunnel. She finished eating her potato, then closed her eyes again. The rumbling and swaying of the train felt good, and her body was suffused with a feeling of drowsiness. Violets were blooming all around Capi, as well as hyacinths and yellow and pink lilies, and wisteria, and irises. The fragrance of the flowers was so overpowering it made her dizzy. Roses were blooming, and camellias, sweet osmanthus and gardenia. The smell of the flowers eliminated the smell of blood, and the dully gleaming eyes of corpses peeked out from among the roots of the flowers.

The conductor, who was checking tickets, woke Remi from his deep slumber. Remi pulled out two tickets from his breast pocket and handed them over.

"Fukuchiyama? That's the next station, so ..." the conductor said, handing back the tickets.

Remi stared at the tickets. Just as the conductor said, they were for Fukuchiyama. Had he been so sound asleep, lying there like a pile of old rags, that he had completely forgotten about buying these tickets? Whatever the case, he had absolutely no idea where Fukuchiyama Station was. He let out a great yawn and rubbed his swollen face with both hands. His whiskers startled him, and then it hit him that he had been on the verge of being killed by cholera or by a pack of rabid dogs, and he cocked his head in confusion. Thankfully, it appeared that somehow he had survived unscathed. The proof that he was alive was the pangs of hunger he felt. He pulled Capi's wristwatch out of the breast pocket of his shirt. 1:30. It was light out, so that meant of course that it was 1:30 in the afternoon. He marveled at how well he had slept.

"We're getting off at Fukuchiyama?"

Remi's heart shuddered for a second at the sudden sound of Capi's voice rising beside his ear.

"Oh, so you're up? I suppose it'll be all right to get off for a while."

"It's raining. Not very hard, though," she said.

Remi glanced out the window. A light rain was falling on the surrounding trees and on the roofs of houses, but it was so light that if he didn't peer closely he would have looked completely through it and not noticed. Remi exhaled, deeply moved that they had come to such a distant place. Even the way the rain fell was different from the rain in Tokyo.

The train gradually began to slow down, and the whistle blew.

The two of them stood up and, pushing their way through the crowded aisle, went out onto the vestibule. It looked as though a lot of people were getting off at Fukuchiyama. Apparently passengers could transfer to other lines there. As usual, many were carrying large pieces of luggage and wearing work trousers or army clothes. They dangled canteens from their shoulders and carried tired-looking rucksacks on their backs. Such people no longer surprised Remi and Capi. Because their own bodies were extremely filthy, they were now like true vagabond orphans, and so could feel at ease around the other passengers, who struck them as rather miserable, vacant-eyed people.

The train gave a great lurch, then came to a stop. Swallowed up in the wave of passengers pressing toward the door, each person struggling to get in front of the others, they were hurled out onto the platform. No matter how far they traveled, monkeys were still monkeys. Remi clicked his tongue in disgust and glanced at the passengers around him. It seemed that no matter where you go in the world—to the real Siberia, or to Argentina, or to the Cape of Good Hope—monkeys will be monkeys, running riot, screaming and shouting vulgarly. He suddenly started to itch all over, and he remembered the fleas.

"Are you itchy?" he asked Capi as he scratched his chest and belly.

"I really don't know. I kinda feel itchy, but …"

"It'd be nice if the fleas jumped off us and onto other people while we were on the train … but there may still be a few left. You should check yourself in the toilet."

Capi laughed and nodded. Apparently it sounded like a joke to her.

They climbed the stairs and headed toward the exit gate. Whenever they arrived at a station, they always went to the toilet regardless. It had become a habit for them. At some point they had come to believe there was no other place where they could feel as much at ease as they did in a toilet at a railway station.

"How are you feeling? Are you still sick?" Capi asked when they arrived in front of the toilets.

The passengers who had dashed into the toilets had formed a queue. The two of them stood a little apart from the queue and settled in comfortably to wait for the wave of people to subside. There was no reason for them to rush.

"I guess I'm feeling better. Maybe the medicine's kicking in now," Remi answered, feeling embarrassed. He felt ashamed about being sick. He was convinced he wouldn't recover. It was cholera, after all, so it seemed somehow more manly and graceful for him to respond nonchalantly to her now … and Capi would likely be more deeply moved that way. He now regretted the self-pitying words he'd spoken last night. But truthfully, he hadn't wanted to die of cholera, so of course he had no intention of lying to her.

"Still, it's best not to strain yourself. Let's not go outside, since we'll get rained on," Capi said, sounding knowing and wise.

"Okay, but we should eat something."

"Let's just get a *bentō* in the station. We're allowed to eat in the waiting room, aren't we?"

Remi nodded. In his heart, he thought, *I'm no match for this spirited child.*

"Is that all right with you? Are you really sure?" he asked.

"Well, we can't be talking about splurging now. At some point, when we can take our time somewhere, I'd like to buy a pot and some rice, and then eat some eggs over freshly cooked rice…. But before we do that, we have to think about expenses. If we keep going like this, we'll soon use up all your money, Remi. Listen, let's do like the real Remi and Capi and become traveling performers and earn some money. If we save up, we can buy a pot and dishes, and if we save even more we can get a futon and a change of clothes, and maybe a radio. We don't have to go back to Tokyo at all. The two of us will always be together."

Capi's face was glowing red with excitement.

"What in hell are you going on about? For starters, how are we ever going to carry that much luggage? On top of that, what talent do you have?"

Remi's spiteful tone of voice was deliberate. There was still a fair amount of money left. Although if they continued traveling and spending like this, they would certainly use it up soon. As it became more and more impossible for them to return to Tokyo, they would have to find work in a town somewhere. He felt anxious, wondering just what would become of them. Still, he had felt strongly that he would deal with that eventuality when the time came. That feeling remained strong for him even now. *Tomorrow's wind will blow tomorrow … You can't see tomorrow's blue sky …* at this moment he wanted to boastfully howl out those phrases, although they sounded like platitudes, like the title of that popular Ishihara Yūjirō movie he had heard about last year. In any case, it didn't seem likely they could ever go back to Tokyo.

"Since I don't have any talent, except for eating, I guess I could sing a little."

"Those Christian songs? Gimme a break."

"But the Salvation Army gets money with hymns."

"You can't call them traveling performers! They do social services. And children's songs won't do either. Let me see, I'm good at telling stories. But then again, they're stories for kids, so that probably won't do us any good at all."

Drawn in by her words, Remi began to think of possible ways of becoming traveling performers. Capi smiled innocently at him.

"Well, then, how about a picture-card show? It can't be too hard to do that. You're good at telling stories, and we can get some construction paper and draw our own pictures. The only other thing we'd need is a box to hold the drawings, and we'd cut out the front to make it look like a stage. "

"Yeah, but the only way people who do real picture-card shows make any money is by selling candy to the kids who come to watch. Kids who are curious will just watch for free, so we wouldn't be able to make much. I don't think this will work."

"Then why don't we make a play of *Mr. Pretty-Heart's Servant, or The Fool Is Not Always the One You Think*? I can be the clever monkey master, and you can play the stupid servant. If we practice just a bit, I bet we can come up with a play that will make us some money."

Remi thought a little, then answered, "But you're not a monkey, you're really a human, and so it wouldn't be nearly as interesting a play. Instead of being a monkey, maybe you should be a dog and mime a dog's tricks. That would work for sure. You wear a leash around your neck, pee like a dog, sit up, tell time by barking … Yeah, that should be good. Then at the end you can put a bowl in your mouth and collect money from the spectators. I'll swagger around and be the foolish master."

Capi pouted and said, "What's wrong with *The Fool Is Not Always the One You Think*? I don't mind imitating a monkey so much."

"C'mon, don't be silly. We don't have to decide everything now, so let's take our time and think about it. We'll come up with even better ideas. After all, we're a team."

Capi nodded in response, grinning broadly.

"That's right. *We be of one blood!* Remi's all better, so there's no worry! Never mind!"

The line into the toilet had finally disappeared. Remi, in very good spirits, headed for the men's room. He thought, naturally, that Capi was right behind him, but she was going into the ladies' room on her own. Instinctively he called out to her.

"Hey, you're going in there?"

"Last night was different. You're all right by yourself now, aren't you?"

"Yeah, I get it."

Remi hurried into the men's room. He was embarrassed at himself for being disappointed and feeling that he had been pushed away by Capi. He went into a foul-smelling stall and tried to take a crap, but nothing would come out. He then pulled off his trousers and carefully inspected his underpants, to make sure there were no fleas inside them. He didn't find a single one. Stepping out of the stall, he went over to the sink, took some medicine, washed his face and neck, and quickly shaved. Remi wasn't very good at shaving yet, and he always managed to leave behind cuts on his skin. This time he cut himself just above his lip. Because his beard was soft and scraggly, it was difficult to shave with a razor. On top of that, he had pimples. After confirming that the acne on his cheeks and chin had gotten worse, he brushed his teeth for the first time in quite a while. There in the cracked mirror was his own pale, unhealthy-looking face, with its drooping cheeks. *Definitely the face of some-one who's been ill*, he thought. Remi sighed and left the toilet. At exactly the same moment Capi came out of the ladies' room. Apparently she'd washed her hair. She'd stuffed her baseball cap and jacket into her bag and was using her hand to wipe away every drop of water dripping from her hair. It seemed that Capi had not found any fleas either, so he decided to forget about them.

They went out the ticket gate and decided on the next train they would board. It looked as though they could catch trains for the San'in Line and for the Maizuru-Obama Lines. They could go either to Kyoto or toward Tottori on the San'in Line. They didn't feel like going to Kyoto, which was way too famous, and the two of them felt a sense of fear at the place-name Tottori. Apparently there were sand dunes in Tottori, and it struck them as very lonely and dangerous. So they decided to head to Maizuru. They had to wait about an hour and a half for the next train there. If they wanted to go on beyond Maizuru to Tsuruga, they would have to wait even longer for a connecting train. In any case, they bought tickets for Higashi Maizuru station.

The sun was out, even though it continued to rain. The sky was bright, but the rain was falling heavier than normal for a sun-shower, and it showed no sign of letting up. Remi and Capi bought four *bentō* and teas at the ticket gate and began to eat in the waiting room. People who seemed to be waiting on the ticket-taker for the San'in Line came in and out of the waiting room. Some wore raincoats, while others were soaked head to foot. A girl with a large medical mask. A wounded soldier with crutches. An elderly couple with the sleeves of their kimonos rolled up, and some middle-aged women carrying on their backs large square bundles wrapped in *furoshiki.*

The windows in the room had been left open so that it would not become hot and stuffy. From time to time, depending on the direction of the wind, fine raindrops, glistening white, would suddenly blow in, and so no one sat near the windows. Instead, several men and women were sitting crammed together on benches against the wall opposite the windows. Remi and Capi were sitting in the space between the wall and the windows, so they could not completely avoid the rain, which misted their cheeks and hands.

While they ate, Capi continued turning over in her mind the play in which she would have to mime a dog. What would it be like, having to put on a leather leash and be pulled around on a heavy iron chain by Remi? Having to run around on all fours? Mouth open, tongue lolling out, snorting, being told *Sit!* and sitting with her tongue hanging down? *Lie down! Stand! Shake! Roll over!* Suddenly, Capi would sniff indignantly, turn her back on Remi, and move closer to the spectators. Remi would get mad and, as he swung a whip around, shout at her. Capi would pretend not to notice and, sniffing at the feet of the audience, would quietly raise one leg and begin to pee, pretending that it felt good.—Of course, she wouldn't really pee. She would just imitate the posture of a dog and make a tinkling sound.—And Remi would scream, with exaggerated outrage, *What the hell are you doing, you uncouth mutt! That's why dogs are always being mocked!* Capi would wag her tail—what would be the best device for that?—and go back to Remi and bark, urging him on as if to say *All right, then, master, let's get to work.* Remi, his eyes wide open, would answer, *What's that you say? Hurry up and get to work? It's all over for people when they start being lectured by dogs!* Reluctantly, Remi would pull a large watch from his pocket—his costume would look like those clothes Dutch people wore a long time ago, black three-cornered hat, black overcoat, and a white ruff around his neck. *Well, now, can you tell me what time it is?* he would ask Capi. *Arf, arf, arf* would mean it was three o'clock, followed by *Arf, arf,* which signaled twenty minutes. Since Capi was actually a human being, this wouldn't be at all difficult. In order to maintain the interest of the spectators, Capi would have to imitate a dog as closely as possible and show that she was ignoring her master's commands. As they were in the middle of telling time, Capi would roll over and lie down. No matter what the furious Remi would say, she would make no effort to get up. Remi would fly into a rage and beat Capi with a whip—it would be unpleasant if he actually beat her, so he would just pretend to. Capi would then grab the whip in her mouth and run off into the audience. Then she would slip off the leash and the tail device and transform into a human. This time she would brandish the whip and scold Remi, take the costume he was wearing and put it on. She would then fasten the leash and tail on Remi. He would sniff about and run around and around in the same spot. *Sit! Shake! Stand!* Capi's voice would ring out sharply. *This damn mutt is useless! What a nuisance! All it does is get bigger! But at least there's one thing it can do—this dog can dance! Please, everyone, if this dog can dance in time to my song, and if he does well and meets your satisfaction, then give us a rousing round of applause! He may be just a dog, but he has a sense of pride, and so he hopes with all his heart that you have enjoyed the show. ...* Capi and Remi would bow their heads, Capi would take a deep breath, and in the clear voice of a boy soprano would begin to sing, *Voices of the angels ring out on high, Gloria in excelsis deo. ...*

Having finished up his first boxed lunch, Remi started in on his second. He was spurred on more by a sense of obligation than hunger. The more he ate, the more his disagreeable illness faded into the distance. *What will become of us down the road?* Remi's anxiety kept rotating around and around, like a small pinwheel fireworks inside his body. If the two of them really could make a life as traveling performers, all in all that would be good fortune. And even if being traveling performers was out of the question, they could switch to a construction camp somewhere, or get hired on as helpers for some trash collector or black marketeer. Still, how long would they be allowed that kind of freedom? They had gone several days without reading the papers or listening to the radio. Not that many days had passed, but it was certainly a sufficiently long time for Capi's mother. If she were a normal mother, she would have worried that maybe there had been an accident and, rather than sit around and wait, would have contacted the police immediately. Japanese police were often said to be slow-witted and incompetent, but in cases like this they moved unpleasantly fast. Photos of Capi's face would have been distributed all over Japan, posters reading *If you see a suspicious-looking person accompanied by this young girl, report him to the nearest police station at once* would be plastered everywhere, and every day on the radio there would probably be calls to the citizenry asking for cooperation in finding the little girl. He wondered if a case in which no ransom was demanded could be called a kidnapping. Every year kidnappings of children take place, and most of those children are murdered. Recently a young man who had run away from home murdered a girl of twelve, the same age as Capi. Sadly, a girl of eight had been murdered in a barley field. If a man kills a child, even if he doesn't demand money, naturally he deserves to be punished by being torn apart. Remi had even heard about some wicked, fiendish monkey who had murdered three little boys and girls. Such things happened constantly in Cold

Lairs. Monkeys who murdered defenseless little ones in exchange for money or to satisfy their own impulses ought to be devoured by Kaa the python. He wanted to go somewhere far away from that Cold Lairs. Except for an imaginary jungle that exists only in a book, no world is protected by the principle that *the rights of the group are the rights of the least of its members.* In Cold Lairs, Remi himself would be considered a kidnapping monkey.

Remi placed his second boxed lunch on his lap. He couldn't eat any more. More than half the food was left. Staring at the contents, it suddenly occurred to him that whenever his stomach was empty he would invariably eat a lot at one time, as he was doing now, believing he would get his health back. But eating like this might cause diarrhea. It was foolish.

Sitting next to him, Capi had eaten about a third of her second boxed lunch and didn't know what to do with the rest. Remi breathed out through his nose and said to her, "Don't force yourself."

Capi nodded and, putting the lid back on her *bentō*, replied, "I'll put this in my bag and eat it later."

"Don't be so stingy about food. It'd be stupid if you got food poisoning. There're all sorts of germs in there."

Remi's voice sounded irritable, even to him. He scolded himself for losing his composure.

A train pulled out and all at once the station grew quiet and people disappeared from the waiting room. But soon others began gathering there again, and it grew noisy in front of the ticket gate. They likely were passengers planning to get on the same train that Remi and Capi were going to board. In the interior of the waiting room a man with stained bandages wrapped around his head and hands was sitting with an old woman. A group of students in uniforms and sailor outfits who had just finished school were making a racket outside. A young woman was sitting right next to Remi and Capi. Her head was down and she was holding a square box wrapped in a white cloth on her lap. She had a patch over one eye. Was she alone, carrying her husband's cremation urn?

Capi silently handed over the lunch box with her leftovers to Remi. He stacked her box with the other three and tossed them all into a garbage can in the waiting room. He then tried smoking a cigarette for the first time in a while. It didn't taste good, but it didn't make him feel sick either.

Capi slid her body up against Remi and asked in a low voice, "Say, Remi, just how did you tell the story of Remi to the children? You said that you shortened the part where he finds his real mother in the end because you didn't want to make the children feel bad."

"Yeah, I actually didn't make a conscious decision about that, but, for example, I'd tell them that Remi and Capi ended up on their own, just the two of them. They were no longer able to meet the family of the gardener, Pierre Acquin, who had been so kind to them, and so they continued their journey. For many, many days they walked on and on, until at some point they reached India. There they met Gandhi, and Remi became his disciple. Remi traveled around India with Gandhi ... he even had an elephant to ride on. Gandhi taught everyone about his ideas, which resembled the law of the jungle. He possessed nothing of his own—he didn't even wear shoes. He wore only rags to cover his body, and ate only peanuts and bananas. He often fasted as well. Amazing, isn't it? Remi trained the elephant to do tricks, they all continued their work as traveling performers, and together with Gandhi they went on making just enough to pay for their food. Then one day a man who hated Gandhi's philosophy killed him. By that time Remi had become a fine young man, and so he became the next Gandhi and, taking Capi and the elephant with him, continued his journey as a solitary but noble holy man who went down in history ... I'd make up stories like that. Pretty moving, don't you think?"

Straining to keep up with the thread of the story, Capi muttered, as if talking to herself, "Would Capi really live that long?"

"Capi's a special dog, and so he will never die. That's how I'd answer whenever the little kids asked me the same question. It made them really, really happy. It made little kids who didn't have parents breathe easier to think that there might be a dog like that somewhere."

"I see. But then *The Swan* doesn't appear anymore."

"If I felt like it, there were times when I'd bring it back into the story. *The Swan* pursued Remi and Capi, traveling down one river after another until it came all the way to India. Mrs. Milligan, Remi's real mother, asked Gandhi for help, saying, *Please cure my younger son, Arthur. Please help me find my oldest child, Remi, who was kidnapped and went missing when he was a baby.* To which Gandhi replied, *You must accept the life that has been given you, just as it is. Discard your riches. You think too much of your own comfort only.* After that, her younger son died, and she gave up on her older son. The lady of *The Swan* shaved her head, became a nun, and spent everyday professing her faith at a temple in India."

"Wow. Of course I've seen a picture of Gandhi somewhere before, but ... an Indian elephant came to the Ueno Zoo, and it was named Indira after Indira Gandhi. I wonder if she was related to Gandhi? Anyway, Gandhi was really amazing. He was like Christ. Christ brought a dead person back to life, he made a thousand fish out of just one fish, and he walked on water. Even after all that, he was killed too."

"But Gandhi wasn't the founder of a religious sect. He was a philosopher, so he's different from Christ. Still, I suppose he resembled Christ. Indira Gandhi—I think she was the daughter of the prime minister, Nehru, but, well, there's no need to be concerned about that, since I was telling a story about Remi and Capi."

As he talked on, Remi began to feel itchy. Capi was also unconsciously scratching her shoulder and thigh with her hands. Thinking that there shouldn't have been any more fleas, Remi was worried. Still, if he were to become a wandering holy man like the Remi in the story he had just told, he couldn't be afraid of things like fleas, lice, or bed bugs. Even though Remi himself could never become a second Gandhi, he thought that maybe he should at least emulate his own fictional Remi a little bit. With this thought, he felt his strength surging back.

The ticket gate opened for the Maizuru-Obama Lines. Remi and Capi got in the queue and went out onto the platform. There were more middle-school and high-school students. It was a local train, and so students commuting to school used it at this time of day. Remi and Capi avoided the crowd of students and continued staring at the tourist posters plastered on the wall. *Amanohashidate*—they had certainly heard of that. It was probably a famous place. *Mikata Goko, Kehi no Ma-tsubara, Wakasa Sotomo*. They had never heard of any of those place-names. There was also a poster for a regularly scheduled ship that left Nishi Maizuru bound for Hokkaido. Setting out from the port of Wakamatsu in Fukuoka, it apparently went as far as Otaru by way of Maizuru and Fushiki. The poster said that it took a week from Maizuru to Otaru. The ship's name was the *Niigata-maru*, and a third-class ticket cost 224 yen. There were also ads for Japanese-style inns. Apparently there were inns here in Fukuchiyama.

A diesel railcar pulled up to the platform. Remi and Capi decided not to go inside, but stood in the vestibule. Since they were going to Nishi Maizuru, it would take only about forty minutes. The poster they had seen a few minutes earlier had excited Remi, who wanted to go from Nishi Maizuru to Otaru, so long as he could go by ship. If their tickets were only about 200 yen, it was unbelievably cheap. After all, it had cost 280 yen, even with the student discount, just to go from Ueno to Fukushima. Maybe he had misread it, and the fare was 2,000 yen. Even at that price, however, it wasn't like he couldn't afford it. At 5,000 yen for the two of them, they could go to Hokkaido, gazing out at the Sea of Japan along the way, without the nuisance of having to change rides. *The Japan Sea! What kind of ocean was it*? Remi's heart fluttered in anticipation. Large black waves heaving, making a dull roar. The wind off the ice from Siberia blowing fiercely. There were all kinds of oceans in the world. Remi thought keenly about his past. Had his life up to now been bound to a narrow, constricted place? If the ship was on a regular route, then surely they would not encounter the kind of circumstances they found on the cholera ships, and there would definitely be food and a bath. If they went all the way to Otaru, then money would become tight, but that was a region where there would likely be fewer monkeys, and he and Capi could go into one of the primeval forests there, and they'd be able to build a modest hut, and if they went to the shore they might even have a chance to go to Siberia. And if they went to Siberia, then of course they would never come back to Japan. He and Capi would become Russians, and continue to wander about like Gandhi. Gandhi had gone around barefoot, but because Siberia was cold it was probably unreasonable for them to do that, and he would have to give up on the idea of including an elephant in their party. On the other hand, couldn't they go about on a dog sled?

The rain was still falling and a dreary landscape flowed by outside the window. Every house was large and had black roof tiles that glistened in the rain. Their eyes were drawn to the pale, light green of the bamboo groves swaying around the houses. They had hardly ever seen bamboo groves in Tokyo.

"There's a lot of bamboo around here," Capi said softly.

"They must get an awful lot of mosquitoes in the summer," Remi whispered back. He still felt itchy here and there. If they went somewhere cold, would the fleas die off?

"I hate bamboo shoots," Capi continued. "I've got lots of really intense likes and dislikes. Hate tofu, can't stand those little *shijimi* clams, or regular clams for that matter, and shrimp and squid. Hate all of them. And soybean flour and fermented soybeans, and that slimy grated yam, and *daikon* radish, and burdock and bananas. And that skinny fish called *sanma*. Yuck! I guess I hate most fish ... except for salted salmon and dried cuttlefish. Like those a lot. But from now on I'll have to set aside my likes and dislikes as much as possible and get used to eating everything."

"If you like salt salmon, well, you don't have much to worry about. You also like potato and curry with rice, don't you? In that case, it shouldn't matter much to you. I don't know what Russian people eat, but I'd guess that at least they eat salted salmon and potatoes there."

"Russian people?"

Remi was flustered by Capi's question, since it wasn't the right time to bring up his plans about moving to Siberia.

"I was just using them as an example," he replied. "Do people around here really eat nothing but bamboo shoots? I'm not very fond of them. From now on we won't be able to eat much good food anyway, so there's nothing to worry about. So long as we can eat station *bentō*, that's good enough."

Remi started to feel itchy again and squirmed in his seat.

"There must be some fleas left. How are you doing?"

"There seem to be a few left," Capi answered offhandedly. "They'll jump off somewhere soon."

"Aren't you itchy?"

"Yeah, but it's not so bad. It's tolerable. Compared to hives, it's nothing at all. Ton-chan often broke out in hives and collapsed. Hives are terrible. Blood came out his ears, and it was hard for him to breathe. His face and body puffed up like a balloon. Whenever he ate protein, he'd get hives. Nothing like that ever happened to me, even though I ate eggs and drank milk."

Remi nodded, recalling that there were children like that at the Children's Home.

"People are weird," he said. "They get hives, or they go out of their minds on account of the slightest thing, or die from the simplest causes—a dog bite, germ

189

infection, getting thrown from a train, getting too cold or too hot. Then again, just when you think that people are really weak creatures, there are times when they stubbornly refuse to die. I don't get it at all. I wonder if animals get hives?"

"Animals usually eat only what they're supposed to. People eat too much of all kinds of things, that's for sure. It may be that people really shouldn't eat things like chicken eggs. It might be best to eat nothing but peanuts and bananas, like Gandhi, but I don't like either one of those things. If you eat just peanuts and bananas, somehow it's like being a monkey."

Capi tilted her head as she gazed out the window.

"Monkeys are greedy, so they eat anything. And people, except for Gandhi, will eat anything to survive. After all, my old man and I even stuffed dirt and moss into our mouths. On the other hand, there are also people who want to die. They manage to live on for years, then throw themselves off the Kegon Falls, or like your father, kill themselves with a knife over a woman. You said it yourself, Capi, that it'd be better if they prepared a hole for people who want to kill themselves. That's okay, I guess, but what I don't understand is why such people are always hanging around. My mom and the rest of my family may very well have burned to death in an air raid. I think my old man may have seen it happen. I was the only one who survived, for whatever reason, and so my father took me and we continued to live as we did. I don't think it ever occurred to him that we should kill ourselves. Maybe he was dazed and couldn't think straight. Anyway, thanks to that, I'm still alive now."

Remi was staring out the window.

"They taught me in religion class that people who commit suicide go to Hell. *My* father is probably in Hell. And your father, Remi, is in Heaven. For sure."

Capi's voice was coolly indifferent, just as if she were talking about bamboo shoots.

Remi, as expected, stammered out, "There's no such thing."

Capi, replied, "If Heaven is the jungle, then what kind of place is Hell? I figure it must be the same jungle. There are times of drought, and the animals die off. The jungle is full of scary things—malaria, poison spiders, scorpions …"

The diesel railcar moved on through the early evening rain. As they passed each of the stations on the way—*Ayabe, Umezako, Magura*—the number of cheerful middle-school and high-school students diminished little by little.

"Well anyway, it doesn't matter. My old man is your old man, Capi, and your old man is my old man. No matter whose parent is whose, it doesn't mean very much."

Capi suddenly broke into a smile and stared into Remi's face.

"Because *we be of one blood.*"

Remi also smiled, and nodded. Capi's brown eyes were glittering. A poignant, keenly felt wish never to be separated from her coursed up Remi's spine, and his body seemed to shiver.

A crowd of passengers had moved out of the car and into the vestibule. As the brakes squealed, the train slowed and slid into the station at Nishi Maizuru. The loud keening of the brakes grew more intense, and the train, seemingly on the verge of pitching forward, came to a halt. The doors opened and the passengers hurried out to the platform. Remi and Capi were swept up in the wave of people and also jumped down onto the platform. This train would continue on to Higashi Maizuru and Naka-maizuru, but there was hardly anyone getting on the train.

They mingled with the crowd and, for the time being, headed for the ticket gate. The rain was still falling. Because they didn't have an umbrella, they couldn't just carelessly leave the station.

Standing alongside Capi at the front entrance, Remi stared out at the plaza. It didn't matter where in Japan you traveled: there was always a plaza in front of the train station, and in just about every plaza was a bus terminal. The atmosphere of each station was different—some big and some small, but there wasn't much to distinguish them. Even the faces of the station attendants looked the same.

"Hey, look over there at that bus. It says it's heading for the harbor. It goes to the wharf. Let's go take a quick look. We can't stand anymore rowboats or cholera ships, but if there's a regular passenger ship, don't you think you'd like to take a look?"

"That poster we saw earlier?" Capi responded. "The one advertising the ship going to Otaru? Are you planning to get on it?"

"Oh, did you notice it too, Capi? I don't know yet whether we'll get on or not, but in any case I'd like to have a look. So let's take that bus, okay?"

They dashed out into the rain. Panting, they got onto the bus, which was standing with its door open, waiting for passengers to board. Two or three minutes later there was a warning whistle, and then the bus pulled out. A female conductor came up to them and asked where they were going. Remi told her they were going to the harbor and, after paying the fare, received two tickets. Remi's money was accepted here. The bus was more crowded than they had expected, and they couldn't find a seat. They held onto the straps, and as the bus lurched, their bodies rocked back and forth, side to side. After repeatedly riding the trains, the swaying of the bus, the size of the interior, and the view out the windows seemed fresh and quite strange to them. Because the bus, unlike the trains, ran through the town, they could see the faces of people on bikes and of people walking along the streets. They could even get a glimpse inside the shops and houses that lined the streets. Two women were chatting in front of a house. An old man was making something in a dark room with a wooden floor. Inside a shop a policeman was talking to the owner. Black umbrellas skimmed past the bus windows. There were people holding their umbrellas up, watching the bus head off. There were also children running along the muddy streets with their clogs in their hands.

They proceeded along the winding road, and when they emerged onto what seemed a slightly larger street, there was the harbor. The rows of houses and shops suddenly ended, and the silvery surface of the harbor could be seen to the left. The real sea spread out beyond that. Remi and Capi got off the bus and rushed through the rain, searching for a building with a waiting room for the ships. They soon spotted a building directly in front of the pier that looked like the right place. A sign that read *Otaru → Maizuru → Wakamatsu* and *Wakamatsu → Maizuru → Fushiki → Otaru* hung from the roof. At the edges of the dilapidated sign, which had paint peeling away here and there, they made out the words "Scheduled service, ticket sales for the *Niigata-maru*." They hurried over and went inside. No one was around, and the ticket window was closed. With nothing else to do at that moment, Remi carefully read the signs hanging above the ticket window, listing the fares and fees for luggage. He confirmed that a third-class ticket was 224 yen. Children were half-price, but apparently there was no student discount. The "harbor fees" were probably the money paid for the barge, which carried freight and luggage and passengers to the main ship. There was also a sign saying blankets could be borrowed for free. Meals were 10 yen each, and passengers needed dining tickets. Remi had no idea what a "dining ticket" was. He felt that 10 yen for a meal was unbelievably cheap, no matter what. But when he considered that the cafeteria on the ship might be like a canteen for company employees, perhaps 10 yen per meal ticket was a reasonable policy. Still, he couldn't be sure about any of this unless he asked directly at the ticket window. Remi put his face up to the window and called out in a loud voice.

"Anybody there?"

No one replied, so he took it on himself to open the frosted glass door of the ticket office and, poking his face inside, yell, "Is anybody here! I'd like to get a ticket for the boat!"

There was no answer this time either.

"It's no use," Remi said. "There's not a soul around."

When he moved back next to Capi, she pointed to the side of the ticket window. "It says there that inquiries about passenger ships should be made at the main office."

Remi had overlooked the poster. Clicking his tongue lightly, he went up close to it. Apparently the main office of something called the Japanese Shipping Control Association was across the street.

"What a pain, but I guess we've got no choice."

"I wonder if it's after business hours? It's not Sunday today, because there were kids riding home from school earlier."

Opening the glass door of the waiting room, they stood under the eaves. The road in front of the building was fairly wide, and on the opposite side a row of stone and wooden buildings stood in the rain. They displayed all sorts of signs—Maritime Union, Cargo Handling, Nautical Equipment Specialty Store, Office of Repatriates Relief Bureau, Japan Mail Shipping Line. There were also a lot of places to eat. But there was hardly anyone around. Remi pulled the wristwatch from the breast pocket of his shirt and confirmed the time. 5:10 in the afternoon. Did the offices of shipping lines finish their business for the day at 4:30 or 5:00? Rain continued to pour, but the sky was still sufficiently light to see.

"You got some business here?"

Suddenly an old man in a black raincoat appeared from behind the building, calling out to them. They were startled and instinctively huddled together.

"What're you doing? Did you come here to ask about a ship?"

Remi calmed down, but Capi was still half hiding herself behind him. Remi asked the old man, "What's the best way to get to Otaru? We came here to find out, but no one's around...."

The old man had no compunction about peering into their faces with his small eyes. Then he laughed, his gold teeth sparkling. When he laughed, his sunburned face, which was dark brown like the color of shiitake mushrooms, became lined with wrinkles.

"Oh, well now, Otaru is it?" he said. "A while ago there was a young man like you, sonny, hanging around here, who kept stubbornly insisting that he wanted to go to Hokkaido. I was so surprised, I didn't know what to say. Anyway, the *Niigata-maru* only comes here twice a month. It's scheduled to get here next on the 16th and leave on the 19th. So you'd have to wait another two weeks. And if you left on the 19th, you'd be going to Wakamatsu. If you're going to Otaru, you'll have to wait until the 30th. It's a lot smarter to go by train. No matter how uncomfortable it may be, if you've got two weeks, you'd be in Otaru by then. So, you'd better give up on the ship."

Remi couldn't help whining to the old man. "Dammit, that's not what I want to hear. We came all this way from the station, and now we've got to turn around and go back."

The old man nodded, but this time he squinted his beady eyes, and laughed mockingly.

"So you really want to go by ship, sonny?" he said. "You got some business you need to take care of in Otaru? If all you really want to do is ride a big ship, there's all kind of ways to do that. The *Niigata-maru's* not available, but that's not the only ship around. There's a freighter and a transport ship in the harbor right now. The freighter will be in port for a while, but the transport ship is scheduled to leave tonight. It's headed for Korea, but it'll stop by Shimonoseki first. It'll be taking Koreans back to their country. Listen, sonny, if I ask an acquaintance of mine, I bet they'll let you ride as far as Shimonoseki. Well, it's against regulations. But if you help out by working in the boiler room or the storage room until you get to Shimonoseki, it should be okay. There's always some kind of work to be done. So what do you say? For 100 yen I can get you on the ship. How about it? Not a bad arrangement at all."

Remi turned toward Capi and, signaling with his eyes, asked her, *Shimonoseki and Otaru are in completely opposite directions, so what should we do? If it turns out like the cholera ship, that would be terrible. On the other hand, if we could go to Shimonoseki for just 100 yen, maybe there's no reason not to take advantage of the offer....*

Remi spoke guardedly to the old man, saying, "But we were really planning on going to Otaru. We don't have any business in Shimonoseki, and I don't feel that it's good to just recklessly board any old ship. I can't even see it from here, and your story—well, I'm sorry if I offend you, mister, but it smells fishy. Maybe you're planning to rob us once we're offshore, and then dump us into the ocean. You'd have to give us a credible guarantee that you definitely wouldn't do such a thing."

The white hairs that were peeking out of the old man's nostrils quivered slightly.

"Well, well, you sure are being cautious. How can I give you a guarantee ... ah, I've got it. I have a wireless phone, so I can contact the ship."

While he was speaking, the old man opened the glass door impatiently and went inside. He had already seen through Remi and figured that the young man wanted to go to Shimonoseki. The old man's position was pretty dubious, so he didn't worry about how suspicious Remi and Capi were acting. Resolving to go, they followed the old man inside. Seeing how the old man walked right into the office, with no hesitation, Remi wondered if he was someone who worked at the Japanese Shipping Control Association office. He couldn't imagine that such a person would help them illegally. Instead, Remi figured that everyone probably knew each other at a place like this, and thus felt no constraints going into other people's spaces.

The office behind the ticket window was a small room, about six-mat size, like a custodian's room in a school. A coal stove was sitting in the middle, and wooden desks were arranged around it. An old-fashioned telephone and some kind of machine they had never seen before were in the corner. Maybe that was the wireless phone. A blackboard hung to the side of the equipment, as well as a shelf that held cups, a cylindrical container for tea, and a kettle. Two black raincoats, of the type the old man was wearing, were hanging from the wall. Cheap-looking boards had been nailed there. The old man first consulted a thick directory on top of one of the desks, then touched the machines here and there and, placing the receiver to his ears, turned to the small, trumpet-shaped transmitter and started shouting.

"Shipping Office here! Shipping Office here! Do you read me? Come in! Over!"

Capi, who was standing at the entrance to the office, was stifling her laughter. Remi couldn't help laughing as well. The old man's laid-back Kansai accent somehow didn't match his brusque manner of speaking on the wireless, and the weird combination struck them as silly.

"Ahhh, are you the correspondence clerk, Mr. Urabe? This is Watanabe from the Shipping Office. Sorry to bother you, but I have an urgent message for Mr. Kondō in the storeroom. Please ... roger. Tell Mr. Kondō that I'll deliver the things he ordered and he should wait on deck. Could you tell him that? Over."

The old man quickly pulled the receiver away from his ear and held up one of the round earphones up to Remi's ear.

"… Okay, I understand. The *Ryūō-maru* is scheduled to leave port in two hours. So hurry. Over."

The shrill, high-pitched voice reverberated in Remi's ear like the rustling of waxed paper. Flustered, he handed the receiver back, then pointed at the receiver to indicate that the old man should quickly reply. The old man solemnly nodded and calmly continued the conversation.

"… Yes, roger that. The *Ryūō-maru* will stop in Shimonoseki, so it shouldn't be a big problem. If you need anything, I'll bring it. How about it? Over … roger that. All right, have a safe passage to Korea. Over."

The old man stood up, removed the earphones, and turned toward Remi.

"Okay then, now you believe me, right? If you do, then we've got to hurry. We can get to the *Ryūō-maru* in just fifteen minutes, but I have to talk to my acquaintance, Mr. Kondō."

He hustled out of the office without giving Remi time to reply. Having nothing else to do, Remi prodded Capi, and the two of them followed after the old man. This situation, which was being manipulated for the convenience of the old man, was getting on his nerves, but he couldn't believe the voice coming from the ship was a lie. Given the circumstances, they might as well give it a try.

Remi made up his mind and whispered to Capi, "It's a weird situation, but that old guy seems set on helping us, so should we try going to Shimonoseki?"

"I don't mind. It sounds interesting." Capi replied, blushing, "But what does it mean that we have to work in the boiler room or the storeroom? What will they make us do?"

"I guess we'll have to carry luggage or coal. Anyway, it's only for a short time."

As they stepped out of the building, the old man pulled on the hood of his raincoat. "We have to walk a little ways through the rain. My boat's at the dock," he said and then walked out ahead of them.

Remi and Capi followed, and as soon as they stepped outside the rain struck every part of their bodies. The old man was sprightlier than they expected, striding quickly in his rubber boots straight along the road that ran beside the sea. Remi and Capi, who didn't have umbrellas, were tired and couldn't keep pace. A gap gradually opened up, but there wasn't anyone else on the wharf, so they weren't afraid of losing sight of him. The sky was finally darkening, but it wasn't so dark that they needed the light of the lamps.

When they had gone about a hundred meters, the old man stepped down onto a separate, smaller pier. Remi and Capi followed after, their legs dragging. They were soaked head to foot again, but because it wasn't as cold as Yamagata, it wasn't uncomfortable. Even so, what if their physical condition deteriorated? If that happened, wouldn't it be best to continue on to Korea, without getting off at

Shimonoseki? Becoming Russian, becoming Korean—either way, it was the same thing. Remi, being seventeen, didn't know how it would turn out for him, but they would surely treat Capi kindly. They were a people who, unlike the Japanese, treated children as something precious. If it turned out that they went to Korea, then maybe they ought to think up appropriate names ahead of time. However, he didn't know any Korean names. He'd have to ask Korean people who were on the ship.

They went down onto the pier and jumped into the small, dilapidated old skiff where the old man was waiting to receive them. It wasn't a fishing boat—more like a barge with a wide deck. In order to get out of the rain they immediately went into the pilothouse, just like the old man told them to, and finally caught their breath. At the same time, the old man turned on the engine switch and began to back the skiff out. For the moment, the two of them pulled their towels out of their bags, wiped their faces and heads, and roughly brushed off the drops of water clinging to their clothes. They were flushed and warm, and they felt steam rising from all over their bodies—though in reality all that rose up was a sickly sweet odor.

When the old man changed the direction of the skiff, the engine noise increased and they began to proceed smoothly over the surface of the sea. Looking back, they could see the reddish-tinged lights of the harbor through the glass window. The lights flickered, like miniature light bulbs, and receded slowly into the distance. The reflection of the lights on the water was diffracted by the skiff's wake and glittered like a rainbow. A shadowy mass of land continued off to the left, and the lights from the houses lined up along the shore looked like those small lamps with paper shades strung up in a shrine. The lights on the opposite side were a little more distant and fewer in number.

Still wearing the hood of his raincoat and staring straight ahead, the old man began speaking to them.

"The bay here is deeply recessed, so it's a perfect natural harbor. Once a ship enters, the waves calm down. However, large ships can't come in. The *Ryūō-maru* is over 4,000 tons, but the ferry from Shimonoseki to Pusan was 7,900 tons. During the war it was normal for an aircraft carrier to weigh 30,000 tons. The *Yamato* weighed in at 70,000 tons. That battleship was a complete folly and didn't do a bit of good. Look, see it? That's the *Ryūō-maru* over there. A fine ship. It survived service in the navy, so it must have been sturdily built."

The two of them caught sight of a black shadow looming above the surface of the water directly in front of them. It looked much, much larger than the cholera ship. It was already spewing gray smoke from the funnel, and it seemed to be making preparations to leave port soon. Lights from the windows were lined up darkly along the hull. The skiff nimbly moved up next to the ship.

"I won't ask you about anything, and I won't say anything to anyone. You two need to keep quiet about me as well. We each have our own reasons. Still, I'm envious of you. You're free to do what you want. Times are terrible, but you young

196

people are energetic. If there's something you want to try to do, then you should go ahead and try to do it. Okay, then, let's climb up that gangplank there."

He cut off the engine of the skiff when they were right under the gangplank. The edge of the gangplank, which had been lowered from the deck, was jutting out, skimming the surface of the water. The old man quickly lashed the gangplank to the skiff with a rope. Unlike the rope ladder, they were able to climb up the plank without any worries. Capi nimbly scrambled up, Remi following after her. Finally the old man, grasping the gangplank in his hands, began to climb up.

When they reached the deck, a younger, taller man was waiting for them. He was also wearing a black raincoat. His narrow eyes and red lips glistened on a darkly sallow face. The old man whispered something in his ear, the man asked something back, the old man replied, and they continued exchanging words in this manner for several minutes. Suddenly, the old man turned back to Remi and thrust out his hand.

"We've reached an agreement about this, so from now on, you listen carefully to what this man says. You promised 100 yen each, so that's 200 yen. Hurry up and pay."

"Sure, let's see. Here you go."

Flustered, Remi pulled two 100-yen notes out of one of his trouser pockets and handed them to the old man. He had to brace himself in case he would be told again that they were counterfeit, but thankfully the old man hardly even glanced at them as he stuffed them into a pocket underneath his raincoat and headed off, just like that, back down the gangplank. No matter how you looked at him, he cut a suspiciously mean figure, like a criminal running away from the scene of a crime. At some point during all this, Capi had taken hold of Remi's arm, without Remi noticing, and pressed her face close to him.

"Hm, still the same disgusting old fart," the man said. "And you two are easy marks, just asking to be swindled. If filthy little tramps like you disappeared, no one would care, would they? Doesn't look to me like the little one here will be of much use. Does look healthy, though. Anyway, go on in. We can't have anyone seeing you here. We'll go down to the storeroom, and then I'll explain your jobs. Don't say a word to the passengers. Even if someone asks you something, just keep quiet. You two are on board illegally, so make like ghosts and stay out of sight."

The man glared, then cut in front of them across the deck, heading toward an iron ladder at the back of the ship.

Scowling, Remi whispered to Capi, "What's up with that monkey? What a jerk!"

"This is just like the story of Anju and Zushiō in *Sanshō the Bailiff*," Capi whispered. "They've made slaves of us. They'll sell us off once we get to Shimonoseki. I'm sure of it. Listen, we've got to get out of here now. If we jump into the sea, we can escape somehow."

The man turned back to face them and yelled, "Stop dawdling!"

As if by reflex, they ran toward the man. Then, looking at each other, they hung their heads. *We're idiots. Why didn't we run away just now?*

"We'll be leaving port soon, so everyone's busy. I have to get back to my own post, so hurry up and go down these stairs."

The man with the red lips pointed at an iron stairway that had been painted white. Perhaps because of the rain, there was no one else on deck. Starting down the stairs, they came to a long, narrow deck that ran around the hold, and they saw some people staring blankly at the sea, while others were standing there smoking cigarettes. They all looked exhausted. About ten children were playing, running up and down the stairs or dashing across the deck. The man went around behind Remi and Capi and pushed them in the back. Panicked, they began to descend another set of stairs to a lower deck, where a large number of people were leaning on the railing and staring out at the lights of the harbor. Were they Koreans returning to their home country? They were probably happy to be going back, but as they moved farther and farther away from Japan, they would probably have mixed emotions as they recalled the days that had passed. Although Remi was getting angry with the man who continued, annoyingly, to push them in the back, he began to consider the circumstances of the "legitimate" passengers on this ship. How many years had they been in Japan? They had been forced to come to here. What kind of jobs had they been forced to do? What kind of life had they lived? On the other side, there were Japanese who, of their own volition, had gone to Korea or China or Sakhalin. And there had been those who, as soldiers, were sent to places like Burma, or Indonesia, or to islands whose names no one had ever heard of before. When the war ended, all those people began to migrate at once. There were also some who had been taken off to Siberia, and recently some people had shipped off to Brazil aboard the *Burajiru-maru*. Those who went to Brazil would likely never come back to Japan, unless, of course, a war broke out between Japan and Brazil. And what would become of Remi and Capi?

With the man still pushing them, they went down stairway after stairway. Just how many levels were there to this ship? The stairs seemed to go on and on. The man announced that they had come to the storeroom, and so they must have descended into the lowest part of the ship. The storeroom must have been the man's "post." The old man, after all, had referred to him as Mr. Kondō in the storeroom. The position of the stairs had shifted away from the hull of the ship toward the interior, and they could no longer see the ocean. They had descended to a level below the water line. The air was gradually becoming more stagnant, and the temperature was rising. The ceilings were low, the angle of the stairs increasingly steep, and there were fewer lights on the ceiling the farther down they went. There were no passengers in a place like this, so close to the bottom of the ship. Instead, there were men wearing dirty undershirts or navy clothes that were too small for them who had begun bustling about, running to and fro. In the busy time right before leaving port, no one paid any attention to Remi and Capi.

"This stair's the end. Walk straight down this corridor. And don't be looking around!"

At the landing of the stairs the man pushed them in the back again, almost shoving them. It occurred to Remi just then, *If we run back up these stairs as fast as we can, maybe we can escape.* An image of them fleeing nimbly up to the deck flitted across his mind. However, what would happen to them if they escaped the man? If they jumped into the sea, they couldn't possibly swim to shore given their current physical condition. And they couldn't ask one of the crew for help either. It was their own choice to board this ship illegally, having paid money, and that reality would simply rebound on them to their disadvantage. If things went badly, they might be handed over to the police. And even if they managed to blend in and hide among the passengers, when it came time to leave the ship, they would surely be found out for having boarded illegally and end up being sent to the police. Remi took a breath and reconsidered their situation. There was no reason to panic, because when they got to Shimonoseki, they would likely be set free unharmed.

There was a large sliding iron door at the end of the corridor. The man opened it and motioned with his jaw for the two of them to step inside. The storeroom, with its tall ceiling, looked like a gymnasium to them. A hazy dust seemed to cover everything, and the light from an uncovered bulb was so dim they couldn't make out the corners of the room very well. Some men, naked from the waist up, were carrying large wooden crates. They were startled by the sound of a dog barking. Apparently a dog that one of the passengers was bringing back to his home country had been locked up here. Wooden crates of various sizes and shapes had been piled haphazardly along the walls. It was difficult to locate the dog.

The man removed his raincoat, wiped the sweat from his face, and, glaring with his narrow eyes, said in a low voice, "All right, then, we'll be leaving port in about an hour, and so you two have no work to do until then. You're going to hide yourself where I tell you, and don't show yourselves to anyone. All you have to do is keep an eye on the most important cargo. If someone comes here and asks you what you're doing, just pretend that you're some passenger's kids who came here to play. They won't know the difference, so it'll be fine. And if they take you to the third-class room, just follow them quietly, and after some time passes come back here. When we leave port, I'll have you haul coal or clean up toilets and showers. You'll also carry up blankets and food for the passengers. If passengers get sick and vomit, then it's your job to clean that up too. You'll work at night, and sleep here during the day. Got it? Just three nights. We'll be in Shimonoseki before you know it. In the meantime, don't you dare do anything on your own without my orders. All right, come this way. You'll be sleeping behind that cargo over there. Don't move a step away from that place, and don't raise your voices either."

The man pointed to a large pile of square wooden crates, each about 30 centimeters in size. They were darker than the other crates and stacked five high. Remi and Capi couldn't bring themselves to ask the man what was in the crates, but simply followed him over near them. Next to the pile of crates was a huge mountain of burlap bags, apparently filled with foodstuffs. They passed through the gap between the crates and the bags, and then went round behind the pile of crates into a space about one square meter in size.

When Remi looked back through the gap at the man's face. The man, who looked irritated, said, "Crouch down in there. Don't stand up, even if someone comes here." He then hurried out. Remi and Capi both took a breath, their shoulders heaving, and looked at each other.

"Shit. Well, let's sit down, anyway."

They sat side by side on the floor, their backs to the wooden crates. A grainy, powdery substance covered the floor, and nails and scraps of rope were scattered about.

"It's cramped and hot in here," Capi whispered, frowning. "And it smells weird too. Is that oil?"

"The engine room is nearby, so I guess it is. This cargo, it's contraband, isn't it? That jerk is probably a pretty bad guy."

Remi sighed again, hugged his knees to his chest, and rested his chin on them.

"He told us not to move from here," Capi said, "but does that mean we can't go to the toilet? Will we get food? I'm hungry now. We should have eaten something before getting on."

"There's no way they won't give us food. Anyway, I'm relieved, since it looks like we can just stay here for now without doing anything."

"There may be rats. If they bite us, it won't be cholera this time. It'll be a really scary disease like typhoid fever, or the plague."

Instinctively, Remi burst out laughing at Capi's words.

"So it's a plague ship this time? If that's how it turns out, what difference does it make? It could be malaria; it could be smallpox. And what else … maybe yellow fever, or radiation. I don't care about any of that. I've thought it over carefully, and the scariest thing in the world is the Man Pack. Radiation and germs are scary, but unlike humans, those things don't think up evil ideas or try to inflict suffering on people."

They heard rushed footsteps approaching from the other side of the pile of crates, and so they stopped talking and ducked down even further. Several people were coming and going around them, speaking briefly to one another. *Hey, over there, put it down gently. A little more—that's no good. More! More!*

Suddenly they heard a loud boom, which washed over them from beyond the wall where large crates were piled. The floor began to vibrate at the same time. The people working on the other side of the crates paid no attention and continued moving around. Since they weren't alarmed by the noise, Remi's and Capi's fears disappeared. Apparently the ship wasn't damaged. The noise and shaking may simply have been the engines starting to turn just prior to leaving the harbor. Given a ship this size, the engine was probably much bigger than average.

Twenty, then thirty minutes passed without anyone leaving the hold. Holding their empty stomachs, the two of them closed their eyes and curled up among the wooden crates. It didn't feel all that different from sitting down in the vestibule of a train packed with passengers. The only difference was that in the vestibule of a train, people's bodies pressed up against your back, whereas here it was hard wooden crates. Sitting there quietly, they gradually began to feel sleepy. As they grew accustomed to the rumbling and shaking of the engine, their space was transformed into a bed where they could sleep comfortably. While Capi was still fretting about rats—*her mother once used a bucket of water to drown a rat she had caught in a trap, and Capi had observed the rat's appearance, its mouth open, crying pitiably and staring at her as it rose and sank in the water, looking like it was dancing as it floundered*—and while Remi was thinking up a way to escape from the clutches of the man when they got to Shimonoseki—*when we arrive at Shimonoseki, new passengers will crowd onto the ship, cargo loading will begin, and during all that confusion the man would have Remi and Capi go ashore, but it was unlikely he would let them go free, since he intended to sell them to a slave trader he knew, so they would pretend to unsuspectingly follow the man right up to the very last moment, and they would have to continue to look stupid, then suddenly take off running at top speed, zigzagging their way through stores and houses, hiding under a veranda, rushing into a rail station, hopping on the first train, it didn't matter which one, and the train would pull out soon after blowing its whistle, and Remi and Capi would be in among a herd of pigs on a freight train, and they could see the man and the slave trader running through the streets, and Remi and Capi, their bodies tickled by the noses of the pigs, would fall over laughing uproariously*—the two of them eventually dozed off quietly, their bodies leaning together.

The ship's whistle sounds in the distance. They are still asleep. The sound of the engine grows louder, and the shaking more intense. But they do not open their eyes. And the man has not yet reappeared.

Remi and Capi do not notice the 4,000 ton class *Ryūō-maru* beginning to slide ever so gently over the surface of the night sea. The *Ryūō-maru* leisurely turns its bow, as if sleepily searching for the best direction to head for the sea. Then, as if it suddenly remembers the way, it begins to proceed out of the bay.

There is something in the water, innocently, joyfully bobbing up and down in the dark sea. Is it a jellyfish … or a mischievous dolphin?

The ship slowly closes in on it.

The water currents pull it back and forth, until it is caught at last in a powerful eddy that draws it to the ship. Just like the numerous jellyfish that bump into the hull. Like large fish and small fish, or like driftwood, or fragments of seaweed, or countless plankton.

201

But that thing is neither plankton nor jellyfish. And the very instant it bumps into the bottom of the ship, it explodes with all its power and rips apart whatever it touches.

The noise and shock, like several claps of thunder striking all at once, assaulted Remi's and Capi's bodies. The wooden crates stacked up above them came tumbling down over their heads, the electric bulb on the ceiling went out, and they were plunged into darkness. Crushed under the weight of the crates, they moaned and writhed. The floor began to tilt, and as it did so the crates around them began to slide little by little down the incline away from their bodies.

"Whoa, that was a shock! What just happened?"

Capi was clinging to Remi's body in the darkness.

"How would I know? Did we run into something? Shit, I've sprained my leg."

A breeze started blowing through the stale air of the hold. A hole had been opened in the hull of the ship. The unintelligible screams of men rang in their ears. Above them the sounds of things falling, the sounds of crashing swirled about.

"It looks like we'd better get out of here. Hey, I can see something strange shining over there. What should we do? Your leg, is it hurt?" Her voice quavering, Capi got up and tugged at Remi's arm.

"That's water over there! My god, seawater is coming in!"

"Stand up! Hurry! We've got to get out of here!"

Capi continued to tug at Remi's arm with all her might. In the darkness the seawater faintly reflected a dull gray light shining on it from somewhere. It made its way toward them in an instant. Several crates were floating in it, and as they spun about forcefully, they were sucked into the depths. The water began to ooze at their feet. Groaning, Remi stood up.

"Where should we run?"

"Let's try going out the iron door we came in through earlier. Which way was it?"

Once more an earsplitting noise arose, the ship shuddered, and the floor began to tilt even more severely. They could hear voices of people screaming. As the floor listed, they began to slide downward together with the crates around them. They tried to stop their slide, but there was nothing to cling to. Instead, they began to slide faster and faster, and the mass of water, shining a dull gray, was coming closer and closer. In an instant Remi removed the belt from his trousers, tied it to Capi's right hand, slipped it through a belt fastener on his trousers, and made a loop.

"At least we won't end up separated. I don't know if we're done for, or if we'll be rescued, but one thing won't change—we'll always be together."

"Yeah, we'll always be together."

At that moment a huge wave swept over them. They were sucked into the giant mass and their bodies began spinning, carried away in the heavily swirling waters.

Why did it turn out like this!

Anger coursing throughout his body, Remi took in the sound of the water. It roared from all directions, like the voices of animals deep in the jungle, and shook his body. Clinging to his arm, Capi opened her eyes and stared at the surging waters. She could only faintly make out what looked like white foam. She still couldn't comprehend what had just happened. To die in this way, to die so simply like this … it had to be a lie! There hadn't even been time to be afraid! It was hard to breathe. *Remi! God!* At the very moment those thoughts came to her, she lost consciousness.

The seawater that surged into the hold of the ship formed a large whirlpool, flowed backward, and expelled the two of them, like small pieces of flotsam, through the gaping hole that had opened up in the hull. Their bodies danced in the sea, swirling round and round as they sank to the depths. All around them the bodies of others danced and fluttered, while wooden crates and lumber and machines slowly sank away.

In due course the final sounds rang out. The *Ryūō-maru* rose up vertically and began to sink to the bottom of the ocean. People fell from the ship. Light luggage, blankets, shoes and planks, dishes, paper, cloth—everything scattered over the surface of the sea and was caught in the giant vortex created around the ship.

It took less than thirty minutes for the ship to disappear from the surface of the water and the vortex to subside. The people who were left on the surface clinging to boards or lifeboats or buoys grew deathly still, and began their wait for rescuers from the harbor.

24 August 1945
The *Ukishima-maru* (4,730 tons), an old naval transport vessel carrying Korean conscript laborers back to their home country, hit a mine as it was putting in at Maizuru Bay in Kyoto Prefecture and sank. 549 people were killed. [The ship was raised in 1954, but the cause of the sinking was never investigated.]

7 October 1945
The passenger ship *Muroto-maru* (1,257 tons), operated by the Kansai Kisen Company, Ltd. between Osaka and Beppu, struck a mine after leaving Osaka Harbor and sank in the offing at Uozaki, Kobe. The death toll was 355, while 227 people were injured, some seriously.

14 October 1945
The passenger ship *Tama-maru* (800 tons), operated by the Kyūshū Steamship Company, struck a mine en route between the port of Izuhara on the island of Tsushima and the port of Hakata and sank in the offing near Katsumoto on the island of Iki. 54 people were rescued, but 246 died.

10. Water Children

A cool indigo blue, like a dawn sky, spreads out before them. It's impossible to tell up from down, but in the distance white sparkles are visible—grains of light, like falling flakes of snow, drifting down over them. Is it the world above? A naked male child is floating amid the seaweed. Another, smaller female child is holding his hand. Their bodies glow an exquisite pearl color. The little girl, fascinated by the beauty of their bodies, laughs with joy. Her laughter rises up—not as a voice, but as pearl-colored bubbles tinkling like bells—and runs off toward the white sparkles in the distance. Tugging on the hand of the boy, who is still asleep, the small girl begins swimming through the seaweed. The boy wakes up and stares around in surprise. Staring at the small girl, a smile finally drifts across his face. He can't remember her name, but her face is deeply familiar and beloved. Pearl-colored bubbles float from the mouth of the boy and, after dancing around his body, are pulled toward the white sparkles. The two naked children stroke, caress, nibble, and lick each other. Completely enthralled with their bodies, the two of them once more feel a sense of great joy. Their bodies had places that were the same, and places that were different. Their own beauty fascinates them. A school of small silver fish draws near and then avoids the children, changing direction and darting off toward the forest of slender seaweed. A school of red fish, catching the light from the white sparkles, passes over their heads. Lush black seaweed and seaweed tinged a reddish hue sway silently. In among the seaweed, blue fish, sea serpents, tiny shrimp, sea snails in their spiral shells, and spiny crabs swim in and out of sight. Holding hands and laughing, the two naked children swim toward the deep indigo depths of the ocean, chasing after red fish, blue fish, running away from moray eels, trying to catch the bubbles that float from their own mouths. No matter how long they play, they never tire, and they never grow sleepy. They don't get hungry either. Huge crags jut out from the bottom of the ocean. In the course of time the two children move close to those crags and cock their heads in wonderment. Those crags aren't rocks, they're objects made by humans. Something humans used to cross the seas. But now those objects have sunk to the bottom and become a Cold Lairs where fish sport and shellfish reside. The children suddenly feel sad; they move away and return to the seaweed forest. On closer inspection, they see people all around them, naked, lambent, pearl-colored, frolicking and swimming at their ease. Apparently they had mistakenly thought the figures moving through the ocean were fish. The children probably looked just like fish to those people as well. A woman nurses an infant while riding on the back of a fish. Children play with the whiskers of shrimp. Men try chasing a sea serpent. The two children vaguely recall people trying to return to their own lands beyond the sea. Those people would likely form schools, like fish, and swim off to the seas around their own countries. The two children look at each other, wondering, *In that case, where shall we go?* For the life of them, they couldn't remember, which made them a little sad again. Holding hands and swimming, they chase after the school of silver fish, they tease the starfish and the sea anemone on the bottom of the ocean, and they greet unearthly looking jellyfish. Then they stare at the white sparkles in the distance. A single silver-colored jellyfish is being drawn into those sparkles. It is transformed into a grain of light like a flake of snow, and then disappears. The children smile. If they go over there, maybe they will learn something. At once they chase after the jellyfish, heading straight for the white sparkles, making their way through the indigo waters. In a flash the white sparkles become a light that is too intense, that shines blindingly into the children's eyes, which have grown accustomed to the gentle, deep light of the water. They begin to feel a sharp pain. Their bodies are also assaulted by pain. Even so, they cannot turn back. They continue to move forward into the brightness, and, in the end, just as they hear the sound of a balloon popping, they unexpectedly appear in empty space. The white brightness, along with a heart-rending scream, rages there like a storm.

… Night. An electric bulb. The light of an acetylene lamp. Sparks scattering from a wire as a tram passes by.

"It's so hot. I'd like to take a cold shower."

It was their mother's voice. Two children were walking hand in hand with her. Two more children, adolescent boys, were following behind. One of them, whose voice had just changed, protested, saying, "It's not hot at all.…"

The other adolescent called out, "Mom, where are we going?"

The woman, who was carrying on her back a fifth child, a little girl, ignored their comments and continued to mutter, "It's so hot. Tokyo is so hot."

The two children holding onto their mother's hands turned to look back at their older brothers. The adolescents, who were wearing school caps over their buzz cuts, short-sleeved shirts, and faded schoolboy trousers, nodded back at them without so much as a smile. Their suntanned faces had the same narrow eyes and cracked lips. The eyes of the shorter adolescent were red from crying.

"Mom, Mom …"

The two children were dragging their heavy legs, and they felt dizzy. They were thirsty, and the ringing in their ears sounded like the hum of insects.

The woman's face was pale. She continued to walk along, her mouth open. Only her eyes were flashing. She couldn't walk straight because of the weight of the child on her back. Her legs were wobbly, and her body was bent and swaying from side to side. Her hair was a mess, and strands of it were plastered across her face, shiny with sweat.

"It's so hot. A cold shower would be so refreshing."

205

The two children could hear their older brothers whispering.

"What's Mom planning to do?"

"Don't make a fuss! Mom's in a tough spot. I don't think we'll have any choice but to sleep outside in a field somewhere."

"She said if we came to Tokyo that auntie would help us some way, but that was a lie, wasn't it."

"Tokyo's such a huge place. It's not that easy to find her."

"We can't live in Tochigi, and we can't live in Tokyo. Dad may have been a good-for-nothing, but we'd be better off if he was still alive."

"Shut up! Stop talking like a girl! Have you forgotten what we swore to each other? We said that from now on, you and me, we'll work to replace Dad?"

The shorter of the two adolescent boys hung his head and rubbed his eyes.

Some red-faced men, drunk on booze, went staggering down the road. Women dressed in summer kimonos and Japanese-style aprons went running by, laughing cheerfully. A woman in a Western-style dress, a cigarette dangling from her mouth, was standing in a space between buildings. A dog was prowling around with its head down, and a cat crossed the road. A trolley that had passed by a little earlier came back the opposite direction. The sparks that scattered from the electric line were blinding. A couple of big American soldiers were walking along together, gawking at everything in wonderment. Some filthy-looking children were running around.

The woman continued to press ahead. The four children, their feet dragging, had no choice but to follow. All sorts of delicious aromas assaulted the children from the stalls lit on both sides by acetylene lamps. The children's eyes were glazed over. They hadn't eaten anything since morning. The rucksacks the bigger adolescent boys were carrying on their backs contained no food. There wasn't a single thing to eat in the bag dangling from the woman's arm. The six of them, mother and children, had eaten up everything on the first day they left Tochigi. They had also used up what little money they had brought with them buying train tickets and children's clothing.

"It's so hot. I'd like to take a bath in this river." The woman muttered and bit her lip forcefully. She had bitten her lips so frequently that they were starting to bleed. She was wearing clogs, and her toes were red and wet with blood. The two children who were walking hand in hand put all their strength into their grip and looked at each other. When they did, large teardrops rolled down their cheeks.

A river was shining to their right. Thin rays of gold and red light danced in the darkness, and it looked not so much like a river as a field where insects were busily swarming. Whenever their feet tramped through fields like that at night, gold and red lights rose as one into space and illuminated the children's bodies.

The little girl on the woman's back began to fret, "Food. I want to eat. Food. Food."

"There, there, don't cry. We'll take a cool bath first. We played in the river back in the country too, didn't we? I'm sure it'll feel nice." The woman stared out at the river, muttering as if talking to herself. The two children, who were still crying themselves, gazed down at the river. Their legs, exhausted from walking, had become hot, heavy lumps. If they soaked their hot feet in the water, it would probably make a sizzling sound.

"Mom, I'm not going to bathe in a place like this."

"Nobody else is bathing here, so ..."

The adolescents boys protested weakly.

For the first time the woman looked back at her oldest sons and smiled. "There's nothing to worry about. This is Tokyo, so no one cares. Come on, you two want to feel refreshed too, don't you?"

The woman spoke, turning first to the adolescents, then to the two children, and smiled gently. Her eyes were flashing red and gold, and her cheeks had grown pale. The two children, tears running down their faces, smiled back at the woman and nodded.

The woman and her five children had come to the end of a bridge on the road that ran beside the river. Small waves were splashing beneath the concrete embankment, flooding in and drawing out. The trolley didn't run across this bridge, and there were very few people about. To the right they could see another bridge. A trolley was crossing that bridge, and there were many pedestrians over there. The river was shining, and the rumble of the trolley echoed. They could hear the sound of a steam whistle in the distance. A moist breeze came wafting over the surface of the river.

"Well then, will you go with Mommy?"

The two children nodded again. At that very moment, the woman pushed them from behind and they both tumbled into the river.

"Now it's your turn!"

The woman gathered all her strength and shoved the two adolescents from behind as well. Bewildered, they did not resist her, and fell into the river. The woman immediately removed her clogs and, with the small child still on her back, jumped in after the other four. Under her breath she murmured the invocation to Amida Buddha—*Namu Amida, Namu Amida, Namu Amida.*

As they fell toward the water, the two children bumped into the concrete embankment. They groaned in pain. It was dark in the water at night, and the gold and red lights on the surface turned to blue and purple and darted along the bottom of the river. The woman with the little child on her back sank lazily, head first. When she saw the two children, a smile floated across her face like rippling water. Her hair, which had a bluish glow, and the hem of her kimono were drawn down into the dark current. Then, her body gently rotating, she floated away into the blue and purple lights. The two children held onto each other in the dark water. Still crying, they began to drift away after their mother, their bodies also rotating in the river current.

At the surface the two adolescents were flailing their arms and legs furiously, kicking up droplets of white water. But in the end, the current pulled both of them under as well. The river water in the city was murky and dirty and had a raw smell.

1947

At approximately 10 p.m. on 16 July a family of six attempted mass suicide by jumping into the Sumida River from the end of the Kototoi Bridge on the Honjo side. The mother and three children died.

The six people involved were Oshida Yasu (age 43) of Sano City in Tochigi Prefecture, her oldest son (15), her second son (12), her third son Akira (10), her fourth son Yasuo (7), and her daughter Teruko (4). The first names of the two older children, who survived, are being withheld.

The children's father died two years ago. Yasu came to Tokyo on the 15th to visit an acquaintance, but she was unable to locate the address and apparently had nowhere else to turn. The next day, after wandering around Asakusa, she told her children that they were going for a swim to cool off. They went to the end of the Kototoi Bridge, and she pushed each of the children, one after another, into the pitch-black river, finally jumping in herself with little Teruko on her back.

The oldest boys were able to swim and attempted to rescue their mother. The river, however, was at high tide, and they were carried about 500 meters upstream, where they crawled onto a stone wall. At around eleven o'clock that evening they asked Sekiguchi Kyōko of Suzaki-machi in Sumida Ward for help.

Yasu's body, with little Teruko still on her back, was discovered in the vicinity of Genmori Bridge. The drowned body of Akira was found near Makura Bridge, but the body of the fourth son, Yasuo, has not yet been recovered.

At about nine o'clock on the morning of 16 July the drowned body of a man aged 44 or 45 was discovered on the bank of the Ōyoko River just above Ishihara-machi in Sumida Ward. Honjo police believe that the man may have committed suicide. He had no belongings with him and has yet to be identified.

At ten o'clock on the morning of 16 July the body of a five-month-old baby girl was discovered under a drain cover in a public toilet at Ginza 4-5 in Chūō Ward. She had been dead for about two weeks.

At around 8 p.m. on 16 July a mother and her young daughter collapsed at the entrance of the H Clinic, located in Kikuzaka-chō, Bunkyō Ward. They were treated at the clinic, but the child, who had ingested poison, died. The young mother, now in critical condition and barely breathing, was able to tell authorities what happened.

The young mother is Mrs. S (age 28) from Ashio-machi in Tochigi Prefecture, and her daughter was named Takiko (3). Her husband returned from the war front gravely ill, so in order to support the family Mrs. S found a job in the Ashio copper mine, where she worked for the next four years. However, following the death of her husband last month, she took her beloved child and came to Tokyo on the 13th to look for work. Before she married she had spent eight years working as a nurse, and she went to the site of the hospital where she had previously worked, only to find that it had since burned to the ground.

On the morning of the 16th, as a final gesture of kindness, she bought her daughter a pretty pair of clogs with red thongs. As her daughter played happily with the shoes, Mrs. S fed the girl some bread laced with rat poison. She also ate some of the poisoned bread herself, hoping to commit suicide. However, at the last minute, she could not bear to see her daughter suffering, so she tried to get help for the child, bringing her as far as the entrance of the H Clinic before collapsing.

A mother wearing a padded kimono was coughing painfully, her small boy asleep on her lap. The boy's grandmother slid open the shoji doors and came into the room clutching three hot-water bottles.

"When the hot-water bottles are ready, you should go to sleep early."

Two older children were seated next to their mother while she held the little boy. They were stretching their legs under the *kotatsu* and drawing pictures with crayons on some old newspaper. The older child, a boy, was drawing a picture of a silver wolf, while the younger child, a girl, drew a blue elephant. Their grandmother was sitting next to a hibachi and carefully filling the hot-water bottles one by one with boiling water from a kettle. She wrapped each of the bottles in scrap ends of old blankets. Setting one of the hot-water bottles beside the two children, she handed another one to the mother and began to speak.

"You'd better get a good rest before your cold gets any worse. It's so chilly today. I think I'll make some hot ginger and honey. Who wants some?"

The two children raised their heads and nodded enthusiastically.

The grandmother opened the shoji again and left the room.

"Ohhh, it's so cold. It looks like it's going to snow."

They could hear the grandmother's voice out in the hallway. The two children looked at each other and giggled.

The mother sniffed and asked them, "What's so funny?"

The older male child said, "Every night grammy says the same thing."

"And she'll say it again tomorrow for sure," the little girl chimed in.

The mother smiled and stroked the close-shaven head of the little boy on her lap.

"You have school tomorrow don't you?" she said to the older boy. "Have you done your homework?"

"Yes. And I've arranged my class timetable. By the way, the day after tomorrow is Setsubun. My teacher told us that in the lunar calendar it was the day before the first day of spring. And she said we're going to go to a temple too, and we'll toss beans to drive out demons and bring good luck. Is it okay if I go? Can I?"

The little girl, still gripping her blue crayon, said, "I wanna go too!"

"I suppose it's all right, but don't say a word to your little brother. If he hears about it, he'll want to go as well."

The two children nodded in unison.

The bobbed-hair little girl said, "I hope his cold gets better soon. I want to teach him how to jump rope." The mother added with a sigh, "Will it ever warm up? When spring comes, his cold should clear up right away.... It was so hard to get either briquettes or cylinders, we had almost no charcoal this winter. How do people who live in colder parts of the country manage?"

The older boy added a black outline as a final flourish to his drawing of a wolf, and muttered, "Kyushu's warmer, isn't it? And Dad's working in a coal mine, so they have lots of coal."

"I'm not sure, but Kyushu's probably warmer than here. Still, he's deep in the mountains, so it may not be all that different."

The mother yawned before she had even finished speaking, and the little child on her lap began to squirm. She peered into his face, placed her hand on his forehead and whispered, "You still have a fever. You'll have to go to the hospital tomorrow. Today was Sunday, so your older brother and sister were home playing, while you had to stay in bed all day with your mother. Poor thing."

They heard the shuffling of footsteps in the hallway, and the grandmother came back into the room, along with the cold air, carrying a tray that held five cups, each containing grated ginger and honey.

"All right, then, drink it up while it's hot, and then go to bed."

The grandmother picked up the kettle from the hibachi and poured hot water into the cups one by one, and then passed them around.

"Look, here's some for the little one too. I made it special, so it'll be delicious."

The two children both complained.

"Not fair. It's not fair. What did you put in his?"

"I want to drink the same thing!"

"Don't be foolish! Hurry and drink it up! After all, your little brother's sick."

The two children hung their heads, glanced at each other, and sighed. Then they began blowing on their drinks and slurping. There was only a little bit of ginger and honey in each of their cups, but even this treat before bedtime gave the two children a feeling of luxury. The little boy's drink had probably just been cooled down a little. At least that's what the two children decided to think. The mother, the grandmother, and the little boy were blowing on their tea and silently drinking it up.

The wall clock rang out. The two children began counting each chime … *bong, bong* ... two, three … seven, eight.

"It's eight o'clock!" The girl with the bobbed hair cried out, as though she were surprised to learn that.

"You really should get to bed …" Just as the mother began to speak, the electric light in the living room went out.

"Another power outage! The lights went out at seven yesterday. Today's Sunday, so I guess we're getting special service," the older boy muttered in the darkness.

The grandmother struck a match with a practiced hand and lit a candle that had been set on top of the *kotatsu* in case of a power outage. Large and small faces, tinted red, came floating up around the *kotatsu*. The grandmother and the mother, holding her little boy, stood up and said in unison, "Well, here we go." The older woman lifted the skirt of the futon covering the *kotatsu* and pulled out from under it a brazier containing a few charcoal briquettes. The charcoal was now almost entirely ash. She then slid open the shoji, took the charcoal out into the hallway, and poured hot water from the kettle over it. The mother got her little boy to stand up. They went over to a corner of the living room and put their hands together to pray in front of the family's Buddhist altar.

"Please protect Daddy, and don't let any accidents happen in the coal mine … Hurry up, you two. Put your hands together."

The two children, who had been forced to move out from under the warm *kotatsu*, came over to stand in front of the altar, carrying their respective drawings of a wolf and an elephant and jostling against their little brother's shoulders. Behind them their grandmother was finishing taking care of the fire in the hibachi.

"Good night, Daddy."

After putting each of their pictures under their arms, the two children put their hands together and began to pray in faint voices.

The little boy, who was wearing a padded jacket over his sweater and a yellow wool muffler around his neck, stared at the gold memorial tablet on the altar and whispered, "But Daddy isn't here. Daddy can't hear us."

"But our ancestors can, and they'll carry our messages to Daddy, who is far away."

The old woman embraced the little boy from behind, then silently put her own hands together.

The mother took the candle and cradled a hot-water bottle. The two children followed behind her, likewise holding hot-water bottles, and finally the grandmother took the little boy by the hand and went out into the cold hallway. Down at the end of the hallway to the right were the kitchen and the bathroom. They had not had a bath in ten days, because they did not have enough firewood to heat water. Off to the left at the front of the house was the family shop—a sundries store where they sold brooms, baskets, and the like. It was closed, however, since they did not have any goods to sell, and now the children used it as a play space. The room they used for sleeping was directly across the hallway from the living room. The mother entered the bedroom and slid open the *fusuma* panels that divided the room into two separate spaces. Three sets of futon and bedding had been laid out there.

The two children placed the hot-water bottles and the pictures they'd drawn next to the futon they shared, and very quickly changed into their flannel robes. Their breath formed little white clouds. Two cloth backpacks were lined up at the head of their futon. The mother had gone to a great deal of trouble to make the little girl's backpack out of red cloth from an old futon cover so that she'd have it when she entered first grade that coming April. The girl had already put ribbons and a picture book and the battledore she had been given for New Year's Day into the backpack. Shivering, the two children burrowed into their futon, and their mother pushed their hot-water bottle in at the foot of their bedding. She placed a hot-water bottle inside her own futon, which was spread out beside the two children's bedding, then got in with the little boy, who was in his robe. The grandmother got into her own bedding alone and blew out the candle.

The two children pushed their icy hands and feet against each other's body, and began giggling. The heat from the hot-water bottle had not yet circulated, so it was still freezing inside the futon.

"If you don't be quiet and go to sleep the demons will come and get you. They'll chew on your heads and eat you up," their mother warned them.

Although she said the same thing every night, as soon as she said it the two children always got scared and, clutching their own little pillows, huddled together and waited with bated breath. Whether their eyes were opened or closed, the darkness spread around them all the same. The mother's coughing continued to beat against the depths of the darkness. The futon presently warmed up inside, and their bodies softly melted into the dark. The two children were already asleep, breathing regularly.

In their dreams the two children had been on the lookout for demons brandishing iron bars coming near the house. There were three demons. They were sniffing the air, baring their fangs, and licking their lips, saying, *There are some delicious-smelling children here!* With their iron bars they broke open the shuttered doors of the shop, smashed the glass doors inside the shutters, and came into the house. At the same time, a freezing wind came blowing in. The bodies of the two children were encased in ice, and their hair, which had turned white, was standing on end. Still sniffing the scent of the children, the three demons proceeded down the hall. They slid open the *fusuma* door to the storeroom; they peeked inside the living room. Then, finally, they slid open the *fusuma* that divided the bedroom and came into the space where the two children and their family were sleeping. The demons lifted up a lantern and counted five heads in the three sets of bedding. An icy wind filled the room, and the grandmother groaned and tossed from side to side. The demons turned to black shadows and came into the room.

At that moment the two children woke up and opened their eyes. Although their dream world should have disappeared, three demons were walking around the room, and an icy wind was blowing in from the hallway through the doors, which had been left open. The two children, unable to move, kept their eyes on the demons. They were fervently praying that the crayon drawings of the wolf and the elephant would turn into real animals and bite and trample the demons and kill them. But the wolf and the elephant did not appear. The three demons had wrapped army coats around their bodies and wore gaiters over their soft-soled, split-toed workman's boots. One of the demons went up to the old woman's futon and picked up a white cord from the pile of robes that the old lady had taken off and tossed there. After handing his lantern and iron bar to his fellow demons, he quickly wrapped the cord around the old woman's neck and pulled on both ends with all his might. Her body thrashed about in the futon and then they heard a low, frothy gurgling sound. After that she stopped moving. One of the other demons wrapped a similar type of cord around the mother's neck and, without a word, pulled it taut. A sound resembling a whistle escaped her throat. The little boy who was sleeping in the same futon suddenly started to cry. Apparently he had opened his eyes and seen the shadow of the demons. The third demon clapped his hand over the child's mouth, then wrapped the muffler around the child's neck and pulled it tight with all his strength.

The two children didn't move a muscle in their futon, and they didn't make a sound. Tears were falling from their eyes, which were wide open. With no difficulty at all, and with no expression on their faces, the demons killed the mother and the child sleeping in the futon. Next it would be the turn of the two children. How painful was death by strangulation?

The three demons gathered around the futon of the two children. They were holding three cords in their hands. They peered together into the faces of the two children and carefully observed the tears that flowed from their eyes down to their ears. The two children continued to cry without blinking at all. The demons wrapped red cords around the children's necks, then made their own faces bright red as they pulled on the cords. Without uttering a sound, without moving a muscle, with no resistance, the two children sank off into a dreamworld. The demons continued to focus on pulling the red cords, as if they were trying to cut off the heads of the two children.

Teardrops were still flowing from the eyes of the two children, who were no longer breathing.

1947

At around nine o'clock on the morning of 3 February the bodies of five people were discovered at a dry goods shop belonging to the K family located at Shindōri 7-chōme in Shizuoka City. The murder victims were the owner's mother, Hama (age 53), his wife Naka (26), his oldest son Akito (8), his daughter Fumi (6), and his youngest son Haruto (2). According to the prefectural detective bureau, the murders were probably committed late the previous evening. Because the victims were all strangled to death and the inside of the building had been ransacked, it appears that a gang of more than two criminals carried out the robbery-murder. The same family had been a prosperous, land-owning household, but at the end of last year the husband, S (36), moved to find work at the Ōmine coal mine in Fukuoka Prefecture.

If an average of 15 million pounds of textbook paper is not manufactured per month, textbooks will not be produced in time for the new school term. Ten thousand tons of coal are needed for this purpose each month, and to accommodate this demand the production of newsprint was cut drastically in half. However, as has been previously reported, the most that can be produced is 1 million 500 thousand tons. At the beginning of the first quarter, textbooks can only be distributed at the rate of one new text for every ten students. Manufacture of all-purpose paper, paper goods like stationery, notebooks, envelopes and the like was also cut in half to 700 thousand pounds, and during the third quarter of the school calendar (from January to March) manufacturers focused their efforts on producing notepaper for school use. Even so, the plan to produce one notebook per student for each term has collapsed, and producing even one notebook per student per year will be difficult.

The two children were standing in front of a house. They had the feeling they had seen it somewhere before—that sliding wooden door in the slightly ramshackle plank fence, that nameplate on the door. The name was written in ink on weathered board, so they couldn't make it out in the darkness of night.

A square-faced young man of about twenty whispered to the two children, "There are no dogs or men in this house. I checked it out thoroughly, so it's fine."

The young man wore an adult soldier's cap, and a soiled hand towel covered the lower half of his face. The two children had their own faces covered in the same way. In place of sneakers, they wore soft split-toe boots. The boots had holes in them.

"But I know this house," mumbled the younger of the two children, a girl of twelve.

"Yeah, it looks familiar to me too." The boy of seventeen was staring at the sliding door. He asked the young man, "Don't you think it's awkward hitting a house we know?"

"Don't worry so much. There are houses like this everywhere. First of all, you two aren't from around here, right?"

The two children had to admit that the young man had a point, and so they nodded.

"It's dark and we can't see anything. So why should this place feel familiar to us? It's weird, " the smaller child whispered to the older child.

"Maybe our minds are playing tricks on us," the boy whispered back, "since we're wandering around at such a late hour."

"Listen, we can't afford to be talking about nonsense at a time like this," the young man warned them. "When we go inside we can't make a sound—not a footstep, not even a sneeze. It's best not to wake anyone up. That's why we chose to come here at two o'clock in the morning, right? Still, if we have bad luck and some-body wakes up and starts to raise a fuss, I'll threaten them with my knife. In the meantime you two collect things that look valuable. In the worst case, I may have no choice but to kill them with this knife. In any case, whatever happens, you two do as I tell you. Don't try to do things on your own."

"We got it," the boy replied. "But please don't kill anyone. That's the one thing we don't want to have anything to do with."

"That's right," the twelve-year-old girl added in a serious tone. "Only demons kill people. We couldn't stand it if we turned into demons."

"I don't want to kill anyone either. I may be dressed like this, but I'm actually a pacifist. Okay, then, let's go. Be careful and stay right behind me."

The young man pulled out from under his shirt a knife, which was wrapped in a cloth, carefully slid it into the waistband of his trousers, and then placed both of his hands on top of the wooden fence. With a bounce he lifted the upper part of his body onto the fence, pulled his legs up one at a time and leapt over to the other side. In a few seconds there was a keening sound as the young man fiddled with the bolt-style lock. The sliding door opened. The two children went inside. The young man held up a box-shaped flashlight, and headed for the glass door of the entryway. Nandina and fatsia shrubs were blooming thickly next to the entryway. The more they saw, the more the two children were convinced that the house seemed familiar to them. Beyond some azalea bushes to the left they could see an alley that led past the entrance to the kitchen. There were cracks in the glass door of the entryway, and those had been patched over with shoji paper. A wooden box tied with a straw rope was sitting in front of the entryway. If a child pulled on the rope, that box could be used as a sled, or a horse-drawn carriage, or a car. The girl suddenly remembered that when she was very small she had played with that box, pretending it was a car and pulling it around. She was now finding it hard to breathe as her memory came to life. She could see broken Western-style dolls and her older brother, with his full, round face, sitting like passengers inside the box. And she could see herself, at the age of five or six, struggling to pull the heavy toy car and glaring back at her own twelve-year-old face, which was hidden beneath a hand towel.

The young man pulled a small rasp from one of his trouser pockets, placed it on a spot on the glass near the lock to the entryway, and began to rub carefully. The boy was now holding the flashlight, pointing it at the spot. The two children had no idea whether or not the young man was an experienced thief, and they couldn't re-member at all just when or how they had met him and become his partner in crime. Had he perhaps called to them a mere two or three hours earlier in the vicinity of an underground passageway? The two children had been terribly hungry.

There was a faint, sharp sound. A small triangular piece of frosted glass was sparkling in the young man's right hand. He handed that to the twelve-year-old girl, stuck his right hand through the triangular hole he had cut in the glass door, and began to turn the key from the inside. It was a simple bolt lock, and he was able to open it easily. Having finished this task, the young man retrieved the flashlight, took a deep breath, and slowly opened the glass door. Preparing for the moment when they would make their escape, he intentionally left the door wide open. On the left of the packed-earth floor were shelves for clogs and shoes, and on top of the shelves was a milk bottle that held sprigs of dandelion and cudweed flowers—shabby-looking flowers that had probably been picked by children.

The three of them stepped up into the house in their soft boots and proceeded on tiptoe straight down the hall. The twelve-year-old child could walk through that hallway with her eyes closed and not lose her way. She knew exactly how wide it was, how long, which floorboards squeaked. On the right was a narrow stairway to the second floor. On the left was a three-mat room. That was the "maid's room" with its half-size closet. The kitchen and bath were further along. On the opposite side was a six-mat room. The mother and her children would certainly be sleeping in there. Beyond that was the four-and-a-half-mat living room with a sunken *kotatsu* and a sideboard and radio set along the wall. However, the main target tonight was the dresser in the six-mat room. The young man only knew black-market operators who dealt in clothing.

The seventeen-year-old boy also had a vague feeling that he already knew the layout of the house really well. He even knew where the family was sleeping. However, he didn't say anything to the young man who was moving ahead of him. Even if he had said that he knew the family, the young man would probably have just said, *So? How is this family different from any other? Why shouldn't we rob them? There's no reason for us to change our plans.*

The young man proceeded to the end of the hallway and, after confirming that the kitchen was on the left, opened the sliding wooden door on the right a crack and made sure no one was in that room. He then opened the door wide and entered the living room. He peeked into the sideboard first and found some dumplings made of steamed sweet potato. He took them out and popped two of them, one at a time, into his mouth under the towel. He gave one each to the two children. The soft sweetness spread in their mouths, giving them the sensation that they were reliving their early childhood—a sweet warmth the girl had savored basking in the sun with her brother when she was four or five years old. The seventeen-year-old boy had never directly experienced that warmth himself, but he had acquired the ability to take the childhood memories of the twelve-year-old girl and make them his own.

The steamed sweet potato, which they had eaten so hurriedly, made the twelve-year-old feel like coughing. To suppress the cough, she placed her hands over her throat and mouth in a panic. The tip of her right finger bumped against a tea canister on the sideboard. It fell over and rolled onto the tatami mats. For a second the three of them held their breath and stiffened up, listening for any signs of movement in the house. Nothing happened. Quietly exhaling, the young man carefully slid apart the

fusuma doors on the other side of the living room and opened them about five centimeters. He put his flashlight up to the crack and peered inside the adjoining six-mat
room. He then slowly but surely opened the *fusuma*—ten centimeters, thirty—and
sneaked in. The two children followed after. A baby was sleeping in a small futon
that had been laid out between two regular futons. An adult woman was asleep in
the futon nearest the three of them. There was a four-year-old sleeping, like a good
boy, with his face toward the ceiling in a futon on the far side. The two children
were bewildered as they stared intently into the one large and two small faces, and
frightened at the thought of who those people were.

They heard something in the hallway. The young man and the two children
stopped still, having only half-finished their job, and concentrated their attention on
the noise. Someone was walking up the hallway toward them. Was that person going
to get a drink of water in the kitchen? The footsteps stopped for a moment in front
of the kitchen, then they came into the living room. The young man and the two
children were dismayed and closed their eyes for a split second. The three of them
huddled together, and the young man pulled out the knife. He unwrapped the cloth
around the knife and struck a pose, thrusting the knife with its glinting blade toward
the living room. At that moment a terrified scream rang out inside the house. The
scream was as loud as a fire alarm, and the mother jumped, the baby started bawling,
and the boy, his face still sleepy, sat up on his futon.

"Shut the fuck up! Shut up!"

The young man spoke in an eerily low voice at the young woman, who was
still screaming, and waved the knife blade so that she could see it. Her robe was
too short, her crinkly hair was messed up to comical effect, and her white chest was
exposed.

"Get in this room now! Sit here!'

She stopped screaming and started to sob instead. She went over beside the
mother and clung to her. The mother was skinny, the young woman was fat.

Holding out the knife blade, the young man went over to the crying infant and
picked it up. Holding the baby in his left arm, he placed the edge of the knife in
his right hand up against the baby's cheek. The mother of the baby and the young
woman, who was working as her maid, both shrieked.

"I don't want to hear a peep out of you! If you try anything, it'll be too bad for
this baby. Be quiet and do as I say. First, the child there is a nuisance, so tie up his
hands and feet. Listen, you, tie him up with that cord over there."

The seventeen-year-old found two cords near the mother's pillow and tied the
hands of the little boy, who was still half-asleep, behind his back. He then laid the
boy down on the futon, and tied up his feet. He tied the cords carefully, not so tight
that they would hurt him, but not so loose that he could easily undo them either.

"Hey, listen up. This sow here is a *maid*. Okay, then, the maid will go to the
kitchen and make as many rice balls as she can from leftover rice. If there are any

217

eggs, then make hardboiled eggs. If there's any *daikon* pickle, then bring out whatever you have. The girl here will keep an eye on you. She may be small, but you'd better be careful, because she has a pistol she snatched from a soldier."

The twelve-year-old suddenly remembered the plans they had made earlier, and, flustered, she pulled a bundle wrapped in a towel from her jumper pocket and thrust it out in front of her. It was actually nothing more than a chipped teapot, but only a small portion of the spout was visible, peeking out from the towel. The young woman headed out to the kitchen. She was crying, and her voice was strained. The girl followed her.

"You. Pull out your wicker trunk and stuff it with all the clothes there. Don't try anything funny!"

After barking his order to the mother, the young man put the infant on the tatami, perhaps because his arm was tired, and sat down. He kept the knife pointed at the baby's chest and continued giving orders. The older child helped the mother with the task. They opened the closet, slid a wicker trunk out, and went through the contents. The clothes looked like nothing but rags. After pulling out a second and third trunk and going through them, they picked out items that looked like they could be sold—a winter coat, a woman's suit, a handbag—and put them into one of the empty trunks. They then pulled everything out of the chest of drawers and, in the same way, picked what looked valuable—blouses, sweaters, trousers, skirts, a kimono, an obi. The seventeen-year-old boy pulled several items out of a small drawer—a bankbook, a mother and child health handbook, and a box containing an umbilical cord, a ring and a necklace. He tossed the ring and the necklace into the wicker trunk. There was a modest Buddhist altar on top of the chest of drawers. When he opened the altar drawer, he found, as expected, a small amount of cash. A photograph on the altar caught his eye. It was the photograph of a man who seemed to be angry, who seemed to be saying, *What are you up to? Who the hell are you?* The man also seemed to be sad, seemed to be saying, *What a foolish thing you're doing.* That face looked familiar to the seventeen-year-old, more intimate to him than any face other than his father's. A face that stared out at him every day from a photograph in a newspaper clipping. He thought, *Don't you recognize me? I'm the child from the graveyard. Before, when I was in the orphanage, you gave me encouragement, but …* the boy felt sad. Now that he thought about it, where was that newspaper article he'd gone to the trouble of clipping out so long ago? He wanted to compare the picture on the altar with the picture in the clipping.

"Hurry up! Don't stand there looking lost!"

The young man shouted, his voice husky. Startled, the boy began to move his hands again as though he had awakened from a momentary dream.

The young woman placed five small rice balls, some pickled radish, and three hardboiled eggs on a plate and returned from the kitchen. The twelve-year-old girl was following her. While the young woman had been preparing the eggs and the rice balls from the leftovers, trembling all the while, the twelve-year-old had kept her mouth shut tight. There was something familiar, nostalgic about all this. The wooden icebox. The holes in the floorboards. The slugs crawling along the sink. The camel crickets hopping around on the packed earth floor of the kitchen entrance. The kettle and pot on the gas rings. The portable clay stove sitting on the narrow earthen floor. If she had carelessly opened her mouth to speak with this young woman, to call her by name, Sumi, the twelve-year-old knew she herself would break down crying as soon as the words left her mouth. She had to focus all her thoughts on her empty stomach. She swallowed her other thoughts deep in her throat, and suppressed her breathing so that she would not let those thoughts carelessly spill from her mouth or nose.

When the seventeen-year-old had filled three wicker baskets, he secured them with some rope they had brought with them. At some point the little boy on the futon had fallen asleep, and it seemed that the baby had exhausted itself crying, for it had started sucking on its own fist. The young woman sat down beside the mother, sniffling, her face utterly exhausted. The mother was sitting up in a formal position on her futon. She continued to glare at the young man with the knife. Her long hair was standing on end, even her lips were pallid, and in the dark room she looked like a ghost.

With the knife still pointed at the baby, the young man put one of the rice balls into his mouth. The two children began to eat hurriedly. The young man and the boy of seventeen ate two rice balls apiece. Because there were equal portions of the egg, they were able to each eat one apiece. They felt ashamed eating while the mother and the young woman were watching, but their hunger was more urgent than their shame. It felt deeply satisfying to eat after having finished their job.

When the plate was empty, the three of them stood up. While the young man kept the knife on the baby, the two children carried the baskets one by one out through the gate. When they picked up the last basket, the young man took the baby in his left arm and, still thrusting out the knife at them with his right hand, began to back out of the house.

"I'll borrow your baby until I get to the entry. So you just sit still."

The two women on the futon didn't respond. As the two children went into the hallway carrying the basket, the twelve-year-old girl looked back and saw the mother staring at them with transparent eyes. Various powerful emotions had sunk to the depths of her being, and her cold eyes, pure and clear, revealed the surface of those feelings. The twelve-year-old at once turned her back on the woman, and continued down the hallway. Her throat began to hurt. Her eyes and nose grew hot. By the time she stepped down onto the packed earth floor of the entryway, her tears were blinding her. They would never be able to recover the time that had passed.

The young man left the baby on the step of the entryway. The wooden step was cold, and the baby started crying.

219

"Run! I'll take that basket, you grab the baskets outside," the young man said, panting. Grabbing the rope on the basket sitting on the floor of the entryway, he tried to run toward the gate. The basket, however, was heavy, and he couldn't run as fast as he thought he'd be able to.

The two children who had been left behind in the entryway looked at each other, then stared at the baby crying on the step. It was completely quiet inside the house. However, they expected that soon the mother would certainly brace herself and come to retrieve the baby, and that the young woman would dash outside and run breathlessly along the street with the trolley line, collapsing in tears in front of the police box at the intersection. The baby was crying, its hands and feet were writhing as though it were in pain. It had been cut by the knife on its right cheek. Blood was dripping, flowing down toward its neck and making a black stain on the collar of its robe. As the baby's crying swelled and grew louder, the two children began to tremble. They had never imagined that a baby that small could cry so loudly. The crying spread through the house, and then outside. It was like the howling of a pack of wolves … no, it was more like a herd of elephants all trumpeting at once.

"Let's get out of here."

"We've got to run away."

The twelve-year-old was now sobbing. She took off the towel hiding her face and began rubbing her eyes violently with it. The seventeen-year-old took the towel off his face as well and clasped her hand. He didn't know why, but tears filled his eyes.

"We've got to run now! These baskets are more important to him than we are, so he won't come chasing after us."

The two children ran outside hand in hand. The leaves of the nandina and fatsia shrubs shone pale blue in the moonlight. The three baskets had been tossed out in front of the gate, and the young man, his face still covered by the towel, was standing in front of them.

"Hey, wait! Where are you going? Idiots! Are you running away?"

The two children kept on running at top speed. When they came out onto the road with the trolley line, they could no longer hear the young man's voice. Perhaps it was all right now. Even so, the two children continued to run, heading away from the intersection with the police box. The trolley tracks glinted beneath the bare light bulbs of the street lamps. But the trolleys weren't running, and there was no one in sight. The road sloped downward, and they gained speed as they ran. They were very frightened. They had no idea why things had turned out like this. The transparent eyes of the mother and the screaming of the baby seemed to be stuck to their backs. They could say they did it because they were hungry, but that didn't matter. They shouldn't have done it. When they reached the bottom of the slope and went through an intersection, the road inclined upward and came to a railroad embankment. Their eyes were bleary, and they were painfully out of breath. They clambered up the embankment on wobbly legs. They squatted at the top and looked down the railroad tracks. Several lines of bluish, shimmering tracks seemed to float before them in their blurred field of vision. At this hour, of course, the trains were not yet running. Bare light bulbs illuminating the tracks twinkled far and near. White flowers were blooming all over the steep slope of the embankment. Lizards, snakes, frogs, and insects were likely hiding in the shadow of the flowers. It wasn't a jungle here, so there were no wolves. There were no bears, no pythons. But there were surely crayfish, and loaches, and diving beetles, and giant water bugs sleeping in the muddy stream flowing along the bottom of the embankment.

"Let's walk along those tracks and find a station."

"Okay. We'll roll down to the bottom."

"Yeah, that'll be fun."

The two children lay on their sides, held onto each other and began to roll down the slope of the embankment. The leaves of the damp grasses stuck to their bodies. Insects were startled and flew off. Lizards chirped and snakes coiled and slithered away. Frogs, shouting in unearthly voices, hopped into the muddy stream below. Crying, laughing, the two children became a single mass rolling along, tumbling down a slope of white flowers.

1946

At around two o'clock in the morning on 28 April a gang of three people, including a child of twelve or thirteen, invaded the home of Mrs. Sugimoto Chiyo of Ehosoda, Odawara City. The group fled with a trunk full of clothing after eating a meal at the Sugimoto home.

At around 2:00 in the morning on 28 April a gang of six thieves invaded the home of Mr. Kyōbashi Keizō of Shimo-Ochiai in Yodobashi Ward, Tokyo. The thieves made off with 800 yen, thirty articles of clothing, and three pairs of shoes.

In the early morning hours of 29 April robbers armed with pistols forced their way into a Tōshiba Materials Company plant located at Kashimada in Kawasaki City. After the gang tied up twenty-one guards and night watchmen, they loaded a truck with sugar used in the manufacture of alloys, and made off with 5,000 yen.

At 7:30 p.m. on 29 April two men threatened Mr. Futakuchi Hidekichi (27) of Tanashi-chō, Kita-Tama District, and took his suit and watch. The incident occurred in front of the Hikawa Shrine in Akasaka Ward.

At ten o'clock on the evening of 29 April two men robbed Tanaka Kōtarō (17) of Shitaya-chō, Shitaya Ward and one other person of 120 yen. The incident occurred in Daimachi in Akasaka Ward.

On the evening of 25 April a gang of three armed robbers broke into the home of Mr. Shimamura Shigeyoshi of Akabane in Ōji Ward and stole a trunk and 650 pearls worth an estimated 40,000 yen at current market price.

At 11:50 on the evening of 4 May two men armed with clubs entered a coffee shop owned by Mr. Takayanagi Yoshio located in Asahi-chō, Kanda Ward and stole items of clothing, 10,000 yen in checks, and 800 yen in cash.

At 2:30 on the morning of 4 May three men armed with scythes forced their way into the home of Mr. Tsunoda Kōkichi of Yaguchi, Inagi-mura in the district of Minami-Tama. They fled with 3 bags of wheat flour, 54 liters of white rice, 18 items of clothing, 2 watches, a bicycle, and more than 650 yen.

At 7:30 on the evening of 4 May Mr. Matsumi Nobuyoshi (38) of Nishihara-chō in Yoyogi, Shibuya Ward was assaulted by three men and robbed of 560 yen. The incident occurred at Hatsudai-chō, also in Yoyogi.

At eleven o'clock on the evening of 4 May a man about 45 years old choked Ms. Nohara Yasuko (25) of Ōji-machi in Ōji Ward and stole 200 yen and some ration tickets from her. The incident occurred at the trolley stop at Ogu-machi 6-chōme in Arakawa Ward.

Unable to endure a ten-day delay in the distribution of food, about 1,000 citizens of Futamatagawa in Hodogaya Ward, Yokohama marched on the prefectural office at 2 p.m. on 30 May. The crowd held up large banners made of mats with big letters reading *Two Cups of Rice for Everyone* and *Don't Starve Us to Death*. Itogawa Niichirō, Satō Shōhei, and more than ten representatives met in the governor's office with Mr. Gotō, a section chief in the Ministry of Home Affairs, and complained about their plight, stating that more than half the prefecture's citizens were barely clinging to life by eating wild greens and parsley. They demanded that the authorities immediately release emergency rations of rice and retroactively distribute the rations that had been delayed until that point.

The prefectural authorities responded by noting that rationing was extremely difficult, given the current situation with rice supplies. The crowd then occupied the governor's office, using mothers who were carrying children on their backs as a vanguard. The situation was volatile for a while, but after the demonstrators demanded something to eat, telling authorities that anything would do since they had not even had lunch that day, the prefecture distributed 500 bags of hardtack....

In a narrow, dark place, the two children clung to one another, trembling. They were small naked babies. The two were wrapped together in rags, and newspapers were wrapped around the rags. Their hands and feet weren't strong enough to be able to free themselves and crawl out from the rags and newspapers. Their hands and feet shaking, they were crying feebly. The only thing they could do was suck on parts of each other's bodies, since there was no nipple for them. The place where the two children were sleeping had been swaying for some time. Apparently someone was carrying them somewhere. There had been a great jolt, accompanied by a peculiar noise, and their bodies had bumped together, and they had cried. They had also sensed the vibrations of the wheels of some vehicle, and the smell of oil had made it difficult for them to breathe. Suddenly a sharp light shone in on them, and they were startled. A cold breeze came flowing over them, and it was painful to breathe. They heard all sorts of sounds. The voices of men and women. A bicycle bell. A bus horn. A brake. Children singing. A bell from a church or school. Footsteps on a sidewalk. A cop's whistle. A radio. Music flowing from a speaker.

The two children had been placed somewhere that smelled slightly of mandarin oranges—not the smell of juice, but of dried peels. It occurred to both of them that they were probably inside a mandarin orange crate. They wanted to believe they were in a cradle made out of a mandarin orange crate, and be satisfied with that belief, but they couldn't help thinking they were like puppies about to be abandoned. Who was trying to get rid of them? Was their mother carrying this crate? Combined with the weight of their bodies, it was probably quite heavy. If they could hear noises from the outside, then that meant their crying could be heard outside the crate, didn't it? If someone heard human babies crying inside an orange crate, surely they would think it suspicious. Were their wailing voices so weak that, even if they could be heard outside the crate, they would sound merely like the mewing of kittens? Or were they already dead? The two children stared at each other, though the space they occupied, wrapped inside the crate, the newspaper, and the rags, had turned to twilight shadows, and they could barely make out the silhouettes of their faces. They were crying just as they did when they were alive, but maybe they only thought they were crying, only thought they were trembling, only thought they were hearing noises and sensing smells. Maybe they were, and maybe they weren't.

The mandarin orange crate began to sway in a regular rhythm. Apparently the person carrying the crate had begun walking again. They heard a car horn. They heard the *clang clang* of a streetcar. Eventually they caught the scent of damp earth drifting up into the mandarin orange crate. There was a sweet odor of wood. Then the bustling noises of the street disappeared. Instead of the scent of their mother's breast, the two children hungrily sniffed the scents of earth and wood, attempting to fill their empty stomachs. They heard the cawing of a crow. They heard the raucous calls of waterfowl. They were probably near a pond. Listening carefully, they could make out the sound of the person carrying their crate walking over gravel. For someone who was exhausted, walking on a gravel road must be trying. That person's feet, already heavy, would feel heavier and heavier. The rhythm of the sound of walking on gravel gradually slowed. The sound of the soles of the person's shoes scuffling along the gravel began to mingle with the sounds of walking, and as it did, the mandarin orange crate began to sag and tilt, finally giving a great pitch to bring it upright again. Perhaps the person carrying the crate was adjusting his or her hold because their arms were getting tired and they couldn't stand it any more. Whenever that happened, the two children were squashed together inside the narrow box, and their heads and chests bumped.

From directly above them came a faint voice that seemed filled with pain. The two children listened intently. A broken voice—was it sighing, groaning, gasping, grieving? They couldn't tell. It sounded like a woman's voice, but it wasn't clear.

Suddenly the mandarin orange crate shook violently left and right and bumped into something with a dull thud. Then it was quiet. The smell of grass came flowing in. The boards above that had been covering the two children were removed, and the newspaper and rags were swept aside. Light shone in directly. The two children shrank from the blinding brightness and squalled. But then they were immediately enveloped in a cool round shadow. It seemed like a woman's face. Wild, disheveled hair swayed like seaweed around the shadow. The mouth shimmered green, the eyes shimmered green, and from the eyes large drops of green water tumbled down, plopping one after another. The two children stared intently back at the woman's face. Was she their mother? She was now a shadow, and they were unable to clearly make out the expression on her face. The sunlight was shining on her hair from behind, and as it softly fluttered, it sparkled. Her eyes were shining green again. Green drops of water fell, wetting the arms and foreheads of the two children. The woman gave a long, deep sigh, quickly covered up the bodies of the children with the rags and newspapers, and finally closed up the mandarin orange crate once and for all.

The twilight the bodies of the two children were accustomed to returned, and their strength drained away. They looked at each other. Had the woman, who was probably their mother, left them here? Had they been abandoned to die slowly but surely? Had the woman been crying? What grief had she suffered? Had she decided on her own that the only thing she could do was abandon them? Would she try to continue living, having chosen something else in their place? Their skin was still wet from the woman's tears. Was she crying even now? Or, was she thinking only about what would become of her own life from now on? Or, having abandoned them, was she smiling happily, bathing in the sunlight, feeling relieved for the first time in a long while? The two children took on the pain the woman had been feeling up to now, and in place of the woman, they began to shed large drops of water from their own eyes. They peed. As the inside of the crate became wet, their bodies gradually grew cold. The two children began to cry weakly from cold and hunger. Or was it simply that they felt that they were crying? Perhaps they had already died, and their corpses had been casually placed inside a mandarin orange crate. Had the woman smothered them with a pillow and killed them first, and then placed them

224

in the crate? How long, exactly, had they been allowed to live after being born into this world? A single day? A week? A month? Their lifetime had been the period of the woman's suffering. Where would the woman likely go now? She would have to continue to milk her swollen, painful breasts. Her milk would be washed away in a toilet, or in a kitchen.

The two children closed their eyes and held onto each other. Their bodies grew cold and hard. They no longer felt the cold. They had no connection with hunger. The two children were at ease. They fell into a silent sleep. Would dogs come to rip their bodies apart, would they be picked at by crows, would their bodies decay and crumble away … for the two children, in their changed state, such thoughts were already meaningless.

1945
Since the beginning of December, 18 infant boys and 14 infant girls have been taken in by foundling hospitals. Some are as young as ten days old. 13 babies who did not have the strength to nurse have died. There are at present 314 orphans in foundling hospitals in the Tokyo metropolitan area.

1946
At around two o'clock in the afternoon on 2 January the corpse of an infant girl about seven months old was discovered beneath the Nakagawa iron bridge on the Jōban Line in Nagato-chō, Adachi Ward.

At nine o'clock in the morning on 4 January the naked corpse of a baby boy who had been dead for two or three months was left on the road in Den'enchōfu, 2-chōme in Ōmori Ward. The baby, who had been wrapped in a burlap sack, had apparently died a week after it was born.

At approximately three o'clock in the afternoon on 19 January, an infant boy about twenty days old dressed in a red padded outfit was left in the smoking area on the third floor of the Denkikan movie theater in the entertainment district of Asakusa Park, Rokku.

At about one o'clock in the afternoon on 27 January, the corpse of an infant boy who had apparently died about one week earlier was left in a public toilet in Tsunohazu 2-68, Yodobashi Ward.

At two p.m. on 28 January, an infant girl about one month old was left in the third-floor hallway of the Tokyo Theatre located at Tsukiji 3-14 in Kyōbashi Ward. At 5:30 that same afternoon an infant boy about forty days old was abandoned in a waiting area at Ueno Station.

At seven o'clock at night on 3 February an abandoned child about one month old was found in front of a maternity clinic located at Nakanegishi 4 in Hongō Ward.

On the morning of 6 February an infant boy about twenty days old was found left on a seat in the Fujikan movie theater in Asakusa Park.

On the morning of 13 April the corpse of a one-week-old infant boy washed up on the bank of the Arakawa River near Hashido-chō 74 in Senjū, Adachi Ward. The body, which had been dead about ten days, was wrapped in cotton cloth, oilpaper, and newsprint.

At around eight o'clock in the morning on 21 April a newborn infant boy died in a vacant lot next to the Metropolitan Yotsuya Labor Exchange located at Wakaba-chō 3-chōme 6-5 in Yotsuya Ward. The baby had a stab wound to the right shoulder that penetrated the chest.

At 9:30 on the morning of 23 April the body of an infant boy was discovered in a sewer just beyond Wakabayashi-chō 543 in Setagaya Ward. Police are investigating the death as a homicide.

1947

The number of abandoned children increased dramatically in July and August. Reports to the Metropolitan Police have come in at the rate of about one child per day since the beginning of August. The police hand these children over to ward offices, where they are given provisional names, such as "Shimoya Hanako," before being sent on to the Tokyo Metropolitan Foundling Hospital in Itabashi, where they are placed in an infant ward. As of 23 August, the ward was caring for 42 babies (12 boys and 30 girls). Most of the babies range from about two months to five months in age. According to Dr. Anno of the infant ward, all the babies have been diagnosed as being less than 80 percent of normal body weight, and thus lacking the strength to survive. The death rate has climbed to more than 50 percent, and the babies are now dying at a rate of one child every two days.

11. The Final Day

That day the sky shone totally blue above our heads. A deep blue. A pure blue filled with light. Squinting and staring up in fascination at that blue sky, we wondered if this was the origin of the color *blue*. It felt as if the meaning of the words "blue sky" was transformed for us from that day on. Even now there are still times that I want to whisper, "Wasn't the meaning of those words transformed?"

We had been riding a train that day on the Iida Line. It was the beginning of June, and already the powerful summer light shone dazzlingly on the scenery along the tracks. The train was a local, moving slowly along, stopping at every station. Because it wasn't pulled by a steam engine spewing smoke, the windows on both sides of the car were wide open. A warm damp breeze drifted through the train, and our bodies melted like honey. We dozed on, luxuriating in that sweet sensation. Because we got on at Tatsuno, where the train originated, we were able to get seats together—of course the train, which consisted of just two cars, was traveling in the early afternoon, so there were lots of empty seats. Other passengers were also napping in the early summer breeze. And so we grew careless.

Suffused with heavy exhaustion, we had thrown ourselves down haphazardly on the hard seats and continued to doze, leaning against one another. How had we come to be riding on the Iida Line? Perhaps we had proceeded east from Maizuru, following the coast along the Sea of Japan, and then moved inland around Naoetsu. But I'm not sure. Because our "journey" was slapdash, we were under no obligation to make sure we planned out every detail. Sometime around the sixth or seventh day after we left Tokyo, making train connections became our only goal, and gradually we no longer cared where the train was headed or where it was passing. We simply entrusted ourselves in a vague way to the trains, and we came to feel that we were carrying out an important responsibility. I no longer felt anxious. Day by day exhaustion seeped ever more deeply into our bodies, so that even moving our eyes became too much trouble. We had gone days without sleeping on a futon. As it turned out, we didn't take a bath, and of course we couldn't change clothes. We hadn't been gone even ten days, and so our travels shouldn't have been all that big a deal. And yet because I was just twelve at the time, I didn't have the physical strength to fight against the exhaustion … or against the strength of my feelings.

And what about the seventeen-year-old "Mitsuo"? He was certainly not very strong or robust, and he did not have a rough personality. Compared to him I feel that I was much more carefree, and had greater powers of resistance. Because I was still just a child, perhaps I was insensitive, or had animalistic strength. Compared to me, Mitsuo got weaker as the days passed, and that undoubtedly heightened his

227

anxiety. If we had continued on the Iida Line, we would have arrived at Toyohashi in due course. Not even Mitsuo had considered where we would go from there. Instead, he told me, half jokingly, how nice it would be if we were to get off somewhere along the Iida Line and live a modest life together. Even though I knew it was unrealistic, it felt exciting, and I laughed and answered, "Yes, let's do that. Let's give it a try. We'll be all right. We can be traveling performers for sure. But if we do, we really should settle at a tourist site, since tourists are usually generous."

"In that case, shall we get off at Tenryūkyō?" Mitsuo whispered. "Even I've heard about the boat rides they take on the rapids of the Tenryū, so it must be a pretty famous place."

We had spotted a tourist poster at Tatsuno. It informed us that the Iida Line ran south along the Tenryū River for a fairly long distance. We remembered the name of a mountain, Komagatake. However, the poster didn't tell us if we could see the Central Alps from the train.

I was excited and said, "Isn't Tenryūkyō full of monkeys? If it is, let's catch one and train it and make it part of our group."

Mitsuo's mood suddenly changed for the worse. He scolded me, saying, "There's no way that's possible. On top of that, I hate monkeys."

His face sullen, Mitsuo went silent. I shut up as well. It seemed that his anxiety over his arrest, which was bound to happen, had returned, and that the childish fantasy of becoming traveling performers was now merely upsetting. However much he tried wishing that the two of us would live together secretly somewhere, his common sense told him that making such a wish a reality was practically impossible for a seventeen-year-old. *What should I do?* Mitsuo was at a complete loss. He grew angry that I seemed indifferent to his concerns. He must have been thinking, *If we hide away deep, deep in the mountains, would we be able to live forever without being discovered? Even a corpse that has been dumped in the mountains will eventually be found by chance. After all, Japan is a small country with lots of people. On top of that, how would we be able to survive in the mountains? Even back when I was a four-year-old in the graveyard, I went out with my father into the town and ate something. I suppose we could catch animals and eat fruit from the trees. But there's no way our bodies could tolerate that kind of diet. We could try running away to a foreign country, but we'd have little chance of success at that. Japan is an island nation, so there's no way we could do as Jewish people did when they fled at night across the border into Switzerland to escape from Hitler. And there's no way we could do as Remi and Capi did in my version of the story—that is, walk all the way from France to India to follow Gandhi.*

Mitsuo had probably been reading the newspapers when I wasn't noticing. It was being widely reported at the time that I had gone missing. Screaming headlines carrying cheap, overwrought clichés had appeared in print: *Whereabouts a Mystery!* or *Another Young Girl Kidnapped!* It was only much later when I first saw them.

228

I instinctively burst out laughing, and then my body trembled. For the first time I directly experienced fear, which felt like the weight of a boulder. Back then no one considered withholding news reports so as not to anger or provoke kidnappers into harming or killing their hostages. Of course, the fear I felt was fear of those icy stares of the "monkeys" who fill the world to overflowing—stares that Mitsuo would definitely be exposed to all the time for the rest of his life. Those stares sharply pierced my body. Had Mitsuo known that photographs of my face, which had no especially distinguishing features then, were being printed in the newspapers?

On that day the sky was refreshingly clear, the grasses and trees were sparkling, and as the sun heated everything, a damp scent wafted up from the leaves and the soil. The temperature quickly rose during the morning, and around noon it felt hot and sticky. An odor rose from our bodies, and we were itchy from head to toe. I couldn't stand wearing the baseball cap, and when, from time to time, I would violently scratch my head, I would catch the odor of my own fingers. Black filth was caked under my nails. Because Mitsuo was as filthy as I, I wasn't embarrassed about it. Instead, I came to feel that because we were gradually coming to smell the same, my safety was assured.

That morning we ate breakfast at Tatsuno. What did we eat? Since we always ate the same foods at the same kind of shops, meals became a blur to me. *Ramen*, curry with rice, set meals, *bentō* we bought at stations ... now that I think about it, where was it that I ate omelet over rice? I have the feeling it wasn't at Tatsuno. They didn't sell *bentō* at any station on the Iida Line. We boarded the train from Tatsuno a little before noon, and we figured that whenever we got hungry on the way, we could get off at a suitable station and look for a restaurant. As we continued on everyday in this unsystematic, disorderly way, the times we ate and the number of times we ate became increasingly random. When we realized there was nothing disadvantageous about an irregular schedule, we became relaxed, and our appetites increased.

Outside the window everything was blindingly bright. The blue of the sky glittered relentlessly, the green of the trees and the river water sparkled, and even the dirt roads glinted sharply. The roofs of houses, the water in small rice paddies, and even white butterflies sparkled. Azaleas were blooming here and there, and yellow and red flowers gathered capriciously. We didn't see any strange birds of extraordinary colors, and of course we didn't spot any elephants or pythons, but I was so fascinated by the scenery along the track that I wasn't at all disappointed. Then the peaks of the Central Alps appeared before us, like masses of light in the deep blue sky. Snow still clung to the peaks, edging the slopes, and the whiteness of the snow dazzlingly slashed and divided the blue of the sky and the blue shapes of the mountains. That blue turned to green little by little as it neared the base of the mountains, and it was overcome by the dark and light greens of the low mountains on the near side of the Central Alps.

"Look at those amazing mountains! I'll bet there are wolves like Akela over there," I shouted in excitement.

Mitsuo stuck his head out the window and said, in a low voice, "Amazing. Why is it that that kind of mountain always brings to mind the word "god"? It looks as if all the answers to all the questions in the world are there. Even the answer to what we're all doing here ..."

"Look, the mountains are chasing us! They're angry, saying, 'You think you can get away from us?'"

When I said that jokingly, Mitsuo settled back in his seat and muttered, "Don't talk rubbish. You've spoiled the moment."

I agreed with him and nodded in response. As the image of Akela running around drifted through my mind, I continued to stare at the mountains towering in the blue sky.

How long were we able to see that mountain range, the mountains of the Central Alps, from the train window? Thirty minutes? Even after we could no longer see the snow-topped peaks, the shorter mountains continued onward. And in the windows on the opposite side we could make out the blue shapes of other mountains, snow sparkling at their peaks. The tracks were sandwiched between the Central Alps and the Southern Alps. As the mountains grew more distant, the bluish-green river drew up closer to the tracks, and the light reflecting off the surface of the water began to flood the interior of our car. I grew sleepy as I stared at that light, and began to doze again. I rested my head on Mitsuo's shoulder and lightly closed my eyes. My head was now completely familiar with the bones of his shoulder, and I was accustomed to his scent. It wasn't a foul odor. It was more like the scent of decaying leaves, or of a clump of grass on a rainy day. It was a smell that had permeated Mitsuo's clothing from the very beginning. I wonder if my scent had become familiar to Mitsuo in the same way? I was such a small child at the time, perhaps my body didn't yet have a scent. Had it never occurred to me, being twelve years old, that I should try to run away from Mitsuo? The only feelings I remember are fear of being abandoned, resignation that, having come this far, I would not be able to return to my former life, and a sense of something like my own responsibility; and so I had started to believe that the only thing I could do was to continue supporting Mitsuo, who had no one else in this world to turn to but me. That kind of reckless pride was natural perhaps, since I was a naïve child. My childish sense of responsibility was no different from my earlier, arbitrary determination to try my whole life to protect my mentally handicapped older brother, the way a wife or a mother might. It was a means to provide an escape for me and Mitsuo.

Steeped in that honey-like drowsiness, I began humming randomly. My song was like a hymn I had just learned at middle school, or like a verse from a song I had learned in elementary school like "When Violets Bloom" or "Summer is Come." There was a time in my life when, if I covered my ears and listened to my own humming, it sounded like the dulcet tones of a flute. I listened intently, enchanting myself. Whenever I continued a verse at random, no matter how I continued it, a beautiful song was born. However, one time my mother, almost screaming, scolded me, saying that there was nothing she hated more than humming, that I should stop, and that I must never hum again. After that, the joy of humming completely left me.

That reminds me, one time I picked up a piece of light blue glass from an empty lot in our neighborhood. I didn't know where it came from. The glass was thick, and because its surface was roughly textured, the blue was tinged with a smoky white. My heart was captivated by the color and feel of that glass. I thought, in my childish mind, that it was like a piece of the Ice Palace from *The Snow Queen*.

I can't help remembering such trivial things now. Of course, before I knew it, that piece of glass had completely disappeared from my possession. Because it was nothing more than a piece of glass, I probably threw it away somewhere. Even so, now, when I remember that light blue tinged with a smoky white and the feel of the glass, I feel a faint excitement, as if something is about to begin.

Each time I opened my eyes, Mitsuo, who had taken the names Akela and Remi, was beside me, was there for me. Even now I remember the joy of waking up like that. Before I'd set out on my travels with him, whenever I got up in the morning and pondered the long day that stretched before me, I'd feel dejected and sad. Such mornings recurred over and over for me. I had to get up when morning came, and, as a child, I would sigh at the thought of that responsibility, which I couldn't escape. But after I left with Mitsuo, those feelings of dejection were all swept away.

The light on the surface of the river reflecting onto my eyelids changed shapes and scampered off in accompaniment to my random humming.

Then, all at once, still in my honey-drenched drowsiness, I was seized and lifted up by violent arms.

Police! It's him, all right, the goddam pervert! Screaming male voices overwhelmed us. At the same time I heard a whispering voice, tickling my ear, "You're little Yuki, right? You're not hurt anywhere, are you? That's wonderful. You can relax now." Squirming with all my might, I looked toward Mitsuo. He had a stricken expression on his face. Sinister-looking men in dark black suits had seized him and put handcuffs on his wrists. He was staring at me, his pale face drained of color. His large eyes were shining blue. Did he say something at that moment? Did I scream something? Did I call out his name? Did I resist and call out *What are you doing? Stop it! Let go!* Perhaps neither of us could say anything. Perhaps we just looked at each other, and then there is no doubt that I started to cry. The thing that we had secretly feared had finally come to pass. And in an instant, I understood, and felt a crushing despair, knowing I would be separated from Mitsuo. And as it turned out, I was never able to see him again. I despaired because I knew our separation would be no different from that brought on by death. The hands of the men pulled Mitsuo out of his seat, and as he looked back at me, he was pushed and kicked violently down the aisle of the train. The men dragged him out, shouting at him all the while. There were no tears on his face. Only fear. His eyes, which shone blue, brought to my mind the eyes of a wolf. It was the last expression I ever saw on his face.

The train remained at the station for a while—was that for the purpose of arresting Mitsuo? Someone continued to embrace me, and I was taken off through a different exit. I was sobbing, and searched the platform for some sign of him. *Where did they hide him,* I wondered, but I couldn't see his figure. Did they whisk him away to a patrol car that was waiting in front of the station? Squirming in the arms of someone who had an unpleasant smell, I had to be forcibly pushed yelling and crying into an unmarked car that had been readied in front of the station, as if some bad guys were kidnapping me. I was sandwiched between a plainclothes detective and a woman police officer. The car took me to Toyohashi. I could hear the sound of a siren in the distance. Was that the patrol car taking Mitsuo away? My car had no siren, and it traveled along the narrow country roads at a normal rate of speed. As before, the outside world was glittering, brimming with a blinding light. I was confused, wondering where all the things I had learned from him—*We be of one blood ... Good hunting all that keep the Law ... the law of the jungle ... Remi and Capi ... Gandhi*—would now disappear. After losing the law of the jungle, just exactly what kind of time would flow from this point onward? When we were separated, both Mitsuo and I were all alone again.

A local passenger who had seen us on the Iida Line noticed that my face resembled the face in the newspaper photograph, and so he quickly contacted the conductor. The conductor passed along the message to an attendant at the nearest station, and the attendant reported it to the police. At first the local police, then the detectives who later came chasing after us from Toyohashi, surrounded the train we were riding on, and several of them came strolling casually down the aisle, and confirmed whether or not we were *really us.* They then designated the station where they would carry out the arrest, deployed a patrol car, and, as soon as the train stopped, overwhelmed us. Apparently that was the course of events. The arrest took place at Toyokawa Station. We had been so fascinated by the mountains, and had been dozing so comfortably, that we hadn't noticed any of those actions at all. We were already being staked out without knowing it. For a long time after that, whenever I thought about it, I couldn't help feeling threatened. We're never aware of real danger.

At the police station in Toyohashi they questioned me informally. For Mitsuo's sake I continued to clearly insist that I had not been kidnapped, that I had followed him on my own. They brushed my assertions aside, saying that a full interrogation would take place in Tokyo. After that they handed back my belongings—the jacket, the baseball cap, the bag. Oh yes, that reminds me—those items had just been left on the seat when I was suddenly apprehended on the Iida Line. The police wanted me to confirm that I had everything, so I looked to make sure, and found the stained towel, the damp toilet tissue, my tooth brush, the tin cup, and the candy drops. Mitsuo's folder, which held the newspaper clippings he treated with such care, was also in my bag. Had Mitsuo intentionally entrusted the folder to me? Or had he simply put it in my bag by mistake? Still, I decided to keep it. Mitsuo probably wouldn't complain. I opened the folder to take a look. The article with the photographs of the graveyard and my father had been mounted on the pages of a scrapbook. Apart from that, about twenty other newspaper clippings had been placed inside a business envelope. All the articles dealt with events from around the time Mitsuo had lived in the graveyard—in other words, from around the time when I was a baby, and when my father died. No doubt he had taken the liberty of tearing these clippings out of the reduced-print editions at the library. When it occurred to me that the library now had a bunch of newspapers full of holes, I wanted to burst out laughing. That was the only time I felt that way. Articles about abandoned children, about families committing suicide together, about wild dogs, about cholera—those things were the entrance to Mitsuo's other world, the monkeys' Cold Lairs.

After confirming that I had my belongings, the woman police officer took me to a hospital in the city. Although Mitsuo was probably somewhere in the same police station, I left without seeing any sign of him. No matter how much I pleaded for them not to treat him as a criminal, I was unable to affect their way of seeing things. I was being "protected," and he was being "arrested." Even though I was just a child of twelve, I knew full well how big the difference was between being "protected" and being "arrested." As a result I realized that, no matter how many times I might tell them I wanted to meet Mitsuo, or how many times I might shout out his name, it would be useless. Thus, I never cried or raised a fuss, saying that I wanted to see Mitsuo, and I continued to follow their instructions. My grieving thoughts, to that extent, had been frozen in the depths of my body.

Even though I was not sick, I was forced to lie down in a hospital bed and undergo a medical examination. My clothes were removed and the nurses cleaned my body. When I put on a white nightgown and lay down, my body was overcome by a drowsiness that was like a heavy stone. I fell into a deep sleep. It was the first time in many days that I had slept in a bed that seemed like a bed.

When I woke up, my mother's face, which I was so used to seeing that I was sick of it, appeared right in front of me. She was staring intently into my face. Flustered, I closed my eyes again. My mother continued to stare at me all the more carefully. From that moment, I was once more back in my mother's time.

I don't remember exactly when we returned to Tokyo—was it two days after the arrest? I did nothing except sleep and eat. At least as I look back now, it feels like that was all I did. I was no longer able to think of anything, no longer able to feel anything. Perhaps I was like a child who has been spirited away. Even though a thorough police investigation in Tokyo must have been carried out, I don't remember it. My twelve-year-old self did not possess the vocabulary that would allow others around me to comprehend the nature of the time I had spent together with Mitsuo. Still, did I offer childish-sounding excuses for Mitsuo's sake—telling the police that he had done nothing wrong … that I had wanted to go with him, and chose to do so on my own … that he had treated me extremely kindly, and had paid for everything … that I hadn't had a single frightening experience? The only thing I remember is that, whenever the detective who was interviewing me laughed, his face looked just like a monkey's. At one point he said to me, "So that pervert called himself Mitsuo? That's not his name." I was so surprised and perplexed that almost instinctively I came close to carelessly asking him, *Well then, is his real name Akela, or Remi?* Why did he have to conceal himself by making up the alias "Nishida Mitsuo?" I began to suspect that maybe even my own name, Yukiko, was an alias. I sensed that by giving me the names Mowgli and Capi, Akela and Remi were ridiculing me. I could no longer call him Mitsuo, and I was angry that I was only allowed to refer to him as *that person.* I had been forced to accept the name Sugi Yukiko, and I had to go on living as Sugi Yukiko. "That person," of course, hadn't committed the crime that the Man Pack, especially the police, wanted to pin on him. Because my mother insisted that it was not a crime, he was only called to account for having stirred up the Man Pack. In the end "that person" was released. However, I continued to resent the crime that had been committed against me, namely the crime of hiding his name in order to live in the Man Pack. *That person* quietly passed me by and became nothing more than a nameless child mentioned once in an old newspaper article in the brief phrase, "A vagrant father and child who were living in the graveyard…." A father with his face hanging down, his back bent over, and a naked filthy four-year-old boy moved on into the distance, away from me, as if sliding over the surface of water.

After returning to Tokyo I continued to carry the cloth bag as before, dangling it from my shoulder, and I wore the dress my mother had brought me. Apparently the clothes "that person" had bought for me had been thrown into the trash in Toyohashi. My mother, accompanied by the woman police officer and two detectives, brought me back to Tokyo. The second-class car of the super-express train we boarded at Toyohashi was different from the slow, local trains I had been riding. It was clean, fast, and I felt that I was about to get motion sickness. We went straight from Tokyo Station to the police station at Sakuradamon, where the first interrogation took place. I was finally released in the early evening, and my mother and I took a taxi. We passed through Ichigaya, and dropped by the school where I had been commuting. Even though it would have been acceptable to make our greetings to the school the following day, apparently my mother, who was a stickler about niceties, wanted to get the bothersome duties over that day. The principal and the nun who was my homeroom teacher looked at me and cried, even though they didn't know much about me yet, since I had just enrolled at the school. I was at a loss and simply stared at them. Some other teachers and a few students who were still there gathered around me. I recognized the schoolyard and the school building, but I stood there feeling strange, wondering *Am I really a student at this school*? My mother bowed her head repeatedly and told them that today, for the time being, she just wanted to pay her respects. Then she took me by the hand and we left.

We got back into the taxi, which had been waiting for us in front of the gate, and headed next for Shinjuku to call on the high school where my mother worked. It was absolutely vital for her to pay respects there as well. Although she was a teacher, her child had become an item in the newspapers, and so she had to take off work for several days. We passed through streets bustling with people and multicolored signs, and finally turned into a quiet, narrow alley with no one about. Although it was close to 6:00, the streets all continued to glow in the early twilight.

We hadn't eaten lunch that day, so I was hungry. My mother was probably hungry too. Although we were by ourselves now, she didn't speak to me. Unlike the mother in *Nobody's Boy*, my mother did not hug me, or press her cheeks to mine. The eyes and cheeks of my mother, who was skinny to begin with, were even more hollow than usual, and her complexion looked even more sallow. However, I couldn't very well say any of that to her. It was difficult for me to imagine how much worry, fear, and grief my mother had been experiencing, and I was afraid to feel the full force of the anger, resentment, and hatred she had for a child who had just come back to her. Still, she *was* my mother after all, and I *was* her child. There was no need to be overly conscious of things, to force ourselves to speak about things that were irrelevant or wide of the mark. My mother and I together felt no hesitation in submerging ourselves in our own fatigue and confusion. And in so doing, we began to return to an earlier time.

I was struck by the fact that there were only male teachers that evening, since the public high school where my mother worked was coeducational. Students taking evening classes rushed past the shoe shelves. Students who took day classes were no longer around. Light bulbs were shining in the halls, and the walls were grimy. That was the first time I had ever seen the place where my mother worked. We went from the teachers' office, where there were a lot of male teachers, to the principal's office. My mother bowed her head and repeated the same line over and over—*I've caused you a great deal of trouble*—as if that was all she knew. No one here cried when they saw me; none of the teachers gathered around. My mother said that because the next day was Saturday, she would like to take one more day off and start work again on Monday. And with that, her visit was finished. Just then I realized that I had completely forgotten what day it was. As my mother and I were leaving the school, the bell announcing the start of evening classes began to ring.

We got back into the taxi. The sun began to set at last. The red sky faintly tinted the ground a reddish color. I suddenly remembered the blue sky on the day that we took the Iida Line. The yellow daffodils blooming in Yamagata. The white flowers blooming somewhere else. The shapes of the mountains … Now I can only recall those things vaguely, like remembering a dream. But still, if those things can be called a dream, I feel as though my life now were a dream. They're both dreams. But if that's the case, then where am I, who's having both these dreams, and what am I doing?—*I don't know, I don't know, someone gave my head a blow! Now I'm foolish, now I'm slow, now my stupid hair won't grow, and all because I just don't know!*— My voice echoes deep in my ears from somewhere. Vague images of Akela/Remi come back to me, and at the same moment, the ghostly figure of my older brother draws near, and I find it hard to breathe, and clutch my cloth bag to my chest.

Surrounded by crowds of people, the taxi has to stop. We're on a wide street near Shinjuku Station. Nothing special is happening; just a huge crowd of people mingling there. Shinjuku is packed with places where people can go out to drink, or enjoy a meal, or see a movie or a play after the day's work or study is finished. And later in the evening, casinos or flashy establishments dealing in the kind of adult entertainment that excites men begin to bustle. However, at this hour there are still a lot of young men about the same age as Akela/Remi mingling on the street. There are few people with black hair. Everyone's hair is dyed gold or white or blue or red, glittering under the light of mercury lamps and neon signs. A man's arm with a silver bracelet bumps the window of our taxi. An English-language song, sounding like so much noise, comes pouring in. The sound of drums reverberate from somewhere. The shouting of men calling to customers at discount shops washes around the taxi like a wave.

The taxi can no longer move forward, even a little. My mother sighs, and decides that we'll get out and take the Yamanote Line home. Clutching my bag, I get out first, and my mother steps out after me. We begin to walk. At that hour there are far more people heading from the station toward Kabuki-chō than heading toward the station, and so my mother and I are walking against the flow of the crowd. We move forward two or three steps, stop, change directions to the side, are pushed back, and then stop again. Hair of various hues comes pushing against us. I can't tell if these people are Japanese or not. Occasionally, men with outrageously large bodies appear. People with different colored eyes and skin pass us, tossing out bizarre words I have never heard before. Chinese. Thai. Korean. English. Vietnamese. Of course, I also hear Japanese. White tourists, cameras dangling from their necks, pass us. And young women, the area around their eyes glittering brightly, their lips and earlobes sparkling. And round-shouldered young men wearing baggy trousers. Everyone walking along, shuffling their feet, their thin bodies bent over. Short skirts that resemble bathing suits. Skirts so long they cover the heels. T-shirts with all kinds of writing on them. All the women's faces look the same—is it because of their makeup? On a gigantic television screen atop a tall building the leaders of North and South Korea are shaking hands. On another screen a volcano in

236

Hokkaido is belching out smoke. People laughing with their mouths wide open are walking beneath those screens. People giggling, people singing, people shouting as they walk along. Everyone trembling. Thin bodies trembling and grating. I can hear people crying. A woman crying. A baby crying. A baby abandoned on the street is crying. Earrings swaying on a man's ears. Women in heavy make-up looking like dolls. White lips. Black lips. Blue lips. Stiletto heels or platform sandals with soles as thick as traditional *pokkuri* clogs. So many people wearing sneakers. High-school girls in uniforms with extremely short skirts. People with what look like electrical cords wrapped around their heads. People with small, flashing cell phones pressed to their ears, talking by themselves. All the bodies shaking, trembling like gelatin, beginning to melt. Their silhouettes indistinct. A baby crying. On the gigantic television screen a huge shot of the leaders of North and South Korea smiling.

A wolf can be heard howling. The *Death Song* of a wolf, reverberating across the jungle. A python slithers away stealthily. The barking of the monkeys in the Cold Lairs swirls around. Gandhi, riding an elephant, and *The Swan*, frozen blue by grief, drift away slowly across the sky. The black shadows of a little naked boy and his father, both dragging blankets full of holes, steal behind the buildings and disappear.

A red moon is floating in the brown, hazy sky of evening. The mouths of the trembling people are open. Their faces all seem to be laughing. Even the red moon is laughing.

23 September 1946
Kigi Kōtarō's analysis

I heard from a friend who works at the Tokyo Metropolitan Police Department that when little Kiyoko received money from her mother in Kyoto, she told her mother "Please wait a minute" and disappeared. After she had given the money to Higuchi and come back, she was asked, "Where is he?" and she answered, "He's a really nice young man, so please, mother, don't let them arrest him."

In the case of girls between the ages of 12 to 14 or 15 who have been abducted, they commonly develop a relationship with the man who kidnapped them and grow close to him—or at least become accustomed to being with him. Based on the exchange between Kiyoko and her mother, we can infer that Kiyoko had already established some kind of relationship with Higuchi, and so I can imagine that Higuchi had Kiyoko completely under his control. Even if you ask Kiyoko where they were and what they were doing during their six months together, she just says, "I don't know." Because she is so young there isn't much that can be done about it, and it is unlikely that the police or her parents will get any further information from her....

Kiyoko's older brother's story

When I went to meet her at Tokyo Station I felt relieved to see that her face looked darker and healthier than before. She had always been thin and delicate, but she had grown strong as a result of living on the road for six months and seemed to have confidence that she could do any job. She's constantly telling us that she wants to help with the housework. Apparently during the period of her kidnapping she wrote something everyday—not a diary exactly, but memos. Those memos aren't in the house now, but my father said he read them and, according to him, she wrote down words of self-examination. Things like "I think I must never use bad words to people younger than me" or "When I return home I'll clean the house on my own."

It made me cry to think that even in the depths of her terrible ordeal, while she was growing stronger as a result of her harsh experience, she was also careful to protect her life and do her best to survive, even though she was a child. My father told me that she wrote a poem in her memos that says "the moon that rises shines the same on everyone."

28 September 1946
The Psychology of an Abducted Girl
Shikiba Ryūzaburō

Young girls who have been kidnapped have not yet experienced a clear sexual awakening, but they already feel an attraction for the opposite sex as a preliminary phenomenon to sexual awakening. The psychology of Kiyoko, which led her to yearn for Higuchi and call him a nice young man, was to a lesser extent present in Sumitomo Kuniko. Thus it is a fact that young girls are attracted to something like love toward their older brothers or their cousins before they awaken to true feelings of love toward the opposite sex. A lack of social education in the family is indicated, but in addition, the adventurous interest of girls about that age in an unknown world may give them the courage to become familiar with a man they don't know, and even take a trip with him without fear.

… These young girls, who didn't know anything of the real world, were given a glimpse into the lives of women and a view of society through Higuchi, and they probably felt a kind of wonder and pleasure. In Kuniko's case, she wasn't with him long enough, but in Kiyoko's case, even though she was still a child, she acquired as a result of Higuchi's training the mannerisms of a housewife who has been taken from a household where she was accustomed to living. For that reason he was considering making Kiyoko his wife, and may have if he had had a little more money.

In the case of Higuchi's kidnappings, or in the case of the serial murderer Kodaira, people find it astounding that girls or young women could be so easily attracted to that kind of criminal. However, when we consider that their method is very gentle and that they make skillful use of psychology to arouse curiosity, it's natural that women are attracted to such men. When you look at the photograph of Higuchi and Kiyoko taken in Kanazawa, you get the sense that it captures a moment on a fun trip being taken by close siblings. The special characteristic of the crimes in this case lies in the fact that, unlike most kidnappers, Higuchi adopted a quiet demeanor and took the girls without being threatening and without frightening them; and the motives of these naïve, docile young girls, which made them easier targets for abduction, are latent. Kodaira was certainly a sadist. As for Higuchi, he tended to enjoy sharing hardships with the girls, a trait that reveals instead a masochistic personality.

ABOUT THE AUTHOR

Tsushima Yūko is the pen name of Tsushima Satoko, an acclaimed contemporary Japanese fiction writer, essayist, and critic. Her accolades include: the Noma Prize for New Writers in 1979, the Kawabata Prize in 1983 for her short story "Danmari ichi" (The Silent Traders), the Tanizaki and Noma Prizes in 1998 for her novel *Hi no yama—yamazaruki* (Mountain of Fire: Account of a Wild Monkey), and the Osaragi Jiro Prize in 2001 for this novel.

ABOUT THE TRANSLATOR

Dennis Washburn is the Jane and Raphael Bernstein Professor in Asian Studies at Dartmouth College. Among his numerous works, the Center for Japanese Studies at the University of Michigan has also published *Studies in Modern Japanese Literature: Essays and Translations in Honor of Edwin McClellan* (edited with Alan Tansman, 1997), *The Shade of Blossoms* by Ōoka Shōhei (translator, 1998), *Shanghai* by Yokomitsu Riichi (translator, 2001), and *A Wife in Musashino* by Ōoka Shōhei (translator, 2004).